I0799431

IMAGES
of America

HARDEMAN COUNTY

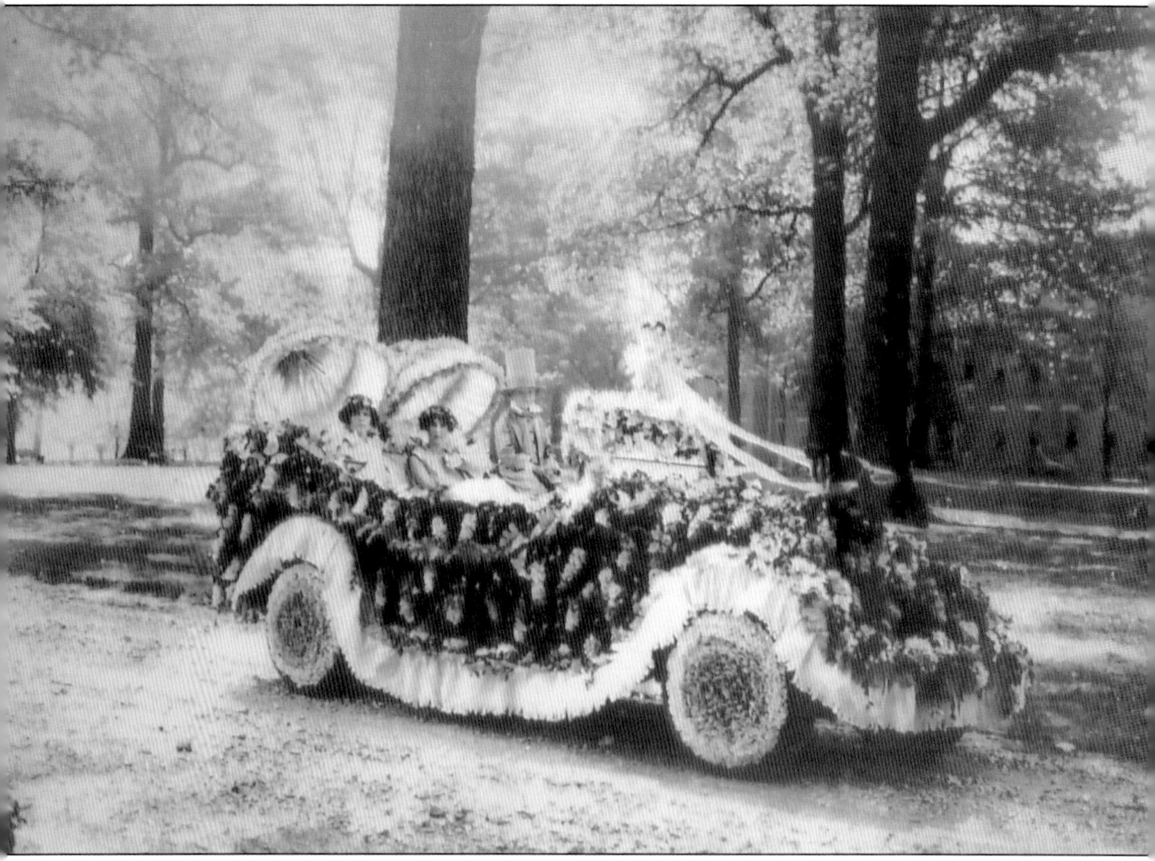

This c. 1926 photograph shows a car decorated in flowers for a May Day parade in Bolivar, one of many events held in conjunction with the celebration. The first prize that year for the "best automobile" was 15 gallons of gas. All decked out in their spring finery are, from left to right, Maggie Lee Goodman Herman, Lucy Farris Keller, and Edwin Cocke Jr., son of Western State Hospital superintendent Dr. Edwin W. Cocke. This image was captured on the grounds of the hospital, and one of the towers of the Administration Building is visible in the background. (Courtesy Western Mental Health Institute.)

On the Cover: Tom Anderson of Cloverport, shown here with his wife, Martha, was known as "The Flying Farmer" because he used his yellow Aeronca two-seater plane, "Champion," to check on his orchard operations in Toone and Whiteville. The orchards and fruit stands produced and sold thousands of bushels of apples, peaches, and pears at one time, and they continue to operate today. (Courtesy Tom Anderson.)

IMAGES
of America

HARDEMAN COUNTY

Lisa C. Coleman

ARCADIA
PUBLISHING

ISBN 978-0-7385-9144-5

Published by Arcadia Publishing
Charleston, South Carolina

Printed in the United States of America

Library of Congress Control Number: 2011939522

For all general information, please contact Arcadia Publishing:
Telephone 843-853-2070
Fax 843-853-0044
E-mail sales@arcadiapublishing.com
For customer service and orders:
Toll-Free 1-888-313-2665

Visit us on the Internet at www.arcadiapublishing.com

To my parents, James Albert and Freddie Kiestler Coleman, and my brother, Chris, who lovingly encourage—and sometimes endure—having a historian in the family.

Contents

ACKNOWLEDGMENTS

Deuteronomy 32:7 says, "Remember the days of old; consider the generations long past. Ask your father and he will tell you, your elders, and they will explain to you." I must first, and always, give the glory to my Heavenly Father, from whom all blessings (and words) flow.

This book is my scrapbook for our county, a place where we may collectively remember our shared days of old. Although my name appears on the cover, this book has been a cooperative project involving many people—the stories and successes I share with all the donors; any shortcomings are my own.

Thanks Mom, Dad, and Chris for your love, support, and encouragement.

Thank you, Hardeman County librarians, for all your help! Thanks to Louise Manhein, Janette Tigner, Cheryl Avent, and Virginia Spencer at Bolivar Hardeman County Library (hardemanlibrary.org); Cynthia Scott at Middleton Library; Loretta Bell at Bobby Martindale Memorial Library; Kristi Marcum and Glenda Doyle at Lee Ola Roberts Library; and Paula Stanley and Julie Fisher at the Saulsbury Community Library.

Thanks to my Hardeman County Genealogical Society friends—your enthusiasm is inspiring and your friendships are cherished. A special thanks to Pat Vincent, who answered all my questions that started with, "Do you know anything about . . . ?" David Smith (birddogfoundation.com), Ken Kowen, Evelyn Robertson, Ken Savage (thepillars.org), Ed and Loretta Doles, and Monita Carlin (www.hardemancountytn.com) have all been most helpful in my search. Darrell Teubner, with the *County Journal*, has been an enthusiastic supporter of this project since our first conversation about it and is a great friend to local history. Thanks also to the *Bolivar Bulletin Times* for assistance with articles and photographs in their paper.

A debt of gratitude by everyone who reads and researches local history is owed to five individuals who have done much to preserve our county's history: thank you Quinnie Armour, Roy Black, Faye Davidson, Faye J. Owens, and Robert Haralson.

Lastly, a special thanks to my editor at Arcadia Publishing, Elizabeth Bray. All first-time authors should be blessed with such an enthusiastic, patient, and kind guide.

INTRODUCTION

To the casual observer, Hardeman County, Tennessee, might seem to be one of those charming, small-town southern places that a traveler passes through, or even passes by, on the way to somewhere more exciting or interesting. However, this casual observer would be wrong, and should be reminded of the old adage of not judging a book by its cover. It is true that the county is rural, small-town, southern, and, yes, even quaint and charming. But a deeper look into this archetypal southern county opens up 1,000 stories—and more—of the people who decided not to just pass by and who stopped to make lives here, making history in the process.

This book will attempt to share some of that history, some of those stories, and some of those images, all presented in the hopes of sparking the marvelous conversation that arises around the words, "Do you remember when?" This book is a starting place to learn or perhaps relearn or remember the people and places that made Hardeman County what it is today. It is by no means an attempt to be the definitive work of the county's history; rather, it is hoped that it will be the starting point for future volumes that will present more of the stories of its people, places, and shared remembrances.

The Chickasaw Indians resided in Middle and West Tennessee long before white settlers set foot in the area. By 1783, England had passed its rights over the area to the United States, but settlers did not move into the area until the Chickasaw tribe formally ceded their claims on the land to the federal government. After the Chickasaw Treaty of 1818, signed by Isaac Shelby and Andrew Jackson with the Chickasaws, settlers began moving into the area of the Hatchie River Valley that would soon be known as Hardeman County, Tennessee. These early settlers were excited by the river, which provided transportation, and by the fertile soil that would produce good crops both to sell and to sustain their families.

A small settlement in what is now the western part of the county began as a trading post in the wilderness—one of the first known settlements on the frontier of West Tennessee. What would those early settlers think if they could visit today and see that their little settlement has turned in to a town that for many years was home to a successful school for African American students? Or of the two prisons that provide employment for many and revenue for the county? What about the early settlers on the Hatchie River who established a small boat landing near Clover Creek? Would they wonder what happened to the boats, traders, and trappers? Would they marvel at the acres of rich land still farmed there today? In the southern part of the county, would they be amazed to see a national park dedicated to the memory of valiant soldiers who fought a war for a cause they held so dear?

Hardeman County was officially recognized on October 16, 1823. The county is located in the upper plateau in the southwestern part of the state and comprises approximately 655 square miles. The Chickasaw word for "river" was "hat-chee" (so saying "Hatchie River" is actually saying "river-river"), and the Chickasaw crossing point on the river became the river port of Hatchie Town. The county was named for Thomas Jones Hardeman, a veteran of the War of 1812 who served his namesake county as its first county court clerk. Later, Hardeman moved to Texas and had a county named after him there as well. The Hatchie Town site was prone to frequent flooding, and by 1825, it was moved slightly south to its current location and renamed "Bolivar" in honor of South American liberator Simón Bolívar. The original port on the river remained active for many years; the first steamboats began to arrive around 1829 and continued traveling the river until the 1850s. There were often as many as 13 or 14 boats making stops at the old port each week. Most of these boats were designed to operate in the often-shallow waters of the river and carried passengers as well as a variety of merchandise to the county.

Hardeman County played an important role during the Civil War and was highly prized by both armies for its proximity to the river and the railroads. Men from every community and corner of the county joined the Confederate forces. The 3rd, 7th, 14th, 16th, and 18th Tennessee Cavalry Regiments, the 4th, 9th, 13th, 21st, 22nd, 33rd, 39th, and 154th Tennessee Infantry Regiments, and Marshall T. Polk's Company of the Tennessee Artillery Corps all counted local men among their numbers. Other units included men who joined Capt. Rufus P. Neely's Company B of the 14th Tennessee Cavalry, Company E of Gen. Nathan Bedford Forrest's 7th Tennessee Cavalry, Company F of the 9th Tennessee Infantry (known as the "Middleton Tigers"), and Company K of the 154th Senior Tennessee Infantry (known as the "Sons of Liberty"). Some men from the area took up arms with the Union Army, while others bravely served in the Union Army's Colored Troops.

Hardeman County's history is rich and diverse and often involved players on a state or national stage, some willing and some reluctant, but all participants in history. Each has added a thread to the tapestry that makes the county what it is today—a work, and a people, still in progress.

Welcome home to Hardeman County, Tennessee.

One

Early Settlers

After the Chickasaw Treaty of 1818 was signed, settlers began arriving in the western frontier of Tennessee, coming primarily from middle Tennessee, Virginia, Kentucky, North Carolina, and South Carolina. The quiet Chickasaw crossing on the river soon was filled with these travelers, and the river would play an important role in the establishment of several new settlements. These earliest settlers in the area paid between 12 and 25 cents for an acre of land.

Early settlers often entered into skirmishes with the Chickasaws, fought off wild animals roaming the area, and endured the isolation and backbreaking work of settling America's frontier. Their tenacity and perseverance paved the way for all who call this beautiful, rural area of gently rolling hills and broad plateaus "home."

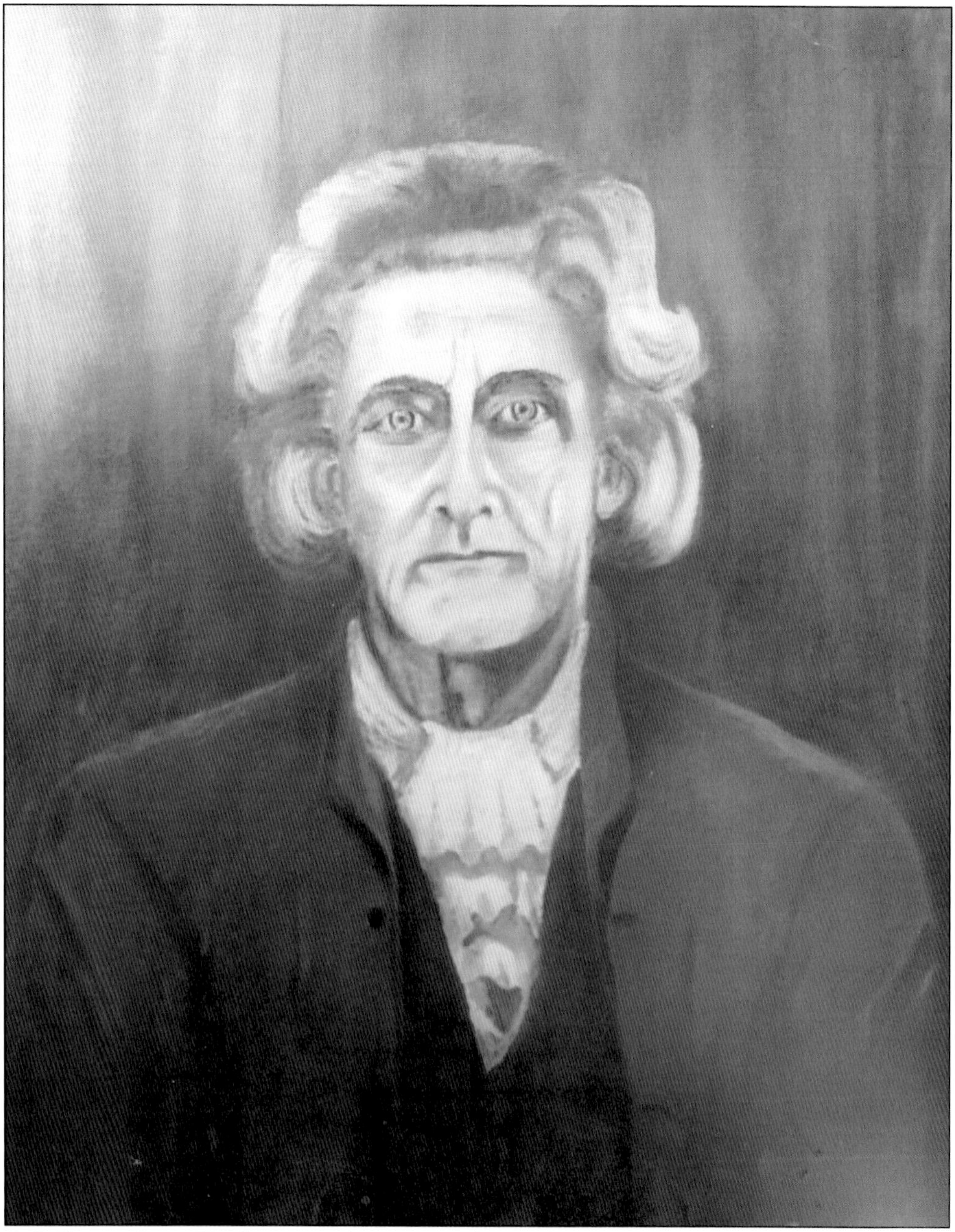

Col. Thomas Jones Hardeman was born in North Carolina in 1788. His first wife, Mary Ophelia Polk, was the daughter of Ezekiel Polk; Thomas and Mary came to West Tennessee with Ezekiel and other family members. Colonel Hardeman served with Andrew Jackson during the Creek War and the War of 1812. He was elected the first clerk of the county and served from 1823 to October 1835; Mary died in September 1835 and is buried in the Polk Cemetery in Bolivar. Hardeman left Tennessee for Texas and, while there, married his second wife, Eliza DeWitt Davis. He and his brother, Bailey, were involved in helping Texas win its independence, and Hardeman County, Texas, was also named for him. He was active in Texas politics and remained there until his death in 1854. (Courtesy Hardeman County Genealogical Society.)

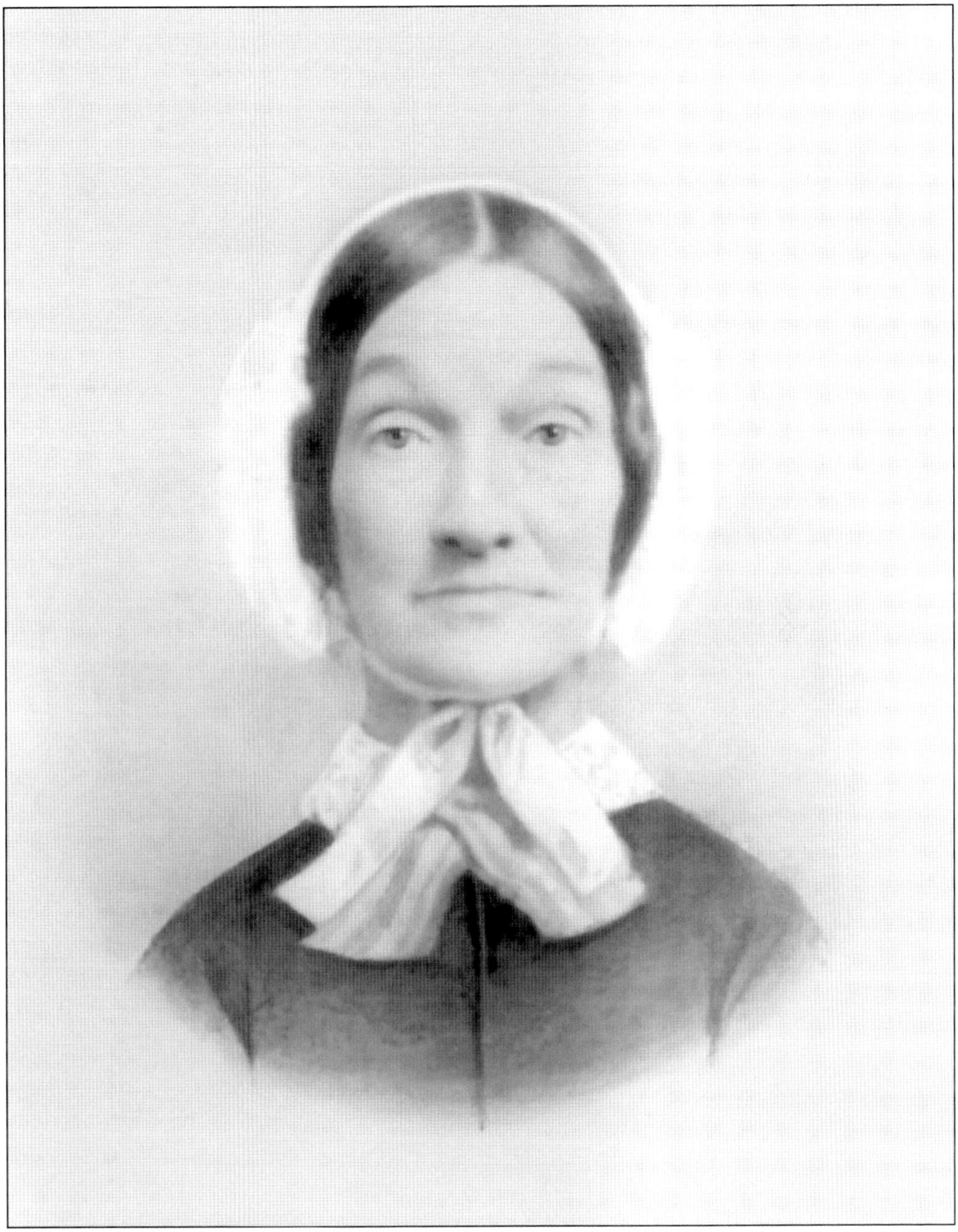

William Shinault settled an area approximately one mile from the present day town of Hickory Valley. His wife, Hannah Youree Shinault (born February 14, 1795, died April 20, 1870), is believed to be the first white woman to cross the Hatchie River. A family story tells of an Indian raid on the little settlement while Hannah was at a nearby spring getting water for the family. Indians took her baby in the raid, but Hannah pursued them and bargained with them to return her child to her, giving them a gallon of "firewater" in exchange, which they agreed to. Her grave marker reads, "A pioneer, the first white woman to cross the Hatchie River, settling one mile east of this place in 1820. A woman of strong character with many Christian virtues; loved by her children, respected by her friends." (Courtesy Hardeman County Genealogical Society.)

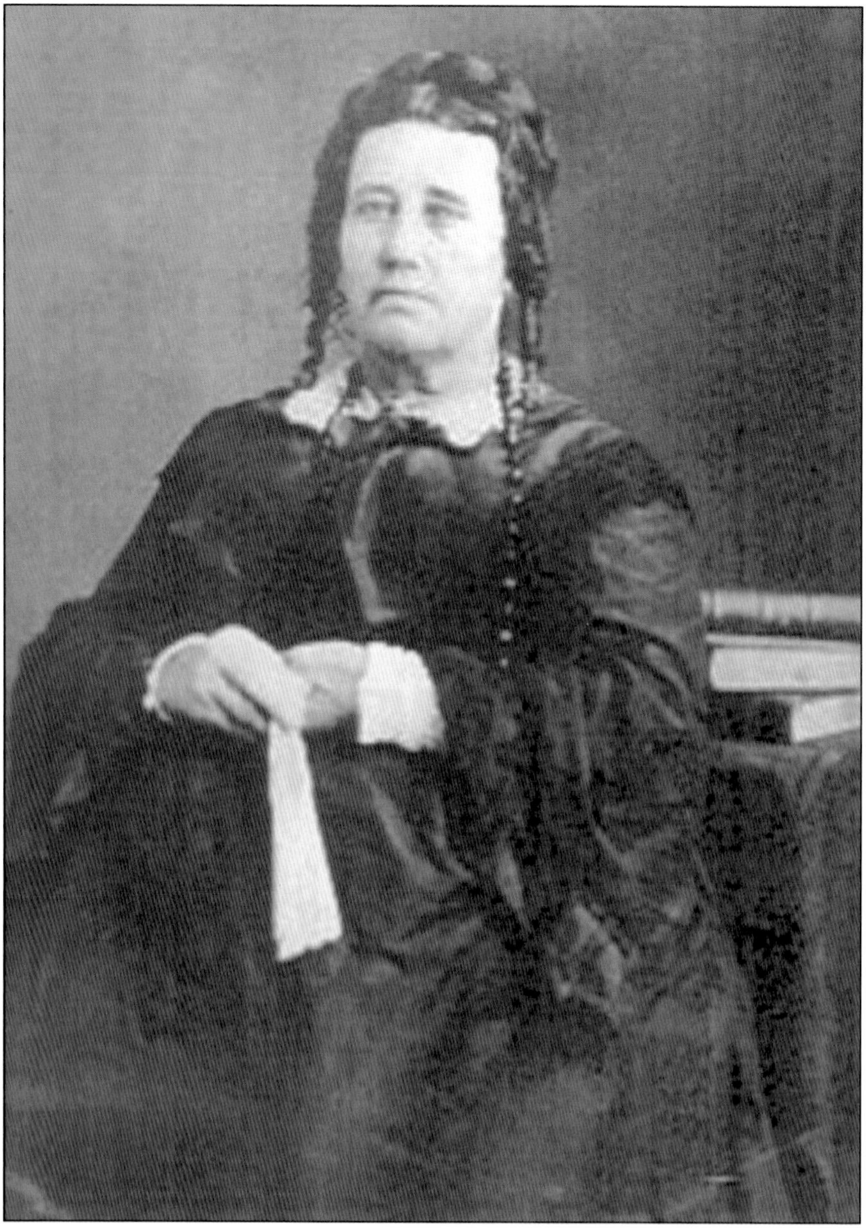

Susanna Wilkinson and Almerion Dickinson were married near Middleburg on May 24, 1829. They later moved to Texas, where Almerion fought and died at the Alamo. The only survivors of the bloody Alamo battle were Wilkinson, her infant daughter Angelina, a Mrs. Alsbury, and Col. William Travis's African American servant, who were all in the fort at the time of the battle with the Mexican Army. Mexican general Antonio López de Santa Anna interviewed the women, giving each one a blanket and two dollars in silver before releasing them. Legend says that Wilkinson displayed her husband's Masonic apron to a Mexican general in a plea for help, and that Santa Anna offered to take Angelina to Mexico, but Wilkinson refused. Her grave marker in the Texas State Cemetery is inscribed "Her name belongs to Texas History. She cast her lot with the immortal heroes of the Alamo. After its fall, with her "babe" in her arms, she carried the news to General Sam Houston at Gonzales." (Courtesy Ken Savage.)

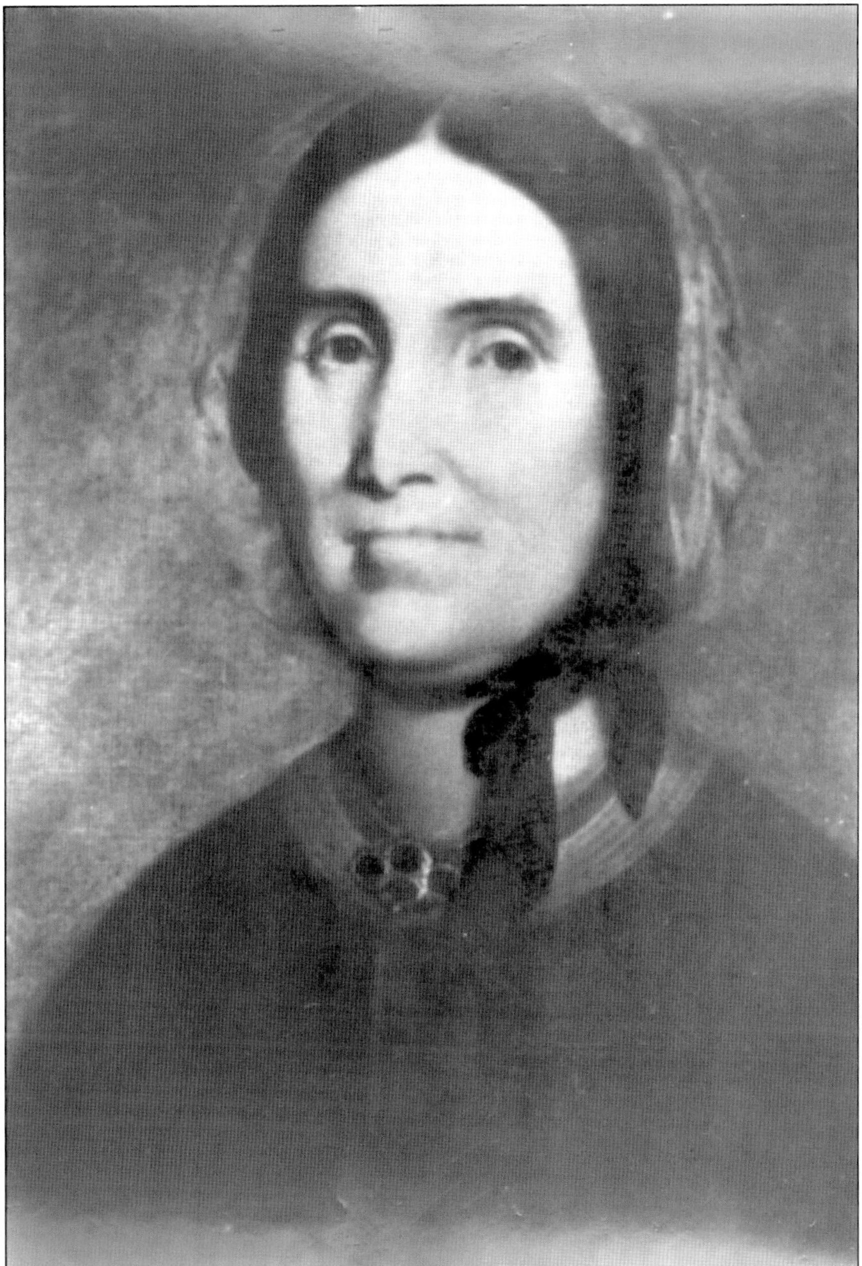

Henrietta Sarah Fitzhugh (1789–1879) and her husband, Henry, traveled by wagon from Fenton, Virginia, to West Tennessee, and she kept a diary during their travels, which took them to the home of her brother Charles and his family in Bolivar. The trip took them about seven weeks, and Henrietta got her first look at Hardeman County on November 2, 1830, noting, "The Hatchie River is not as wide as I expected, however, the waters are unusually low. We ferried over. [Bolivar] is a very pretty, flourishing looking place, far superior to Jackson in appearance, although we had to drive with the utmost caution to avoid stumps in the streets. [Bolivar has] some very pretty buildings." She lived in West Tennessee for only a short time and eventually settled in Ravenswood, in what would become West Virginia. (Courtesy Pat Vincent.)

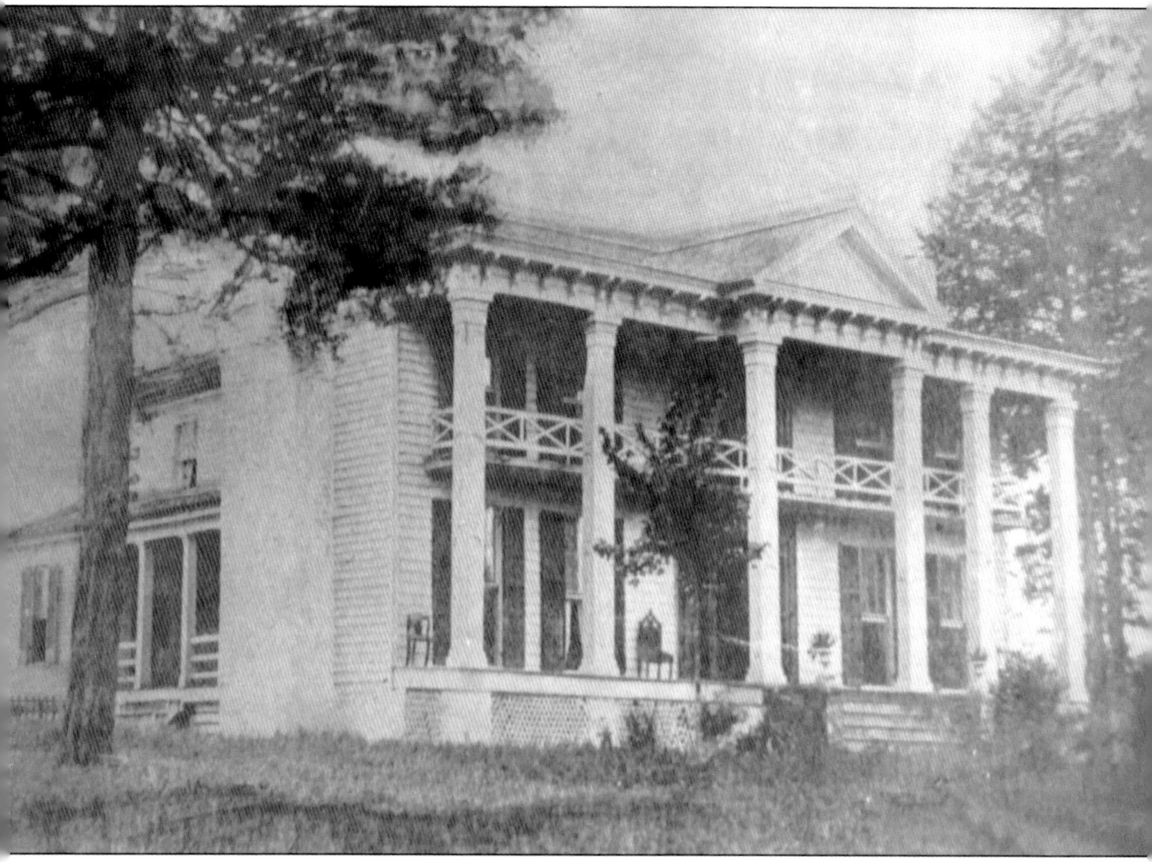

Ezekiel Polk (1747–1824), born in Pennsylvania, spent his childhood in Mecklenburg County, North Carolina, and helped to settle parts of Middle and West Tennessee. By 1820, he moved to the western frontier of Tennessee with his sons Samuel and William, and sons-in-law Col. Thomas J. Hardeman and Thomas McNeal, and their families. They were some of the first white settlers in the Hatchie Town settlement. Polk built a home west of Bolivar named "Mecklenburg" that burned down in 1962. "Old E.P.," as he was known, was the grandfather of Pres. James K. Polk. He wrote his own epitaph prior to his death, and generations of Hardeman County youngsters made rubbings of his tombstone during scavenger hunts, especially the line, "And Methodists with their camp brawling," which was considered so controversial during his grandson's presidential campaign that it was removed and later replaced. (Courtesy Gary Fish.)

Two

The Three Courthouses

Only a few years after the first settlers began moving into Hardeman County, they recognized the need to be more formally organized and to have a proper county courthouse. The first courthouse was built near the location of the current court square in Bolivar. It was a log structure with two floors—the first floor was the courtroom, and the second floor served as a temporary jail. This modest log structure was only used for a few years.

When this first structure was moved around 1827, a second, larger courthouse was built to serve the county, and as the centerpiece of the town of Bolivar. Very little is known about this second courthouse. It was built around 1830 and was used for 34 years until the retreating Union army burned it down on May 7, 1864. Quick thinking and planning on the part of a clerk preserved the handwritten county deed and other record books. There are no known drawings or photographs of the second courthouse.

The third courthouse, which is in use today, was built in 1868, only three years after the end of the Civil War, and was designed by architects Joseph Willis and Fletcher Sloan. The cost of the entire building was $25,000, and it was referred to as "a magnificent Hall of Justice" in a *Bolivar Bulletin* article on November 23, 1867. The county commissioners appointed J.H. Bills, E.P. McNeal, P.T. Jones, and E.G. Coleman to superintend the work on the building.

Additions made to the courthouse in the mid-20th century nearly doubled the size of the original structure. Many feet have traveled up and down its well-worn front steps and the staircase inside while taking care of a variety of business in the building's courts and offices.

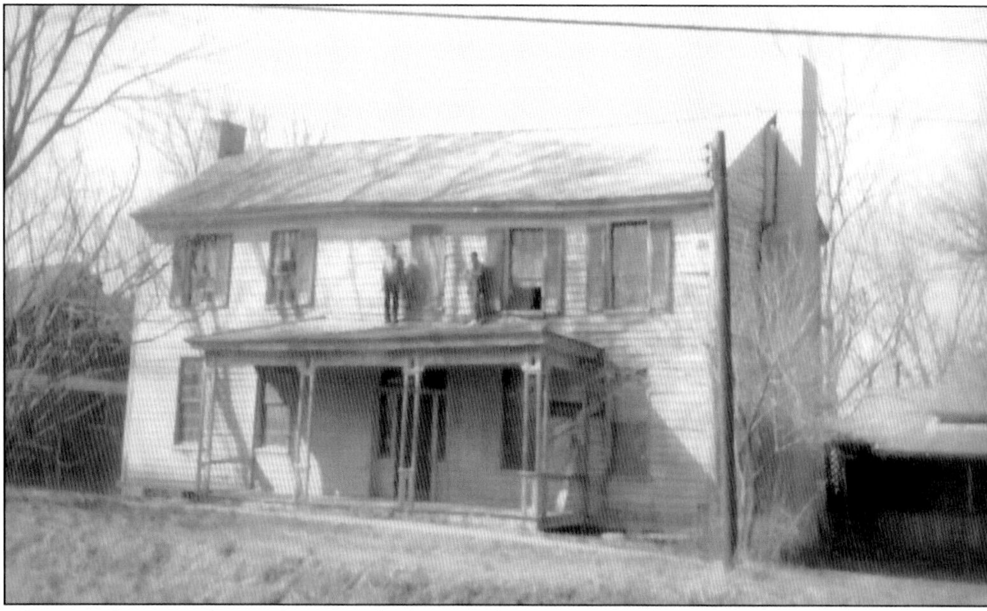

The 1824 log courthouse became the home of the Levi Joy family; it was later purchased by Judge Barry, and the judge's widow sold the house to Dr. Thomas E. Moore in 1849. Dr. Moore made many restorations to the structure, adding rooms to the house and placing weatherboard siding over the exterior logs. The Moore family lived in the house for over 100 years. In 1967, the descendants of Dr. Moore's granddaughter, Jennie Hardaway, sold the house to the county. The Hardeman County Chapter of the Association for the Preservation of Tennessee Antiquities (APTA) began extensive restorations on the house, including returning the interior to the old logs. (Both, courtesy Gary Fish.)

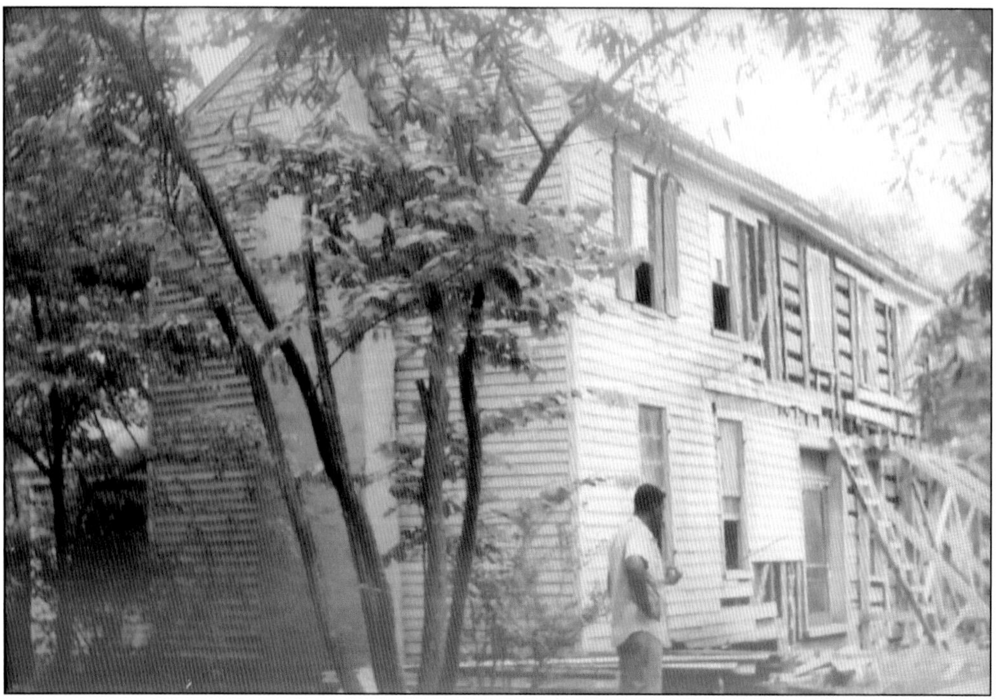

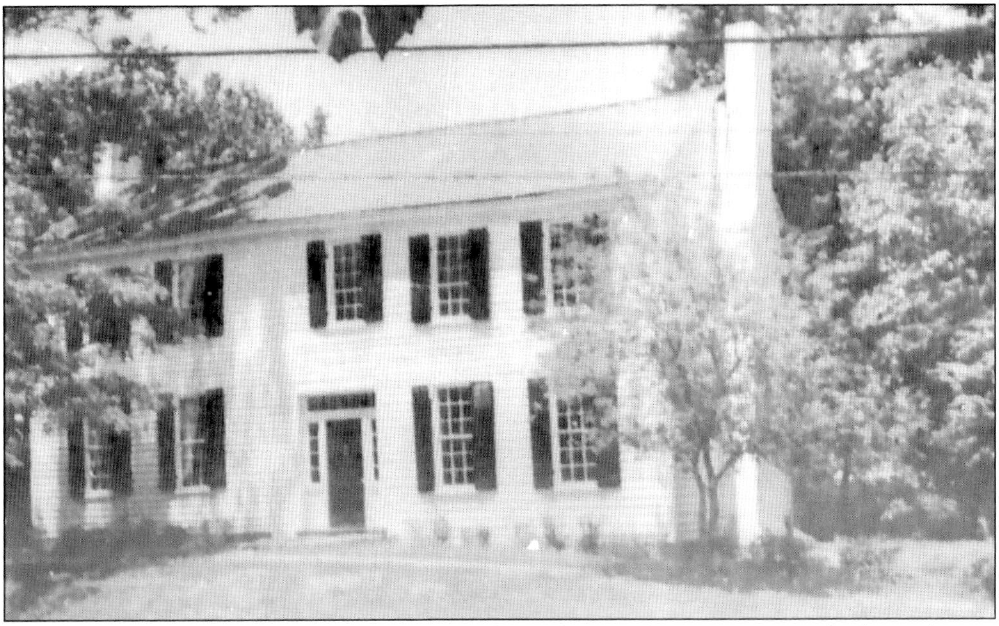

Today, the Hardeman County APTA operates the Little Courthouse Museum, which now houses county artifacts and photographs. The courtroom has benches and other furniture from the early days of the third (current) courthouse. Special displays and programs throughout the year highlight different areas of the county's history. (Courtesy Hardeman County Genealogical Society.)

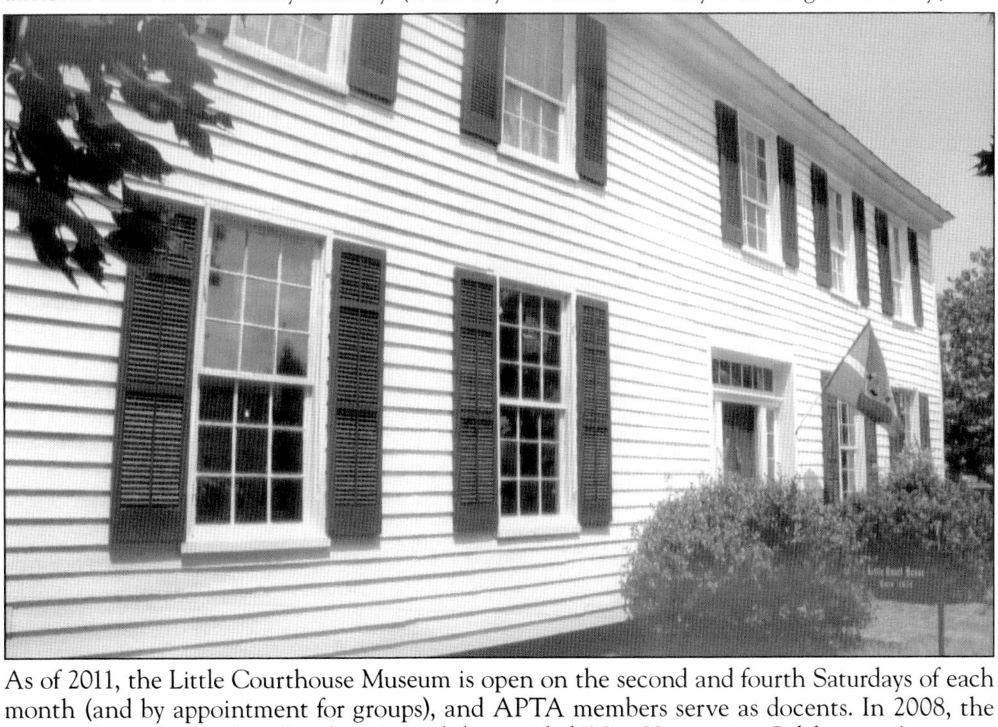

As of 2011, the Little Courthouse Museum is open on the second and fourth Saturdays of each month (and by appointment for groups), and APTA members serve as docents. In 2008, the museum hosted a traveling Smithsonian exhibit entitled "New Harmonies: Celebrating American Roots Music." Visitors, including several hundred local schoolchildren, toured the museum and received hands-on lessons from area musicians. (Lisa C. Coleman.)

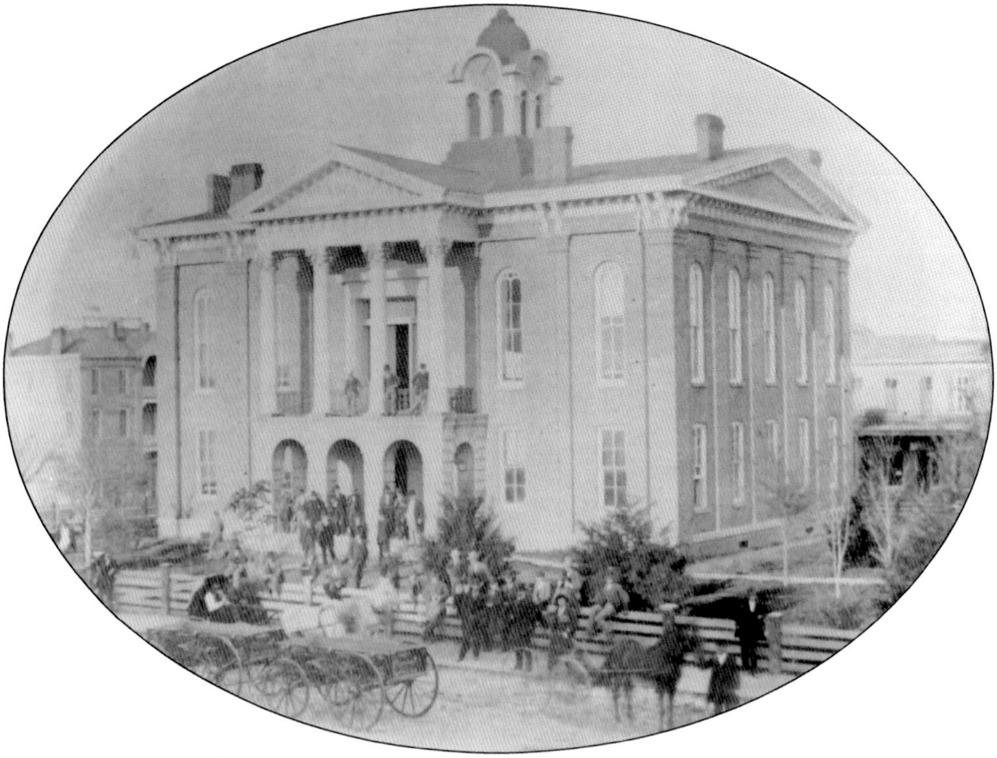

Believed to be one of the oldest known photographs of the current courthouse, this image shows a busy scene on the square, both at the courthouse and at the many businesses surrounding it. The wooden fence was later torn down and replaced with a wrought-iron fence. (Courtesy Arthur Jr. and Esther Wheeler family.)

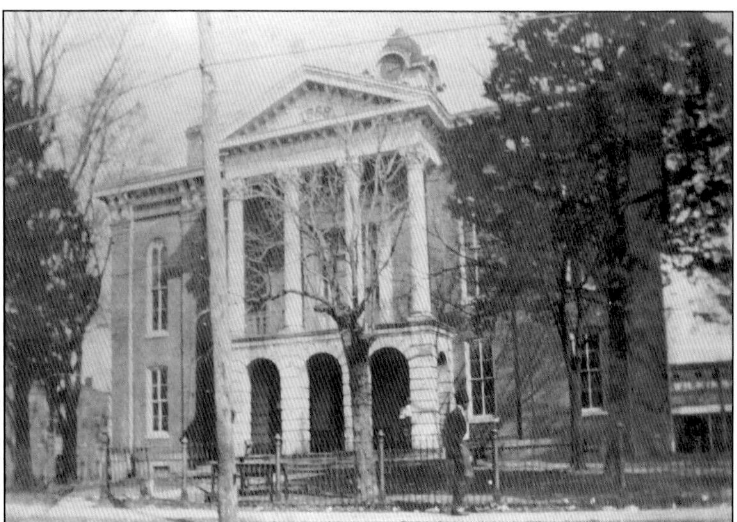

A man strolls down the sidewalk on the Main Street side of the courthouse in this early-1900s photograph. The old Bolivar Hotel (left) and Wilkinson's Store (right) are visible in the background. The wrought-iron fence is visible in the foreground. (Courtesy Arthur Jr. and Esther Wheeler family.)

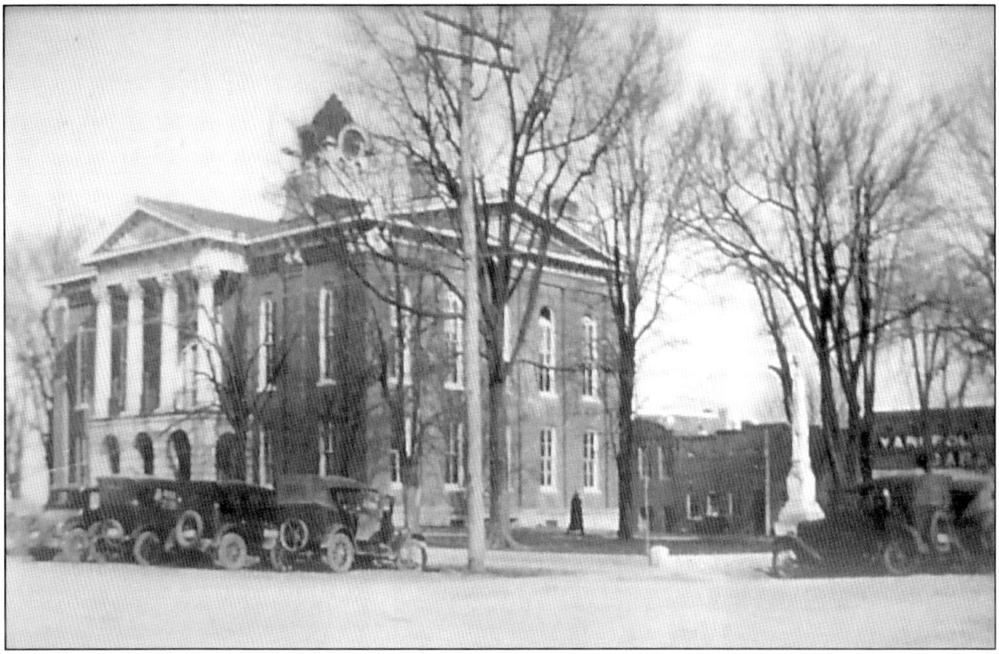

This late-1920s/early-1930s photograph shows the "new" technologies that became part of the court square scene—automobiles and electric power lines. The Confederate Monument is visible on the lawn on the courthouse. The court square has long served as a gathering place for county celebrations and remembrances. (Courtesy Hardeman County Chamber of Commerce.)

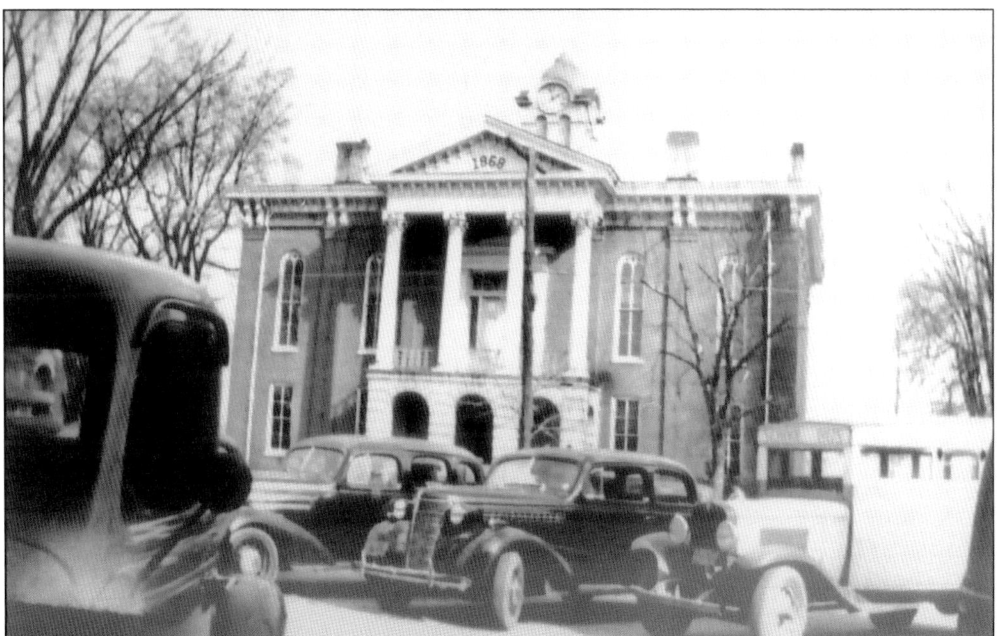

Judging by the number of cars (and even an old school bus) lining both sides of Main Street, this was a busy day on court square. The Main Street side of the courthouse, with the "1868" beneath the clock tower, is considered the "front" side of the building. (Courtesy Hardeman County Genealogical Society.)

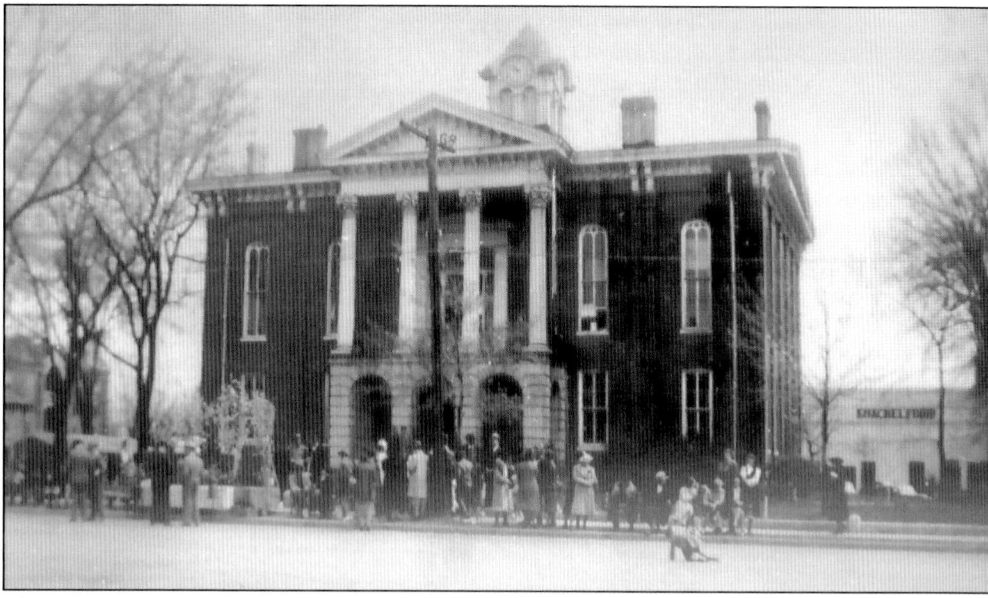

This 1940s photograph shows a different court square neighbor in the background at right—Shackelford Funeral Directors, located behind the courthouse on Warren Street. A group of men, women, and children gather on the courthouse lawn (and even in the street) on a busy day. Benches around the square provided a place for "local commentators" to express views—and to tell a story or two. (Courtesy Hardeman County Genealogical Society.)

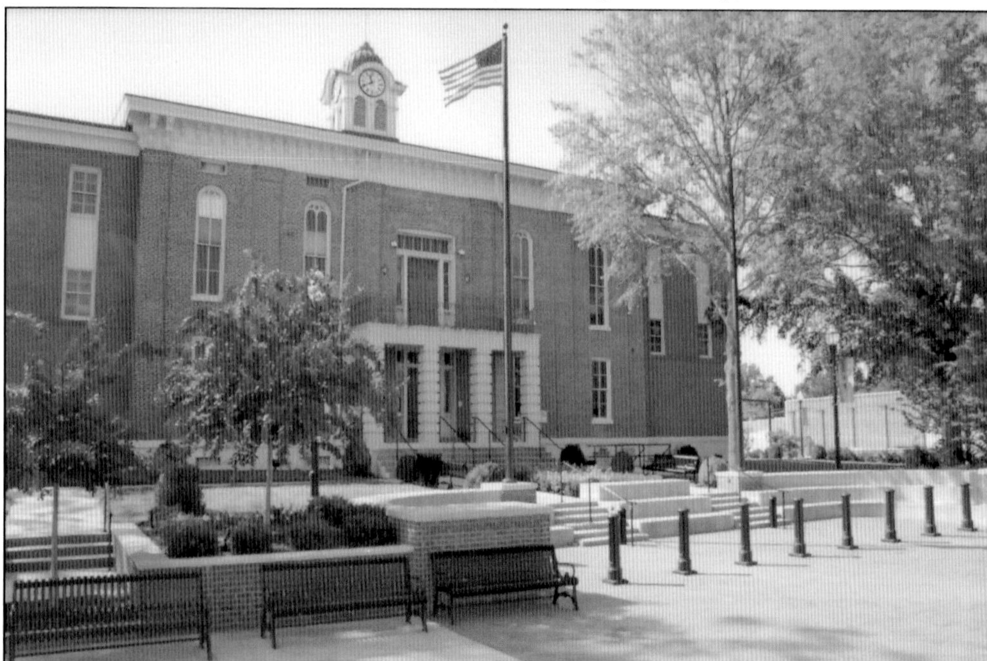

In the 1990s, Raymond Russell spent many hours disassembling, repairing, and reassembling the clock in the tower. An amphitheater added onto the back, or Warren Street, side of the building in 2008 has become a popular venue for live music on Tuesday, Friday, and Saturday nights. (Lisa C. Coleman.)

Three

School Days

Almost as soon as the early settlers came to Hardeman County, they began building schools. Edwin Crawford and Henry Thompson are credited as being among the county's first schoolteachers. Prior to 1873, there were several "academies" in the county: the Bolivar Male and Female Academies, the Lafayette Male and Female Academies, the Enon Academy, the New Castle Female Institute, and the Middleburg Male and Female Academies (there is some question as to whether Enon and Middleburg's academies were ever operated after being chartered).

In 1873, the state's first public schools came into existence, and Crainsville (now Hornsby) operated the first such school in the county under the tutelage of John W. Wilson. Another nine academies flourished until a second change was made to Tennessee state law in 1891. During the Civil War, many slaves joined the camps of the Union army, and in 1865, the Western Freedman's Aid Commission sent teachers for the children, establishing the first school programs for black children in the county.

A.G. Freed established the Freed School at Essary Springs in 1888. Freed, D.S. Nelms, and the community raised money to build and furnish the school. An advertising circular from 1892 boasted that the school had "already surpassed the expectations of its best friends. Over four hundred and fifty students from four states were enrolled in the last session. The prospects for the future are flattering in the extreme. High, dry, and healthy. Pure Air. A nice, quiet place four miles south of Pocahontas on the Memphis & Charleston R. R." The Freed School, later known as the Southern Tennessee Normal College, was the predecessor of Freed-Hardeman University, which continues to operate in Henderson, Tennessee.

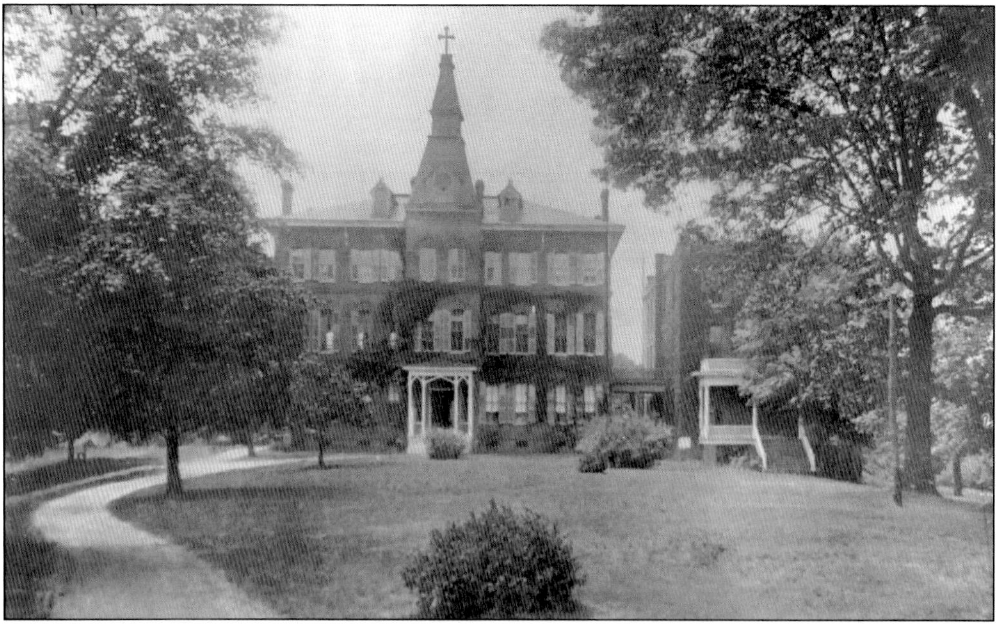

The Episcopal church built St. James School for Girls (later renamed St. Katherine's School for Girls) between 1872 and 1875 for approximately $10,000. The buildings were destroyed by fire on April 6, 1944. The 1916 graduating class of St. Katherine's included, from left to right below, Mary Bodkin of Memphis, Lane Winfrey of Somerville;, Evelyn Tate (Buchanan) of Bolivar, Cornelia McGehee of Como, Mississippi, and Jimmie Jacobs (Mitchell) of Bolivar. The class mascot (standing in front) was Christine Wright of Bolivar. An oft-told story about this class is that another young lady did not stick around for the photograph, instead choosing to slip out of a window and elope with a young suitor! (Above, courtesy Louise McAnulty Manhein; below, courtesy Hardeman County Chamber of Commerce.)

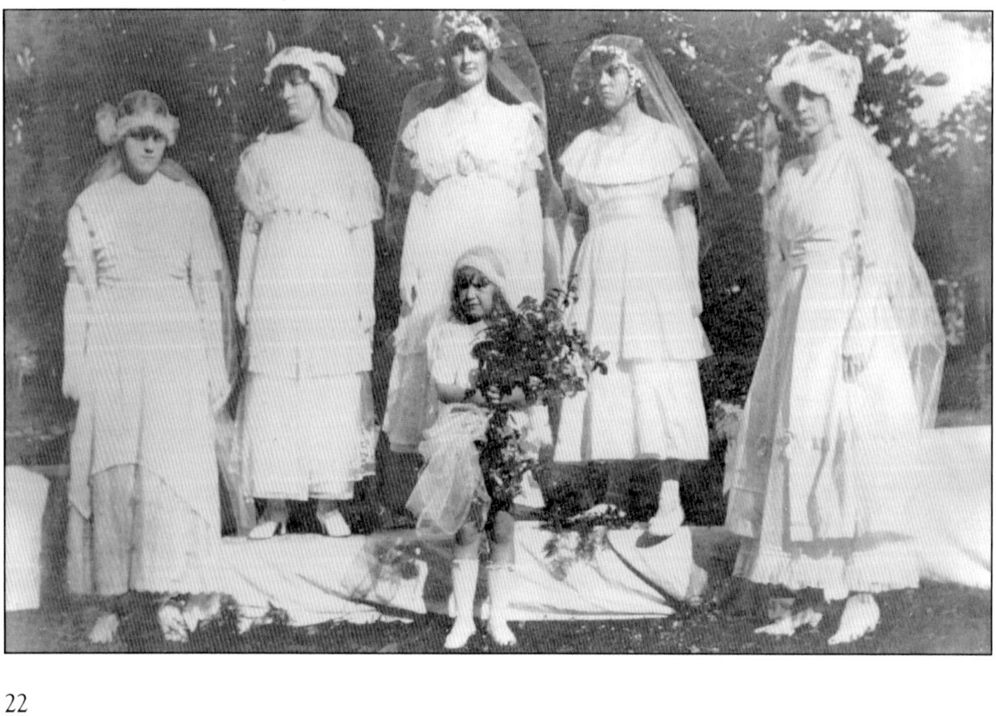

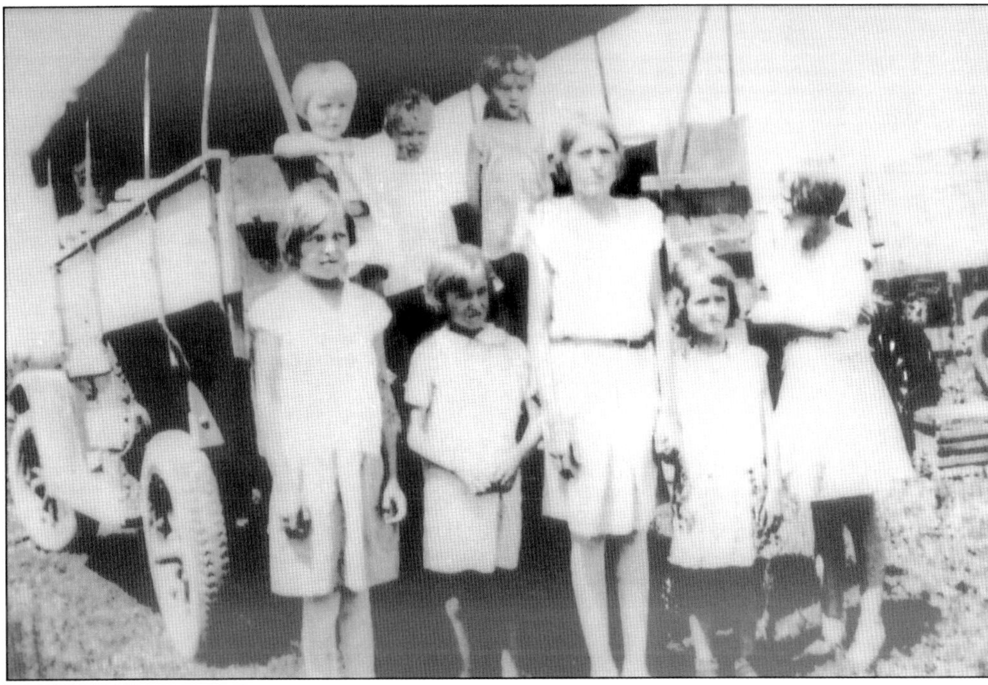

Transportation was often a problem for students, and around 1925, parents pooled their resources to begin subscription transportation services in the county. Wagons served as the first "buses," but by 1928, this group of Toone schoolchildren was traveling in a more modern form of transportation. (Courtesy Hardeman County Genealogical Society.)

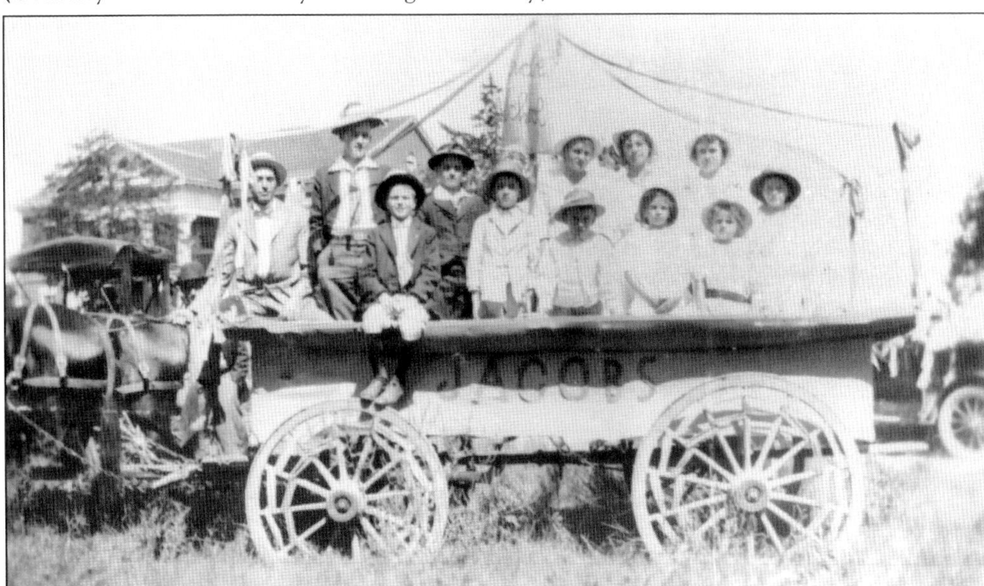

Although numbers vary, from the late 1920s through the mid-1930s, there were more than 80 schools in the county; many were one- and two-teacher schools held in churches, small one- or two-room schoolhouses, or even vacant buildings. This group of students from the Flatt Plains School displayed school pride on a float for an early May Day parade. (Courtesy Hardeman County Genealogical Society.)

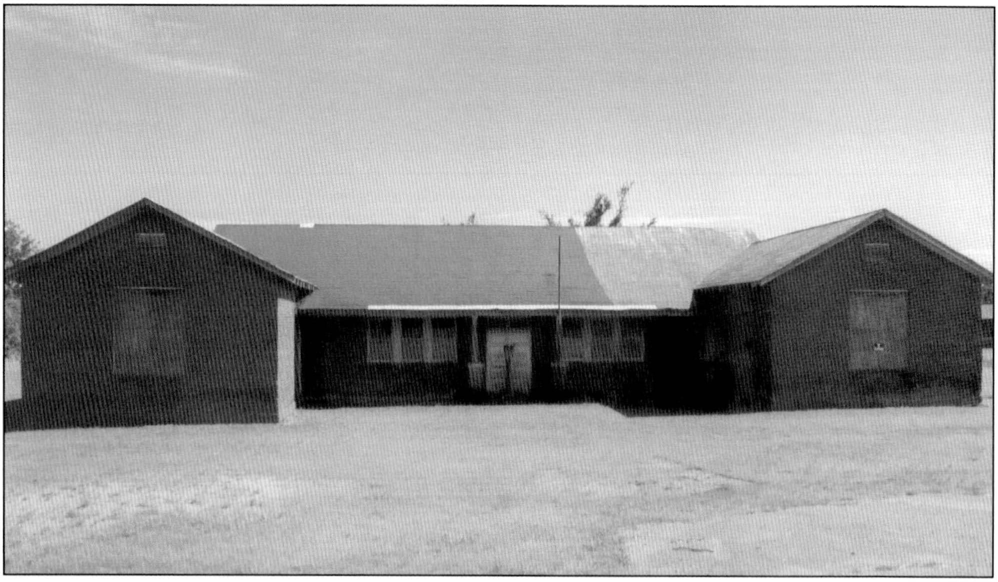

Many students have fond memories of the old Pocahontas School (above), including Lee McAlpin (below) and classmate Josephine McClintock Brewer-McGee, who remembers, "We started each day with the Lord's Prayer and the Pledge of Allegiance. I remember I never saw Lee until he got up each day to empty the pencil trimmer into the wastebasket. I thought that nobody else but Lee knew how to empty that trimmer! Trips to the outside toilet always took longer when the weather was pretty. The trips in the wintertime were cut shorter because the wind would be whipping around the corners of the schoolhouse. I cherish the years I spent learning at Pocahontas Grammar School, and all the friends I made the years I was there." (Above, Lisa C. Coleman; below, courtesy Esta Lee Lamberth.)

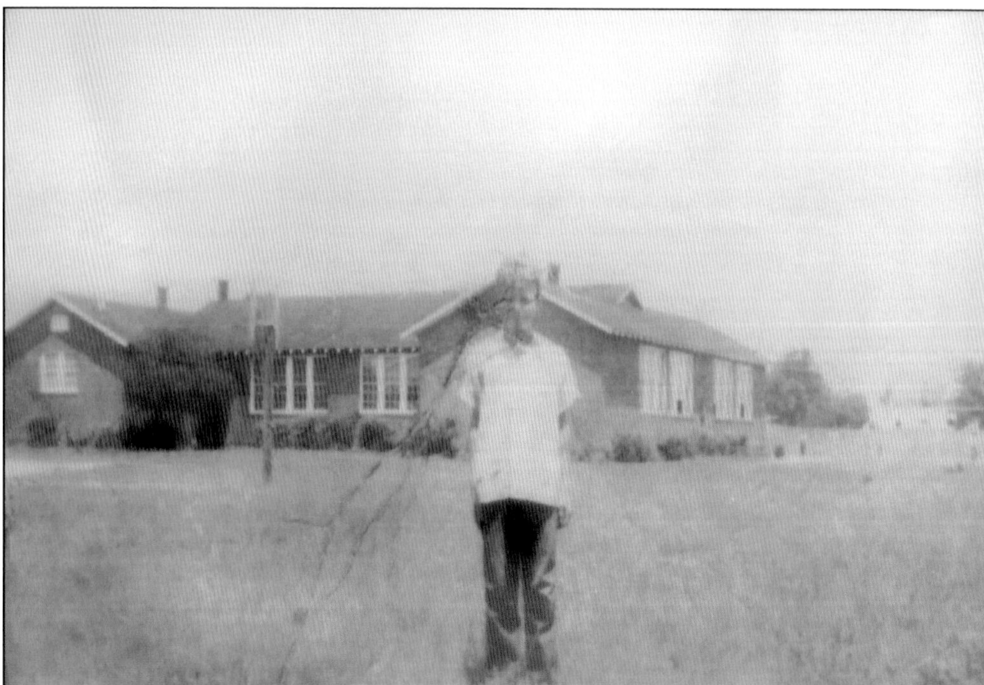

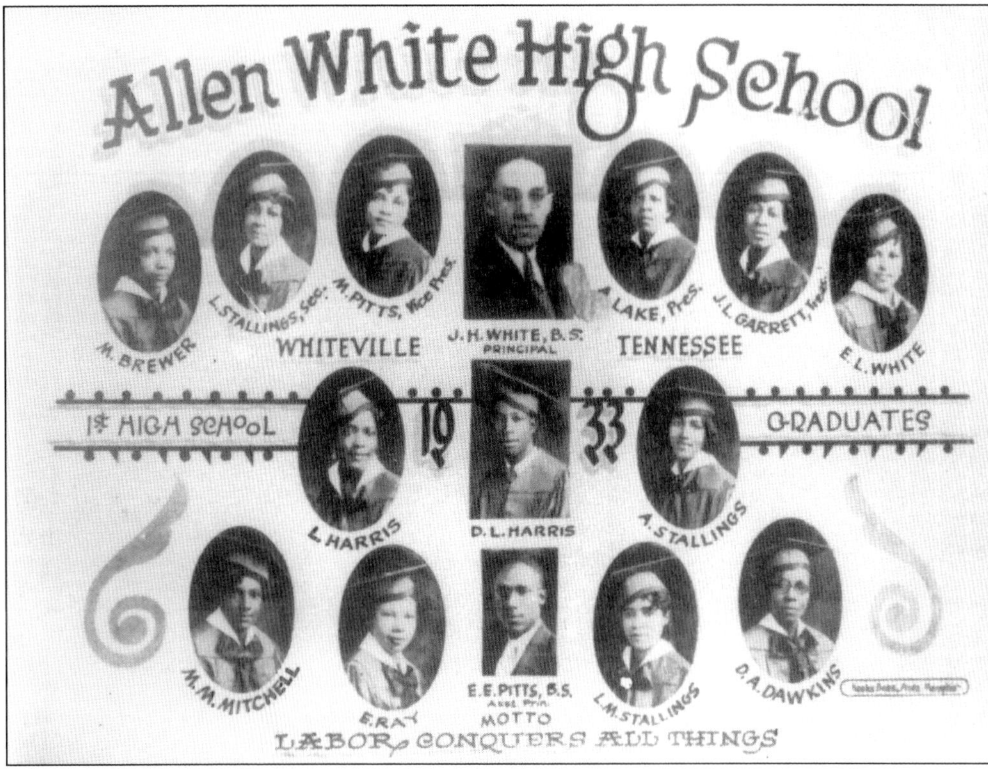

Allen White High School's first graduates (above) completed their studies in 1933. Pictured are, from left to right, (top row) M. Brewer, secretary L. Stallings, vice president M. Pitts, principal J.H. White, president A. Lake, treasurer J. Garrett, and E.L. White; (middle row) L. Harris, D.L. Harris, and A. Stallings; (bottom row) M.M. Mitchell, E. Ray, assistant principal E.E. Pitts, L.M. Stallings, and D.A. Dawkins. In 1970, the last class (below) graduated 31 students. That year, M.A. Jarrett was the principal, E.C. Robertson was the assistant principal, and Clay F. Morrow was the president. The school closed because of the integration of Hardeman County School System. (Above, courtesy Evelyn Robertson Jr.; below, courtesy Curtistine O. Gatlin.)

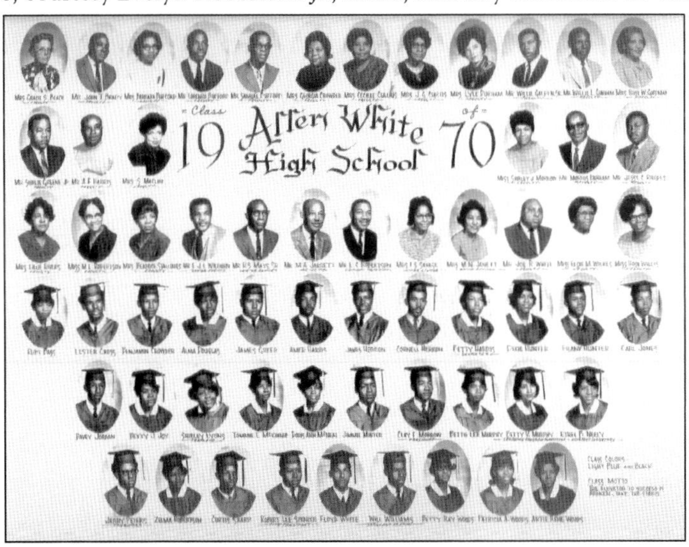

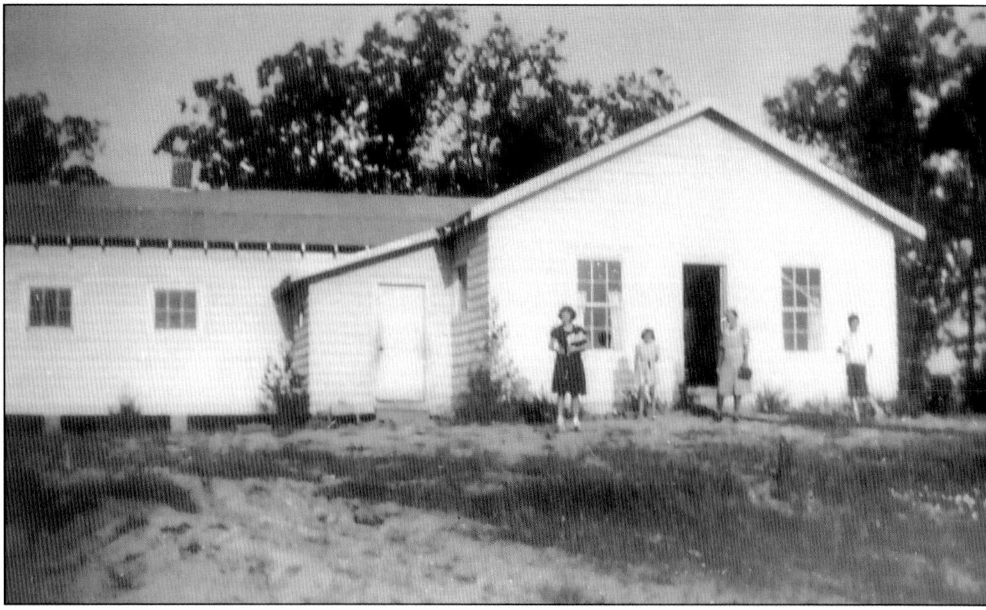

By 1928, these children were students in the old Ebeneezer School building. At a reunion in 1984, former students and teachers remembered the large pot-bellied stove in one of the rooms and reminisced about reciting scripture verses and learning to do "figures" in their heads. Teachers at the school included J. Simon Smith, Elta Dorris, Ruth Holmes Powell, Mary Matthews Pulliam, Ester Doyle Burkeen, Mildred Ross Mitchell, Nelle Holloway Buford, Louise Ross Hanna, Mary Pulse Vaughan, and Willie Margaret Johnson. (Both, courtesy Hardeman County Genealogical Society.)

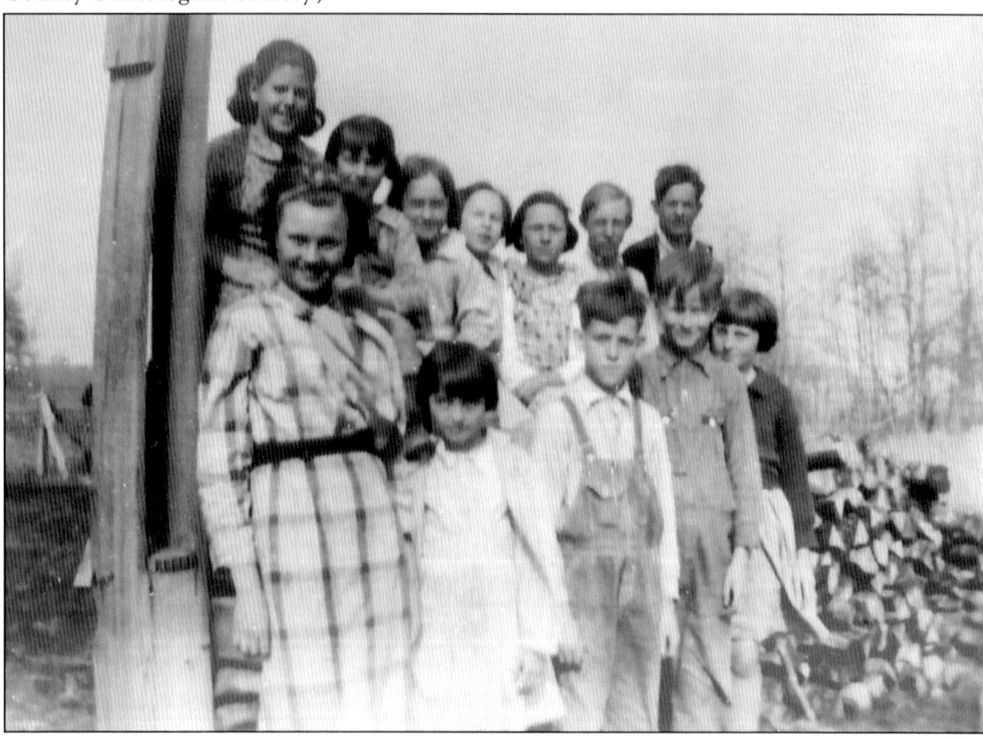

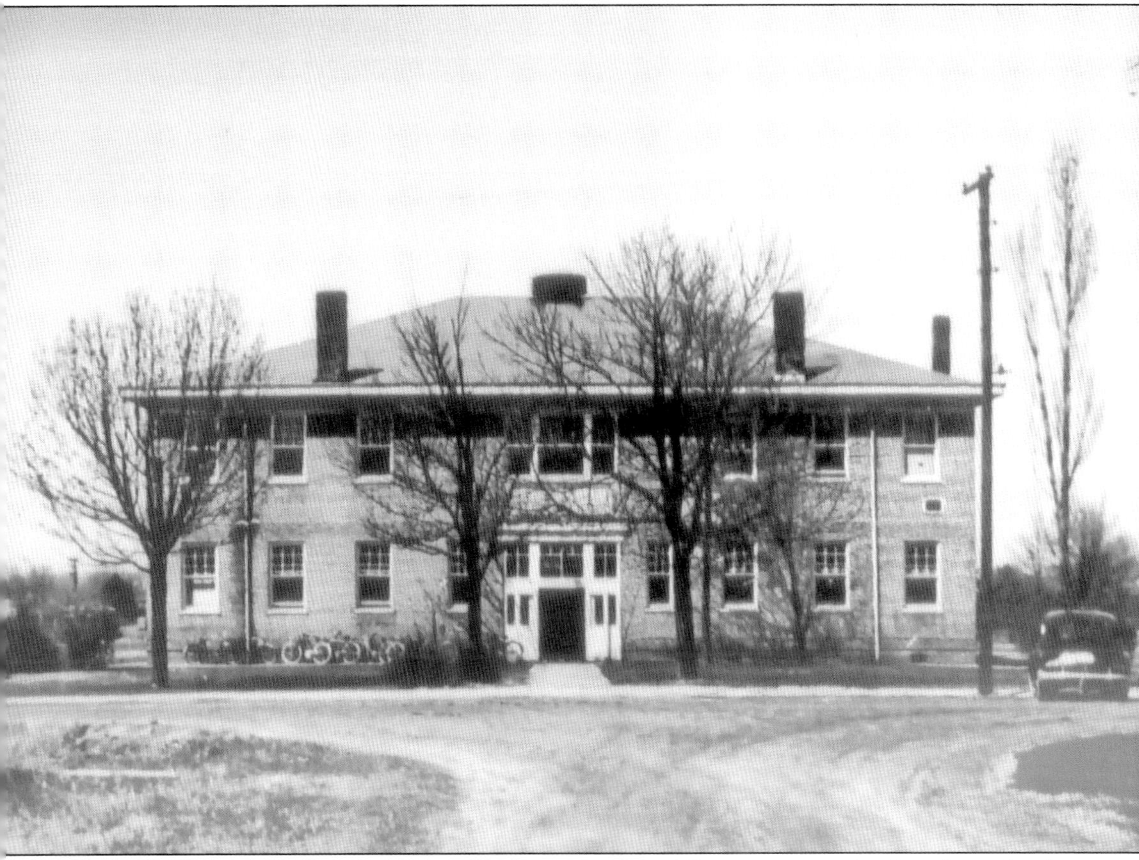

Although there were several private schools in the Grand Junction area, the first free school was not opened until 1898. Enrollment grew to 125 students, with three faculty members. In 1915, the townspeople constructed a new, nine-room brick building funded with $10,000 in bonds issued by the town. The school awarded its first diploma in 1921; this photograph shows Grand Junction High School around 1930. During World War II, several faculty members were called up to military service and local pastors stepped in to teach students and help keep the school open. Grand Junction High School closed in 1972. (Courtesy Hardeman County Genealogical Society.)

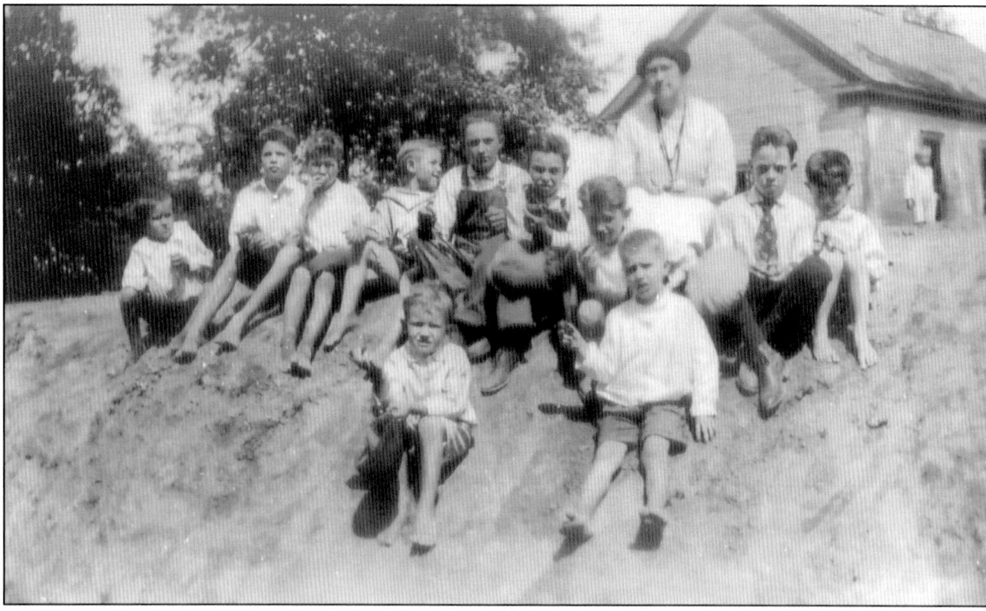

Christine Kelley was an early Hardeman County teacher who spent much of her career teaching in schools all over the county during school terms, which varied from one or two up to five months. Kelley is shown at an unidentified school with several young scholars, enjoying a few minutes of recess. (Courtesy Hardeman County Genealogical Society.)

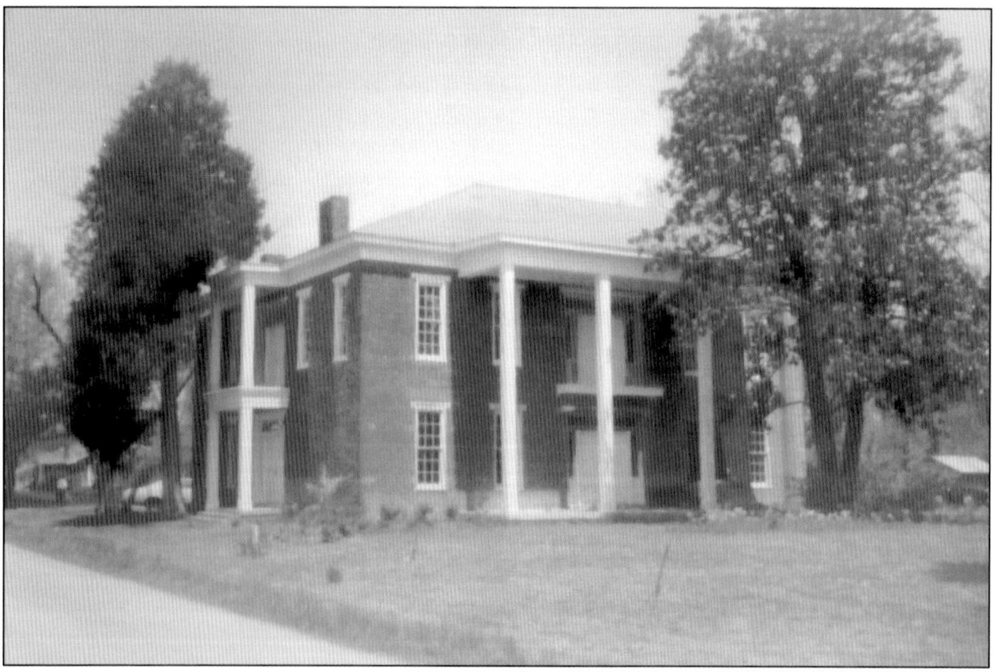

One girls' finishing school in Hardeman County was located in Pocahontas, at the Joyner-Carr house. Young women from West Tennessee and North Mississippi attended to learn how to be "proper young ladies." The great-grandmother of Pres. Bill Clinton, Frances Ellen Hines (Blythe), originally from Tippah County, Mississippi, attended the school as a young girl. (Courtesy Esta Lee Lamberth.)

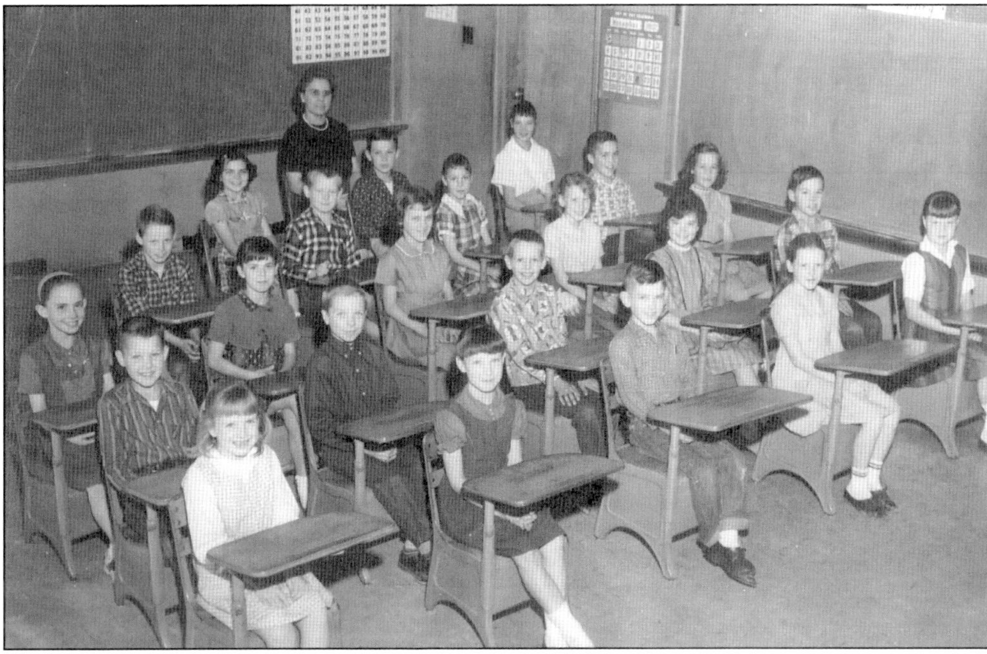

This picture shows a class of third and fourth graders at Hornsby School in 1962. Pictured are, from left to right, (front row) Debby Vandiver, Helen Diane Freeman, Jeff Young, Martha Frances Wiggins, and Charlotte Whitman; (second row) Dennis Barnes, Junior Wiggins, Daniel ?, Susan McClure, and William Wilson; (third row) Diane ?, unidentified, Debbie Hodge, Janette Tigner, and Patsy Hooper; (fourth row) unidentified, Mike Parsons, Sharon Mathis, and Tommy Cox; (fifth row) Betty Ervin, Terry Mayfield, and Linda Mathis. Seated in the back is the teacher, Louise McClintock. (Courtesy Janette Tigner.)

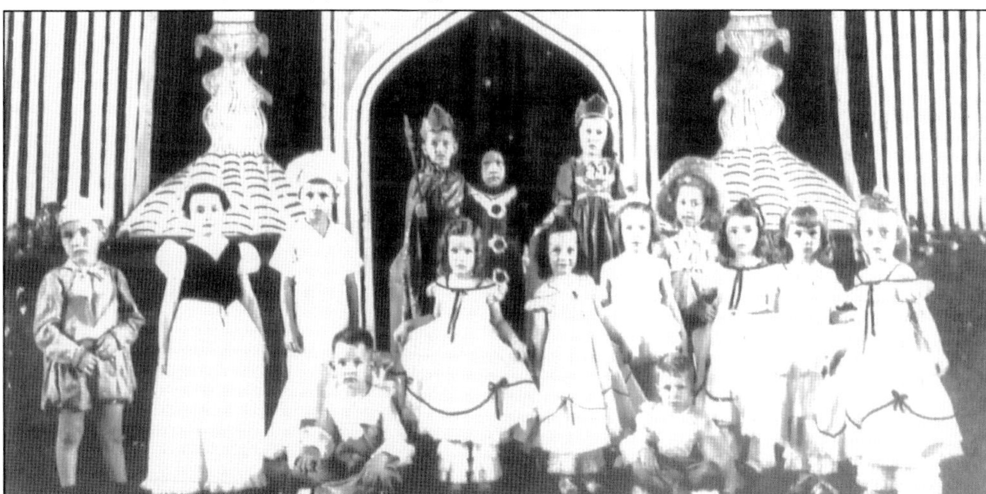

A performance of *The Gingerbread Boy* was part of the kindergarten graduation activities in Miss Elizabeth Ingram's School of Childhood in Bolivar in 1944. Pictured from left to right are (first row, seated) Lee Porter Butler and Eddie Hazlegrove; (second row) Don Alphin, Sandra Williams, James Armour, Ewlene Harris, Eva Lynn Newton, Donna Vaughan, Nancy Whitehurst, Joyce Brint, Nancy Orr, and Jane Kirksey; (third row) Marion Creekmore Jr., Don Shackelford, and Carolyn Smith. (Courtesy Hardeman County Genealogical Society.)

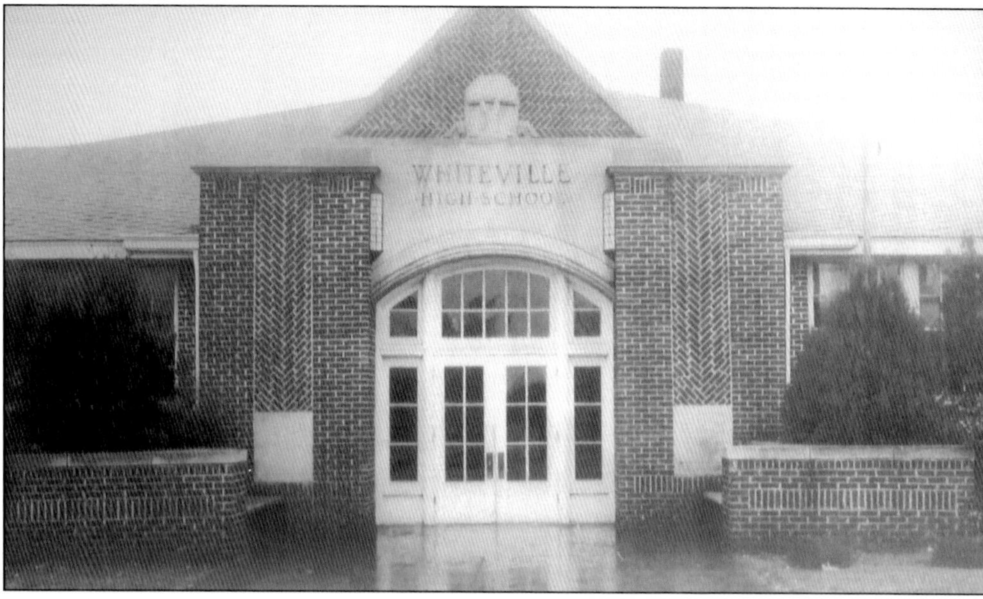

Whiteville High School was built in 1932 (after a fire destroyed the old school) and operated as a high school until 1970, when grades nine through twelve were bused to Bolivar and the old school became Southside Elementary School. In 1979, a fire destroyed almost all of this building; today, the facade and cornerstone are located at the Lee Ola Roberts Library in Whiteville. (Courtesy Bettye H. Perry.)

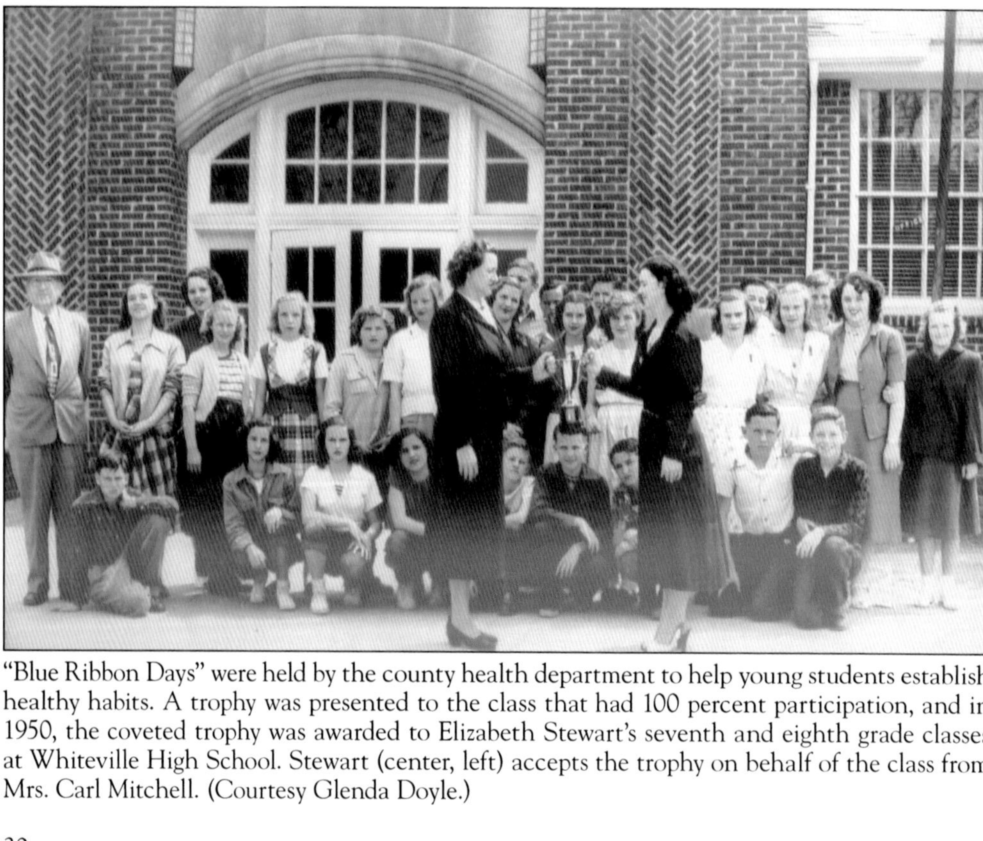

"Blue Ribbon Days" were held by the county health department to help young students establish healthy habits. A trophy was presented to the class that had 100 percent participation, and in 1950, the coveted trophy was awarded to Elizabeth Stewart's seventh and eighth grade classes at Whiteville High School. Stewart (center, left) accepts the trophy on behalf of the class from Mrs. Carl Mitchell. (Courtesy Glenda Doyle.)

"Tom Thumb weddings" were popular for many years, and Hardeman County hosted its share of these, usually as fundraisers. The bride and groom at the 1928 Whiteville Tom Thumb wedding pictured at right were William Thomas Hazelwood and Elizabeth Ann Gibson. Below, a 1940s Tom Thumb wedding in Bolivar included, from left to right, (first row) ? Keller, Jane Vaughan, Gerald Granger, Ann Vaughan, and Gaither Smith; (second row) unidentified, Winston Doyle, Billy Joe Majors, Mike Inlow, Emily Weiland, Beth Carter Bradley, Beverly Emerson, Frances Ann Harris, Dewey C. Whitenton, and J.C. Jordan; (third row) Gwendolyn Doyle, Charles Frost, Clara Hanna, Billy Keller, Betty Lou Clifft, unidentified, Lelah Ann Gee, J. Hall Brooks, Mary Frances Young, Forest Shearon, Lucy Patrick, Katharine Black, Max Massengill, Joanne Warren, David Adams, and unidentified. (Right, courtesy Bettye H. Perry; below, courtesy Frances Ann Scott.)

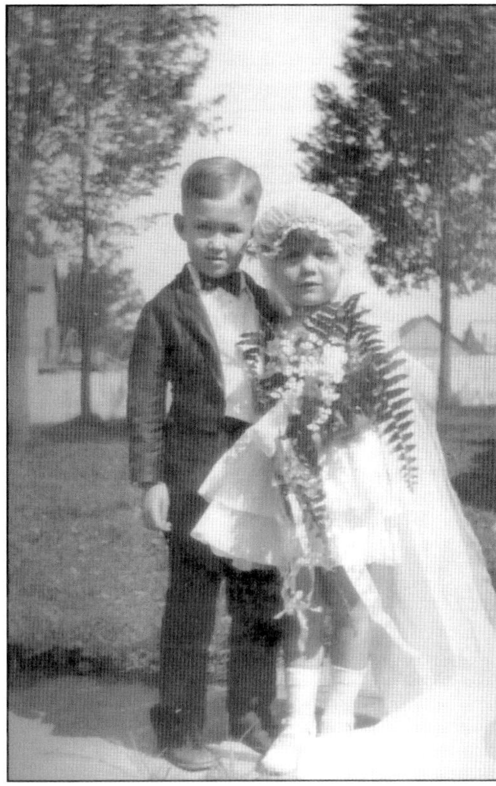

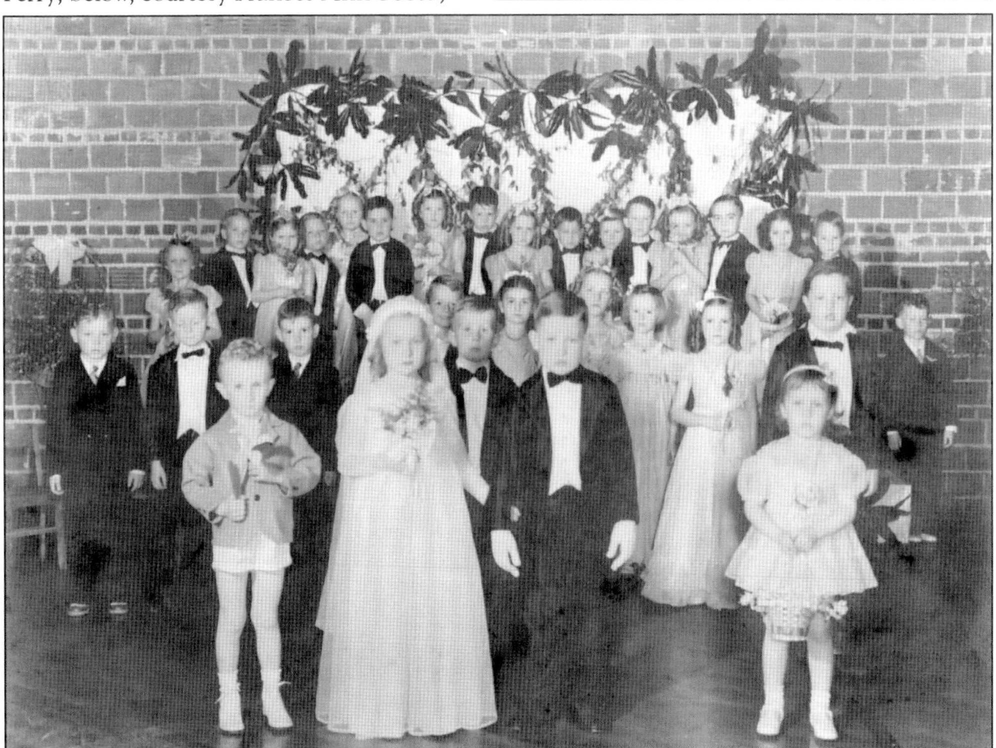

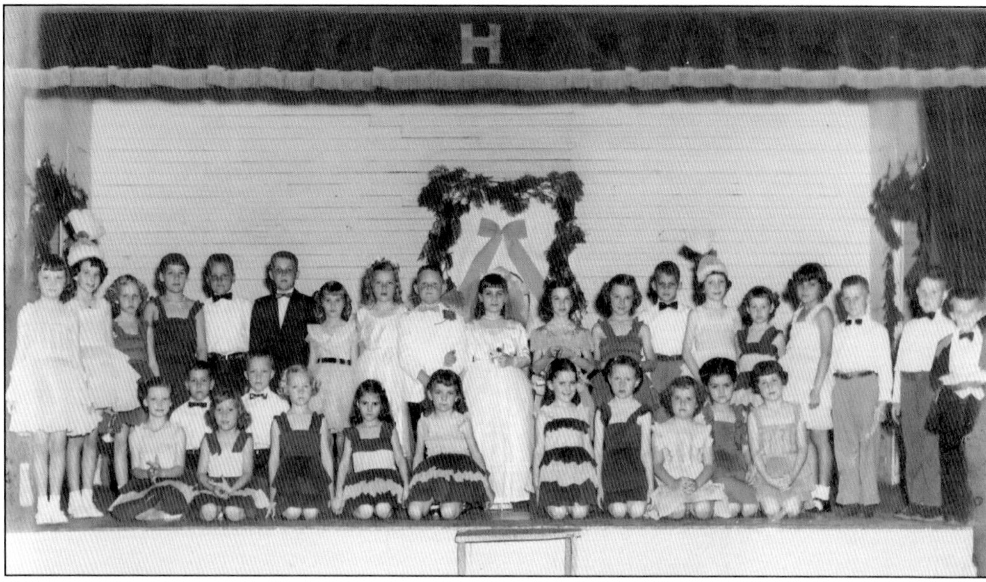

A 1950s "wedding play" at Hornsby School included, from left to right: (first row, kneeling) Gaylon Cox, Doug Jernigan, Carol Starnes, unidentified, Leatha Doles, Carolyn Hawthorne, Linda Wiggins, Virginia Doles, Janet Baker, Terry Ervin, Pat Willoughby, and unidentified; (second row, standing) Ruth Ann Pierce, Tommie DeBerry, Shirley Tigner, Brenda Vaughan, Ray Whitloe, Joseph Johnson, Wanda Derryberry, Carolyn Baker, Ricky Chandler, Rita Baker, Judy Crowley, Betty Kirk, Ronnie DeBerry, Pamela Talley, ? Doles, Kathy Morris, Bill Linam, Russell DeBerry, and Lynn Morris. (Courtesy Pat Murphy.)

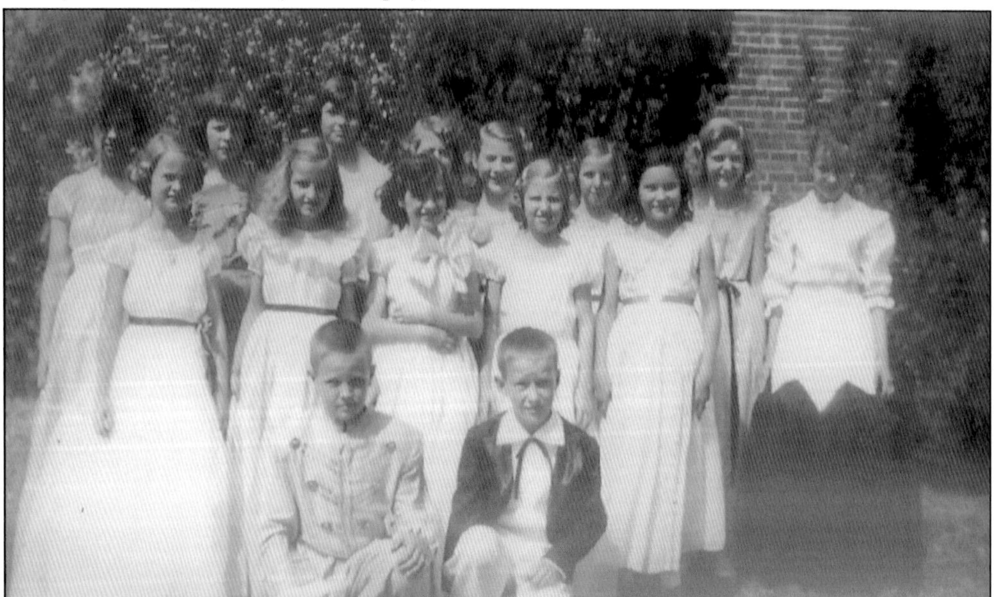

Cinderella made an appearance at the Grand Junction School during the 1954–1955 school year in the form of a play starring, from left to right, (first row) Charlie Bryan and Jim Nunally; (second row) Lynn Parham, unidentified, Billie Jean Drew, Ann Brown, and Gerald Vickers; (third row) Carolyn McKinnie, Jane Maclin, Marianne Strub, Linda Dunn, Betty Nunnally, Margaret Brown, Kaye Yager, and Joanne Drew. (Courtesy Jane Maclin Moore.)

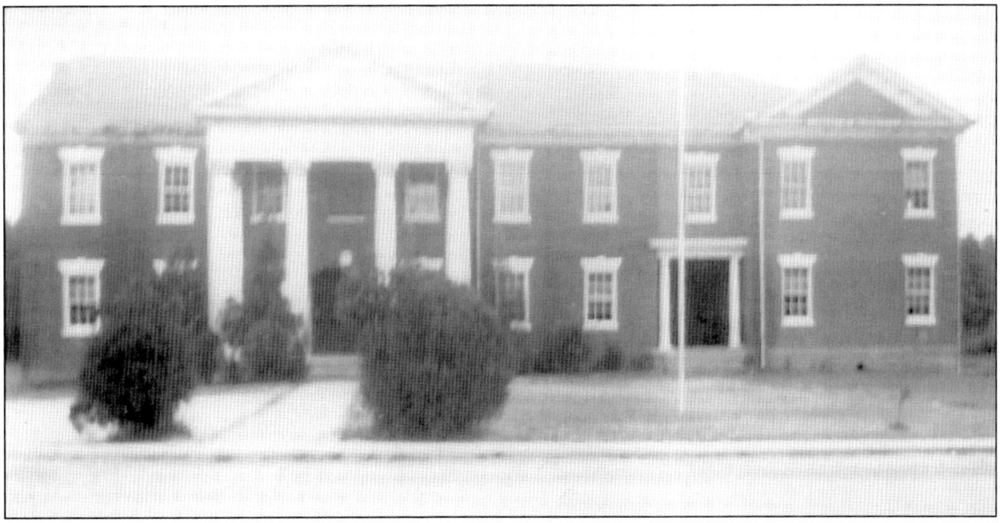

The old Bolivar school was built in 1899 and served grades one through twelve until it was replaced with a new school in 1950. That year, the high school students began the year at the old school, and when classes resumed after the cotton-picking season, they went to the new school. The class of 1951 was the first to graduate from this building. (Lisa C. Coleman.)

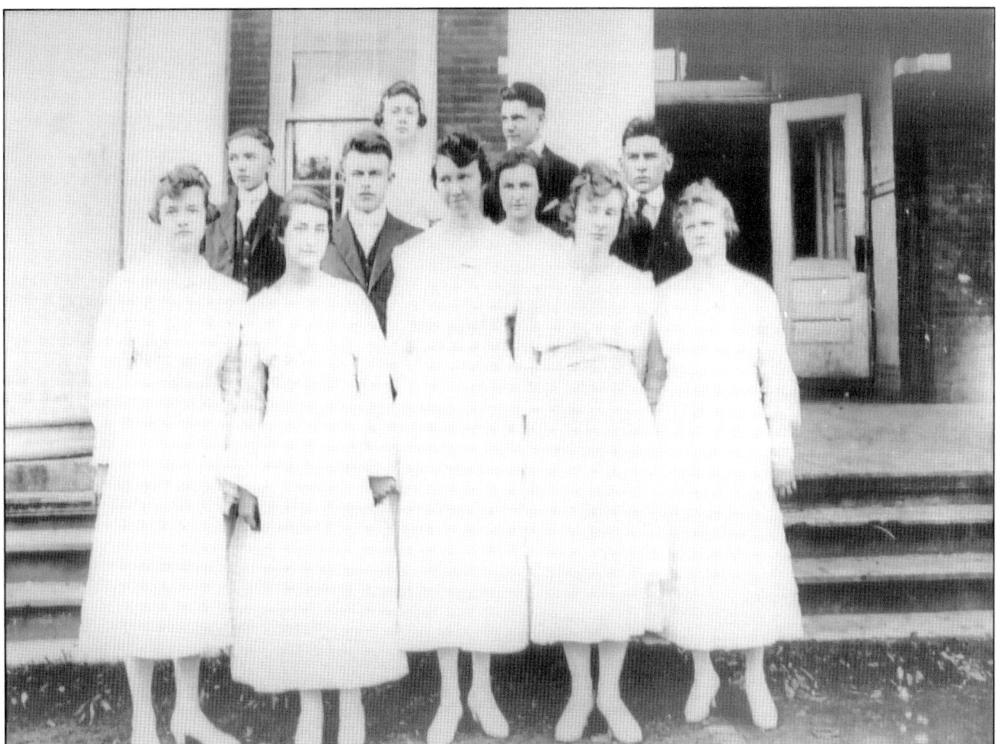

These students in Bolivar High School's graduating class of 1919 are believed to be the first to graduate from one of the county's public high schools. Pictured from left to right are (first row) Charlene Harris, Estelle Keller, Mattie Harris, Margaret Thomas, and Clayte Harris; (second row) Earl Dorris, J. Simon Smith, Nancy Morrow, and John Reaves Stroupe; (third row) Ollie Mae Fish and Robert Boyd Cox. (Courtesy Hardeman County Genealogical Society.)

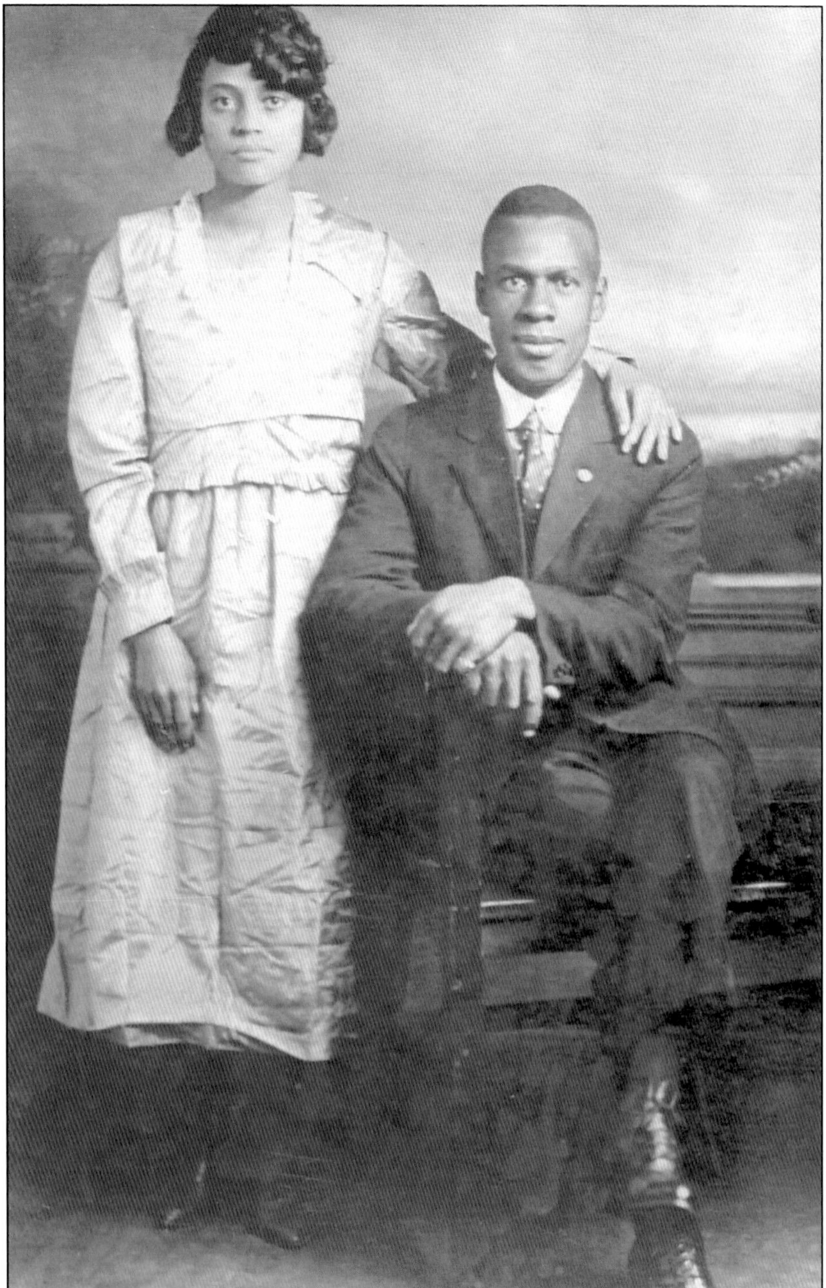

Jeff McKinnie Sr. (1895–1979) was born and raised in Hickory Valley. He attended Rust College and, later, graduated from Lane College. All six of his children had either finished their college degrees or were in college at the time their father completed his college education. He and his wife, Rachel, also a graduate of Lane College, were teachers in the Hardeman County school system for over 40 years. Jeff was a veteran of World War I, served as a deacon in the Mayes Hill and Springfield Baptist Churches, and was a 32nd degree Mason. Rachel was a member of the Eastern Star, and they were both active in many church activities. This family, with roots in slavery, has produced educators, soldiers, nurses, lawyers, and entrepreneurs. (Courtesy Audrey McKinnie.)

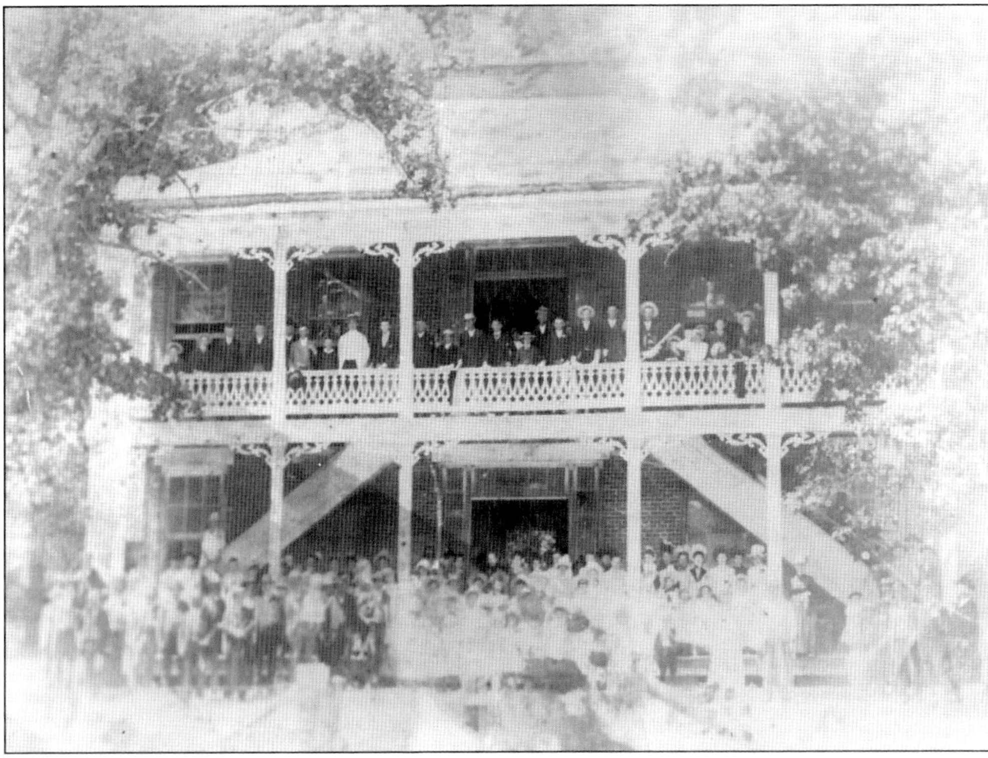

One of the best-loved schools in the Saulsbury area was the old Woodland Academy, known for many years as "one of the best and most useful of its kind." It was established by Hugh Gwynn in 1857 about one mile west of Saulsbury. Fred M. Malone was the school's first principal. Until 1900, this academy welcomed and trained young men and women from the surrounding countryside. Dr. F.H. Malone (right) was a teacher at Woodland Academy for many years. Dr. Malone later left Hardeman County to serve as a doctor in Caperville, Tennessee. (Both, courtesy Cissye Pierce.)

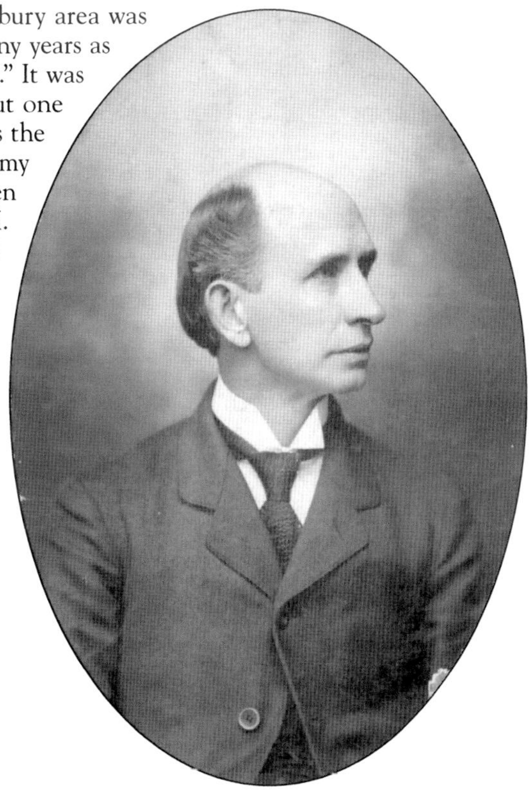

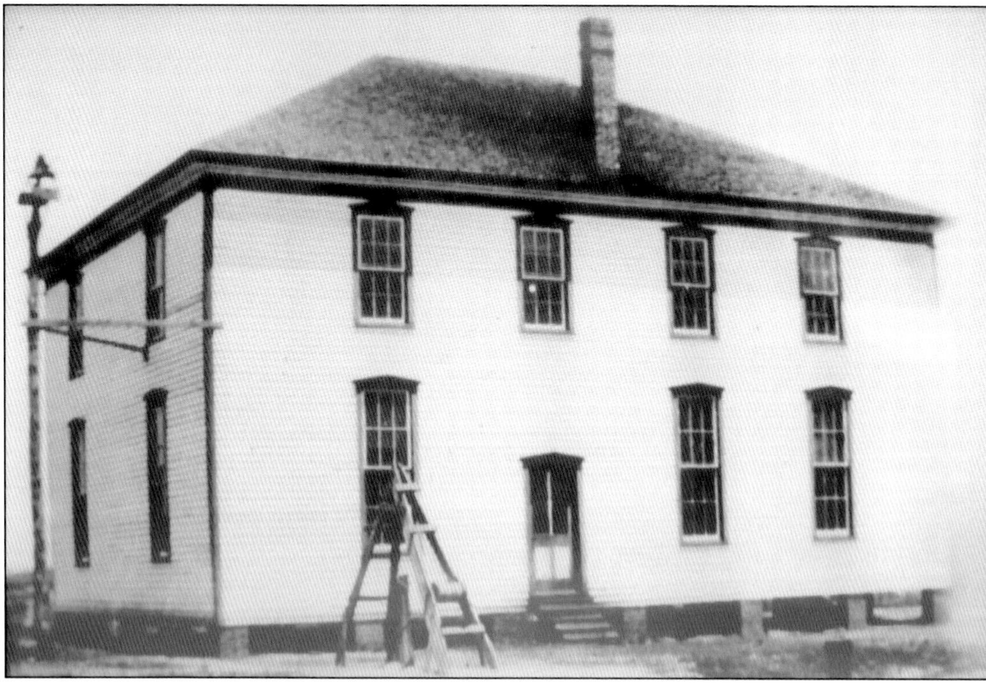

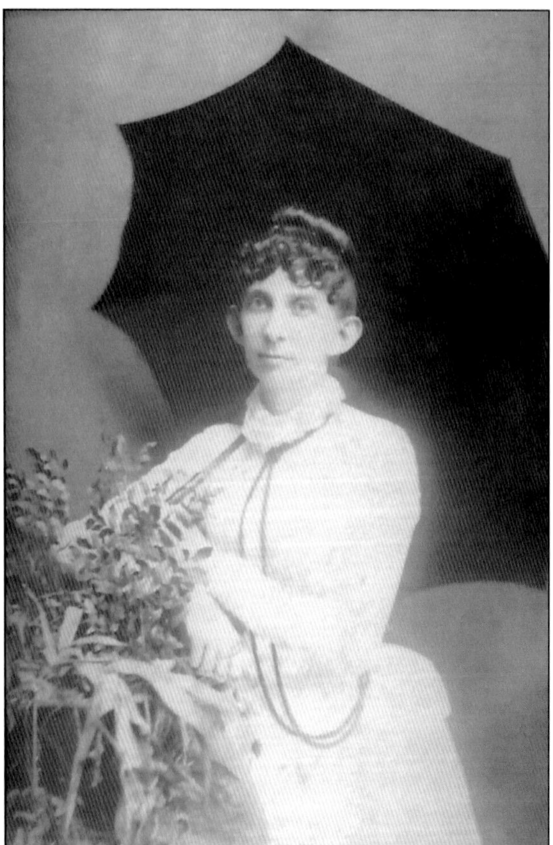

This building, originally the community church, was located in the northern section of the town, facing the railroad, and eventually became the Hickory Valley School (which operated from the 1870s until around 1900). When the building became the public school, Dr. Pat McKinnie served as its principal. The old well is visible in this photograph. (Courtesy Hardeman County Genealogical Society.)

Fannie Norment was one of the county's early teachers. She boarded with the David W. McAnulty family while teaching in Hickory Valley, a common practice at the time. In the winter of 1889, Norment helped nurse area children who had typhoid fever. She later taught at Black's Academy, near Bolivar. (Courtesy Hardeman County Genealogical Society.)

Four

Time for Church

Early settlers in Hardeman County founded churches almost as soon as they moved into the area. "Camp meetings" were held in the area as early as 1824, and by 1830, citizens had organized the Methodist Episcopal Church in Bolivar, which was on the preaching circuit by 1837.

Rev. Daniel Stephens arrived in Bolivar in 1833 with an idea to establish a congregation in Bolivar and realized his dream when the Saint James Parish was organized in April 1834. Vestrymen appointed to serve were William B. Turley, James J. Williams, W.H. Wood, David T. Brown, Thomas C. Jones, Calvin Jones, John Houston Bills, Pitser Miller, Allen Hill, and W.W. Bomer. One of the most loved and respected ministers to preach at Mount Comfort (near Hickory Valley) was Robert A. Moorman, who came to the area around 1827 and attended to the spiritual and physical needs of those who settled in this part of the country as both a minister and physician.

One of the early influences of the Baptist faith in this area of West Tennessee was a preacher named Obadiah Dodson. He preached throughout West Tennessee and helped to establish the Big Hatchie Association, and was instrumental in establishing churches at Middleburg and Clover Creek. No photographs or sketches have been found of this tireless and influential minister of the Gospel, who later left Tennessee and founded the Louisiana Baptist Convention.

The first church in the county for African Americans was Union Church, located in a brush arbor near Bolivar; Baptist and Methodists alternated hosting services there. In 1866, Piney Grove Baptist Church had 65 members, and Mount Salem Missionary Baptist Church was organized by 1868. All of these churches—and many more today—continue the spiritual legacy of the early founders.

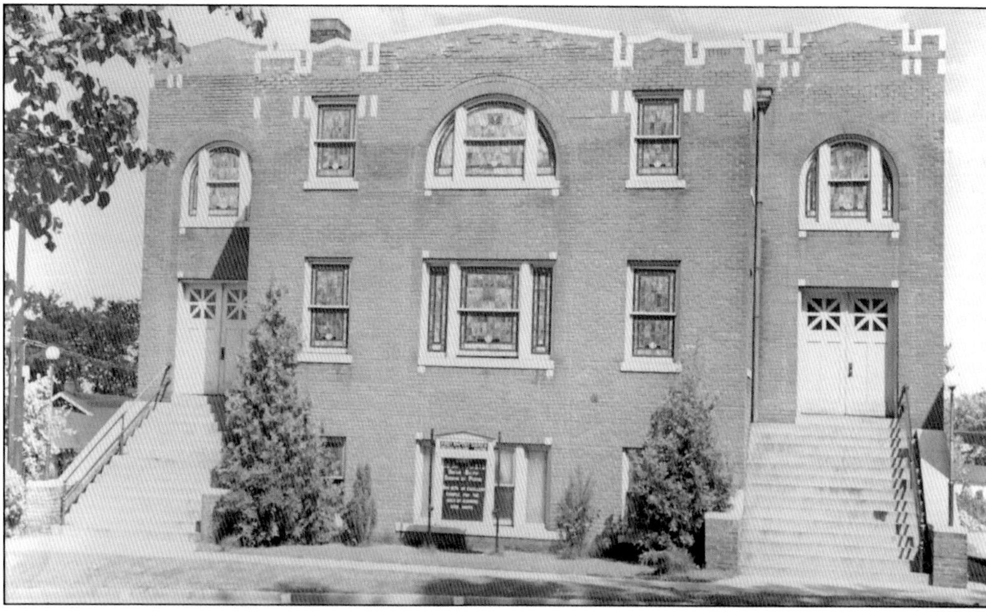

First Baptist Church of Bolivar's first deed was recorded in 1837 for a lot at the corner of Jackson and Water Streets, and it remained in this location until a move to West Market Street in 1961. The Sunday sermon title in this photograph is: "Man Sets an Excellent Example for the Child by Acquiring Good Habits." One of the first vacation bible schools (VBS) in Hardeman County was held here about 1922. Below, a VBS group is pictured sometime between 1949 and 1952. Rev. W.R. Woodell, the pastor at the time, is pictured at the top of the steps in the center of the doorway. The church continues its VBS tradition each summer. (Above, courtesy Arthur Jr. and Esther Wheeler family; below, courtesy Pat Vincent.)

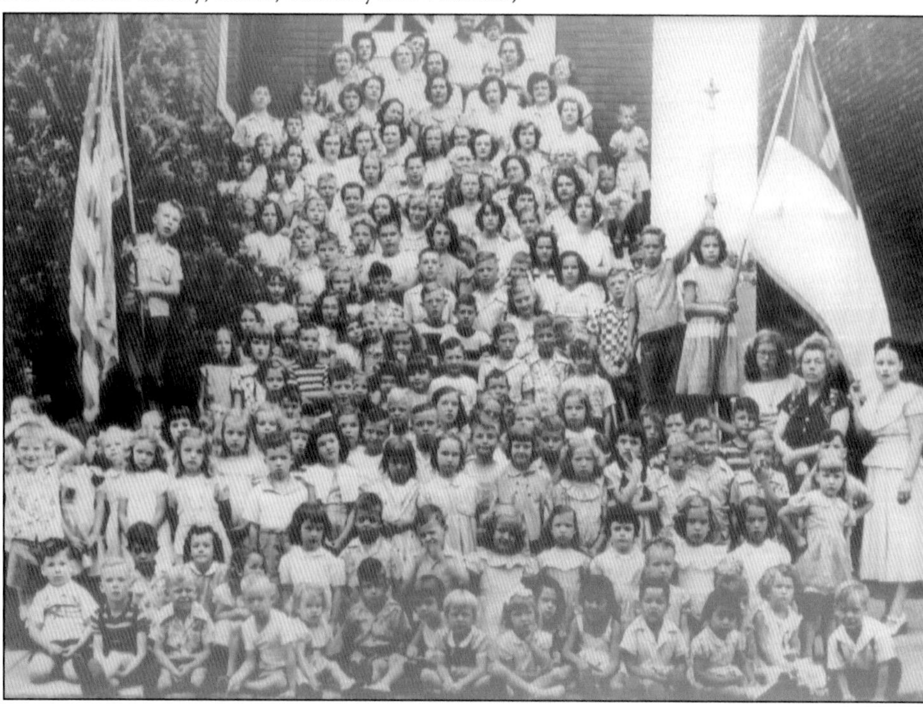

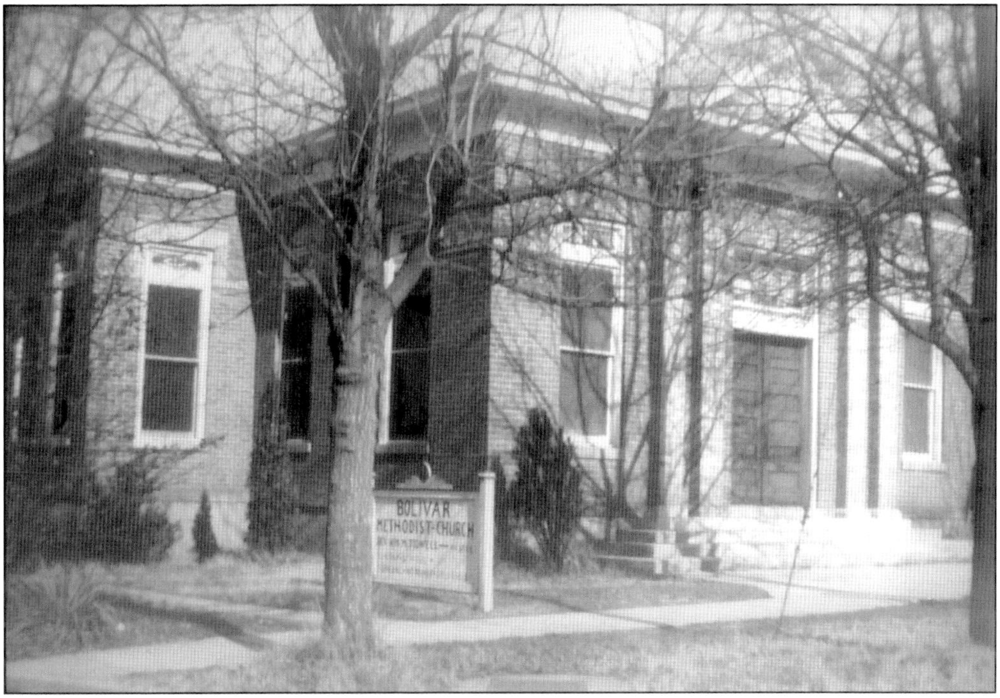

The first Methodist church in Bolivar was located on Market Street and was used as a hospital during the Civil War; its church registers and building were lost in the fire of 1864, but members rebuilt after the war. Pictured below on the steps of the old Bolivar Methodist Church are, from left to right, (first row) George Carter, John L. Roach, Mack Frost, and Will Cobb; (second row) Vernon Carter Jr., Ellis Deming, Edwin Cocke Jr., Bonds Frost, Billie Daniel, and Keylon Barrett; (third row) Lawrence May, Hunter May, Jack Stevens Brown, Woodson Savage Jr., unidentified, Mack Frost, and Tom Ryan Prewitt. (Both, courtesy Anna Laura Bledsoe.)

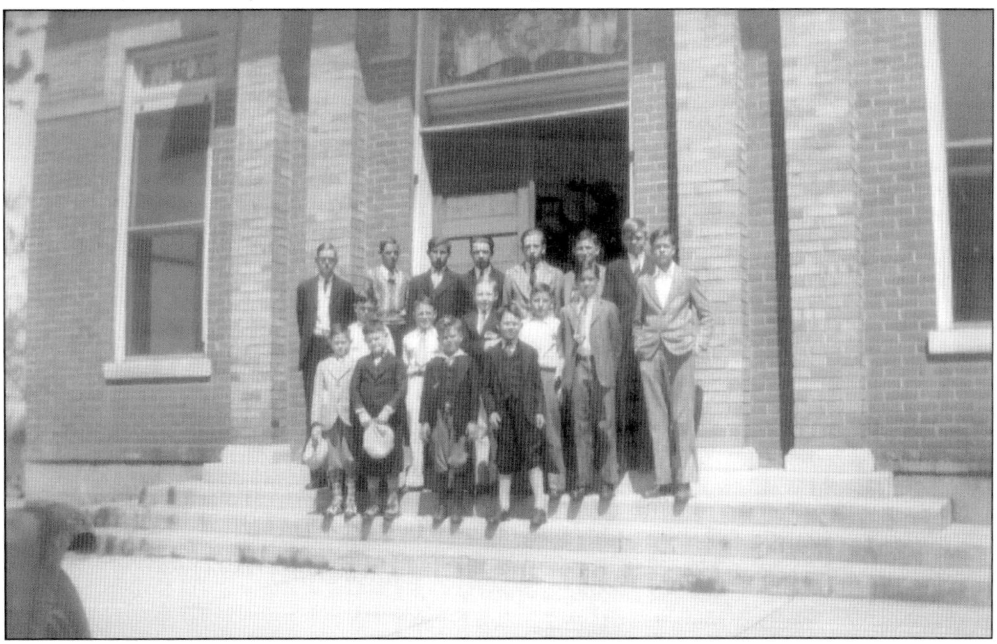

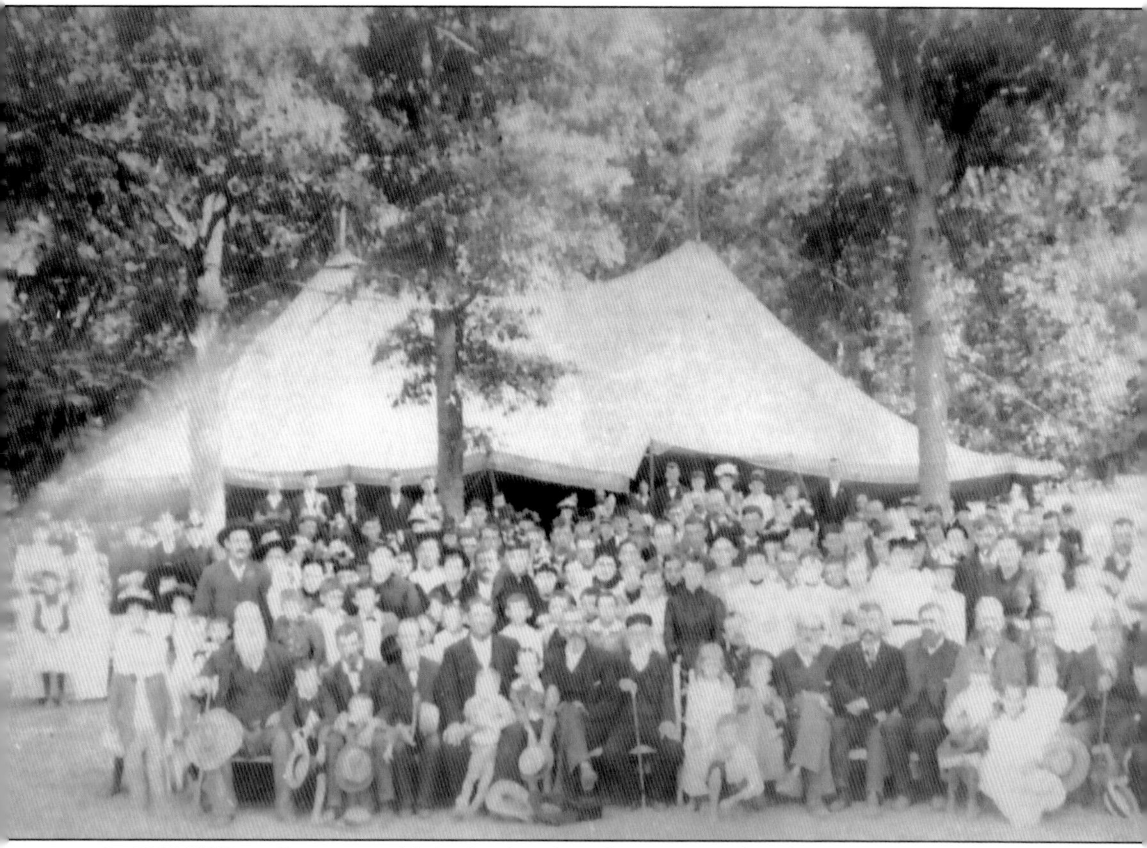

In 1827, William Barnett established a church and campground in the Mount Comfort area (near present-day Hickory Valley). Barnett was an ordained Cumberland Presbyterian minister who reportedly preached sermons of such power that his audiences trembled under the influence of his overwhelming appeal. He died during a revival camp meeting in 1828. The summer camp meetings continued to be popular for many years; the Bush Camp Ground hosted this meeting in 1891, with Rev. W.H. "Wild Bill" Evans spreading the word to the faithful. (Courtesy Hardeman County Genealogical Society.)

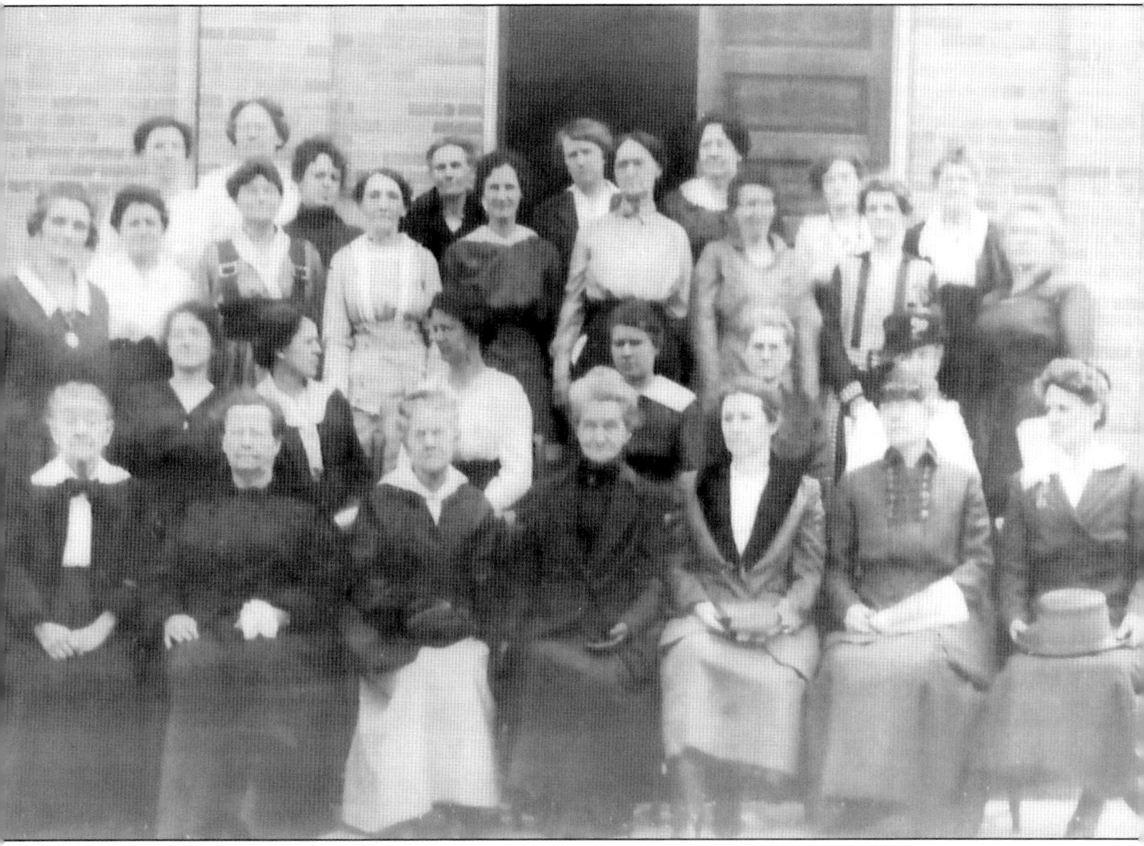

Nineteen individuals organized the Whiteville Baptist Church on July 28, 1892. This group of ladies comprised the 1912 Women's Missionary Society of the church. Pictured are, from left to right, Patty Daniels, Mellie Keller, Minnie Prewitt, ? Rhodes, Mrs. David Campbell, Mrs. J.R. Webb, and Mrs. Johnson Seddens; (second row) Mrs. John Nuckolls, Mrs. F.T. Blalock, Mrs. J. Pettigrew, Neely Woods, Hattie Crawford, and ? Irby; (third row) ? Chapman, Katie Howse, Mrs. John Cross, ? Pepper, Mrs. W.H. Hizer, ? Pepper, ? Edwards, Mrs. Ernest Parker, and Mrs. I.H. Hornsby; (fourth row) Mrs. Clarence Nickolson, ? Lindly, Eula Priddy, Mrs. A.B. Jones, Mrs. Clyde Hunt, Mrs. Joe Doyle, Mrs. Josh Bently, and ? Pearson. (Courtesy Hardeman County Genealogical Society.)

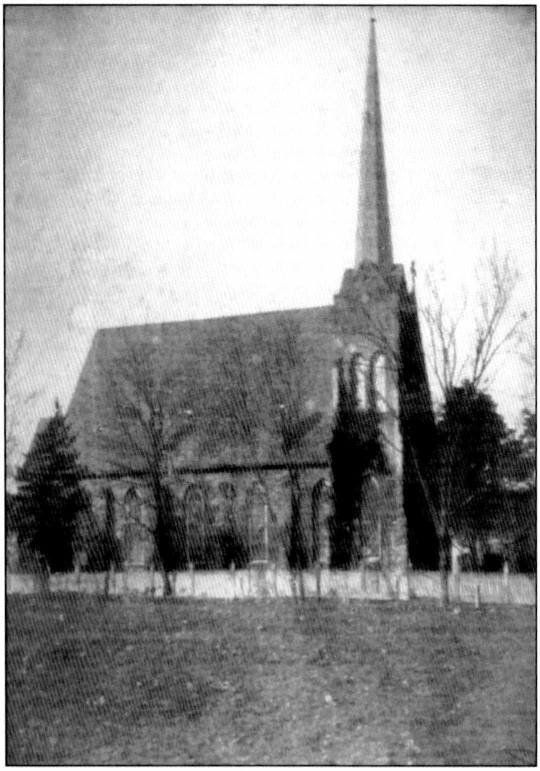

In his 1834 letter to Episcopal bishop Right Reverend James Otey, Dr. Daniel Stephens wrote: "They have hitherto not been in the habit of going to hear any kind of preaching, neither men nor women, and on a certain occasion some ladies said they would rather go to the ball than go to hear Old Stephens read." The congregation Stephens began remains active today. (Courtesy Gary Fish.)

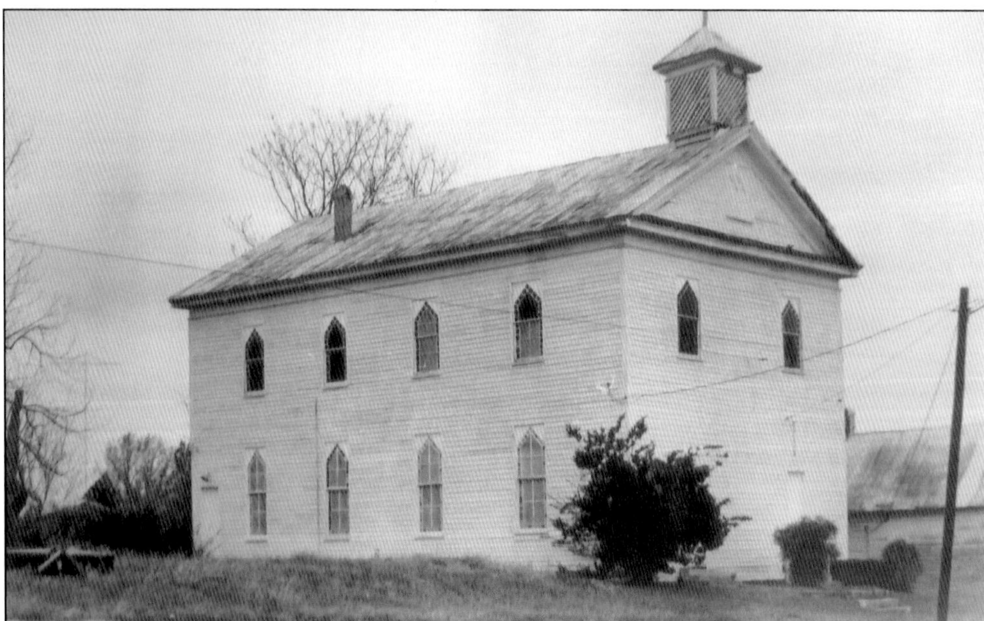

The Middleton Methodist Church was built around 1869 and was jointly constructed by the Methodists and Masonic Lodge No. 264. Members of this lodge, which was chartered on October 8, 1857, were John W. Harrison, John D. Jones, Will T. Yopp, R.W. Biggs, William A. Nance, T. Hall, Thomas T. Harrison, A.A. Myrick, J.M. Bowling, and W.L. Harrison. (Courtesy Gail Mills.)

In this 1963 photograph, children at Powells Chapel Methodist Church are looking cute in their Easter finery (and ready for the annual Easter egg hunt). Pictured are, from left to right, (first row) Sandy Thigpen, Glen Tigner, Gary Tigner, and Greg Cox; (second row) Pat Cox, Vicky Tigner, John Raymond Thigpen, Tommy Sparks, Ricky Tigner, and Steve Cox. (Courtesy Tim Cox.)

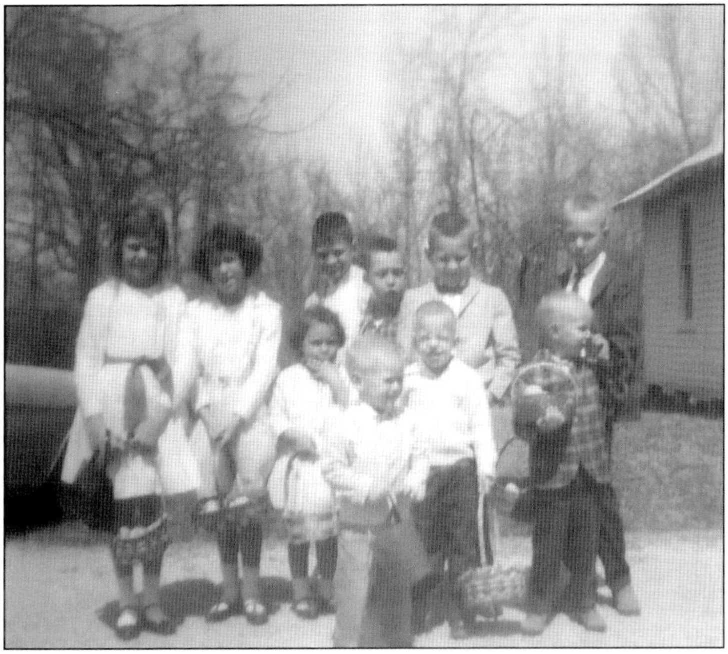

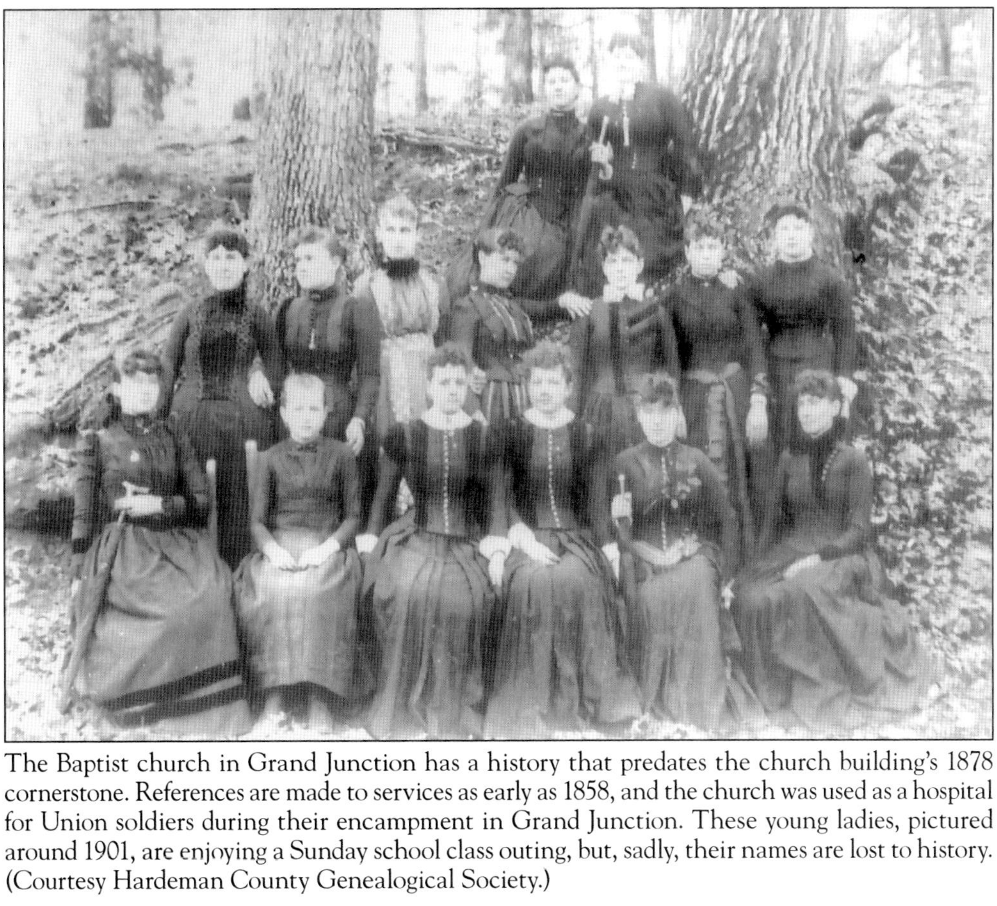

The Baptist church in Grand Junction has a history that predates the church building's 1878 cornerstone. References are made to services as early as 1858, and the church was used as a hospital for Union soldiers during their encampment in Grand Junction. These young ladies, pictured around 1901, are enjoying a Sunday school class outing, but, sadly, their names are lost to history. (Courtesy Hardeman County Genealogical Society.)

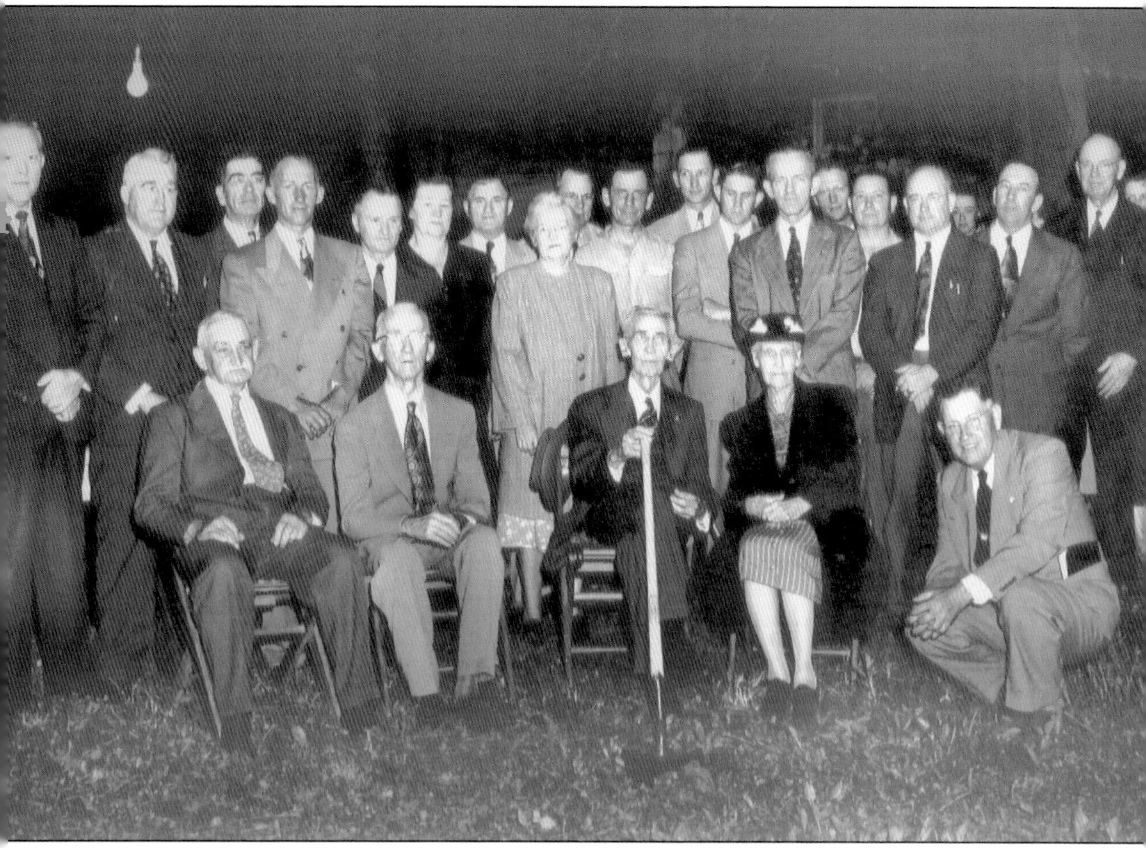

Methodism came to the county with its earliest settlers. One of the earliest Methodist ministers in Bolivar was John H. Holland. Bolivar's first Methodist church building was a one-room house that could seat up to 200 worshippers. A ground breaking for a new Methodist church was held on April 29, 1949. The church held its first Sunday school in the new building on Easter Sunday, April 10, 1955, with an attendance of 192. Pictured here are, from left to right, (first row) T.H. Williams, John Mitchell, Dr. B.V. Hudson, Maggie Hudson, and unidentified; (second row, standing) Dr. R.A. Butler, Frank Hanna, Roy Keller, S. Kirksey, Dewey Whitenton Sr., Sarah Mitchell, Alsey Young, Margie Hudson Young, ? Warren, Mahlon Brown, ? Brown, Bert Kay, George Carter, Robert Mitchell, two unidentified, Roy Prewitt, ? Carlton, Gruner Porter, Elizabeth Butler, and Lizzie Dickson. (Courtesy Anna Laura Bledsoe.)

A crowd of members, worshipers, and friends from the Pleasant Grove Missionary Baptist Church, located near Grand Junction, gather on a Sunday afternoon on the banks of Goddard's Pond to witness baptisms. The church was organized in 1872 in a brush arbor. Founders of the church were S.J. Hunt, Jordan Hunt, Ephriam Pugh, and Cornelius Pugh. (Courtesy Bobby Martindale Memorial Library.)

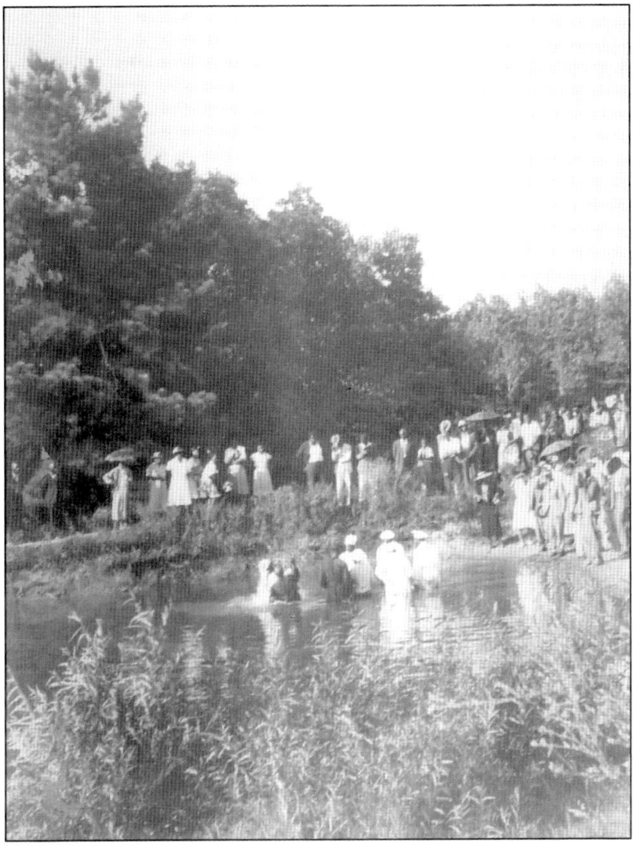

An early photograph from the town of Saulsbury shows, from left to right, the Methodist, Presbyterian, and Baptist churches. The Methodist church was used as barracks for Union army soldiers while they were in the area; today, the building is home to the Saulsbury Community Library. (Courtesy Saulsbury Community Library.)

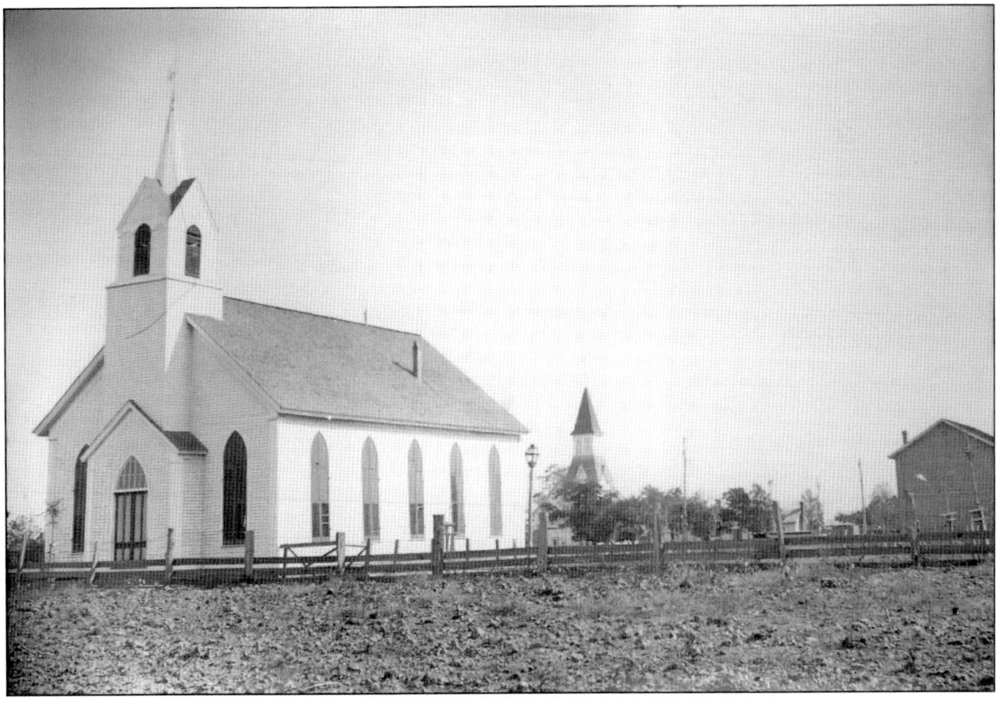

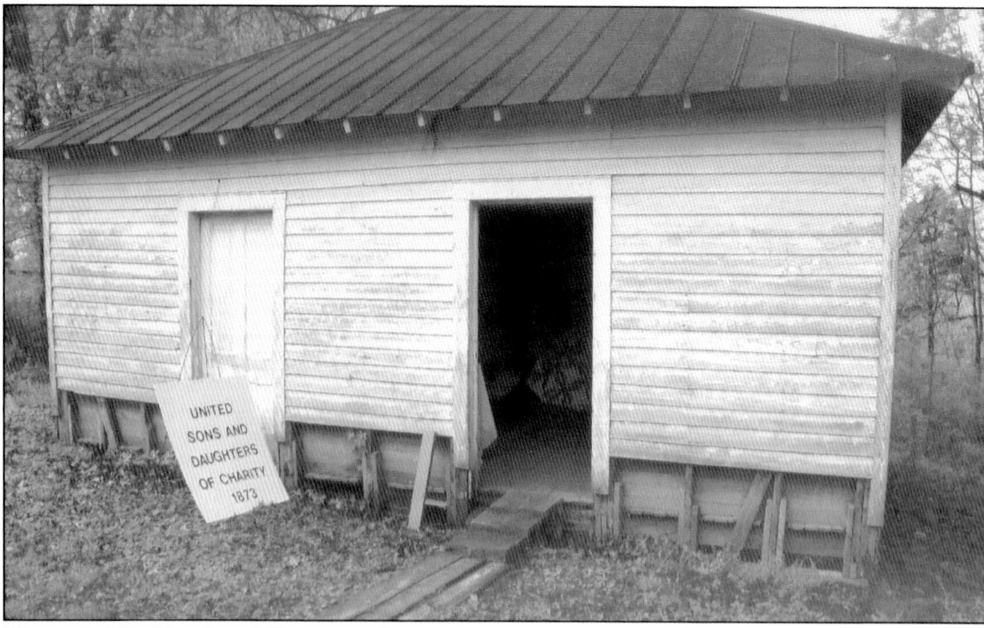

The end of the Freedman's Bureau and Reconstruction left a void in the lives of African Americans emancipated during the Civil War. In January 1873, they formed the United Sons and Daughters of Charity, a local service and benevolence organization, in Bolivar. Founding members were Joseph Bright, Nathan Bills, William Miller, Abraham Miller, and James Smith. Around 1909, the group decided to expand its services and built a lodge hall on East McNeal Street, an area in the heart of the African American community at the time. This first building burned down, and the present building was constructed in 1928. The building was used as a school, and ministers of all denominations held church services there. Area churches also used the building for box suppers, fundraisers, choir practices, and other events. The United Sons and Daughters of Charity Lodge Hall was added to the National Register of Historic Places in 2005. (Both, Lisa C. Coleman.)

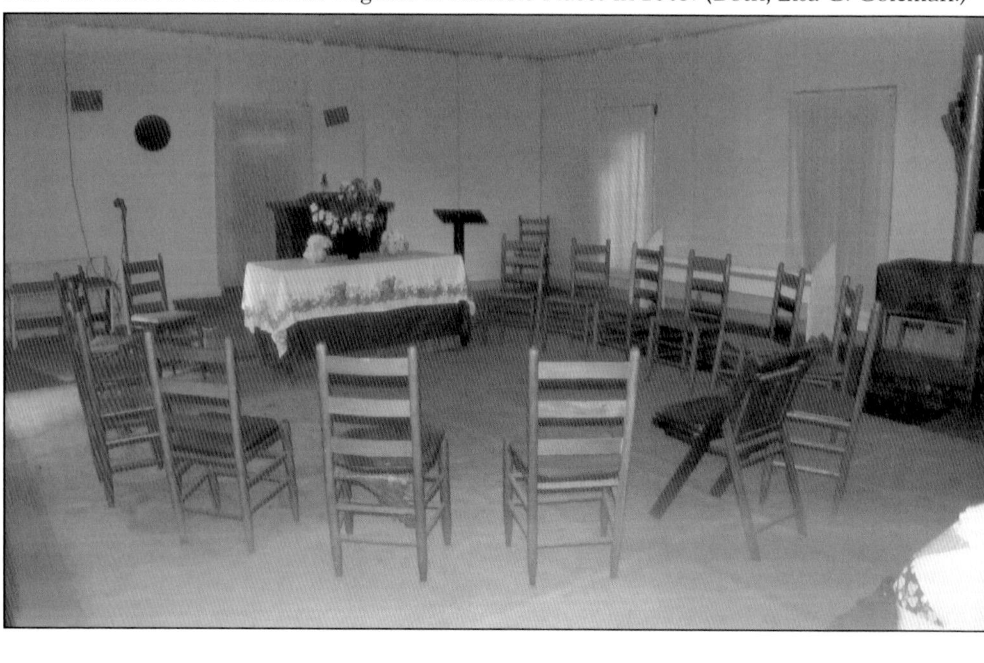

Five

On the Job

The earliest settlers in Hardeman County appreciated the fertile soil and abundant wildlife and quickly set up trading posts that became some of the county's first businesses. Farming, both to feed the family and to make a living, flourished, and, as in many Southern states, cotton reigned as the "king" crop for many years. Farming continues today as a way of life for many families; Hardeman County boasts six Tennessee Century Farms, which are properties that have been owned and farmed by the same family for at least 100 years.

Bolivar became the center of Hardeman County's river trade at the old "Hatchie Town" site. Vessels ranging from keelboats to steamboats made their way up the Hatchie River, bringing goods and people to the county. Stagecoaches, popular modes of transportation and business, created at least two towns—Middleburg (the midpoint of the Bolivar-LaGrange route) and Slab Town (along the Memphis-Corinth, Mississippi, route), later renamed Middleton.

The railroad's emergence in the county brought a faster mode of transportation for goods, services, and passengers. Grand Junction's name came from its importance as a junction for the Memphis & Charleston and the Mississippi Central Railroads. Crainsville lost its standing as a town when the rails bypassed the village by just one mile, creating the new town of Hornsby. The village of Matamora Hill was moved closer to the rail line and renamed Pocahontas. The village of Berlin was abandoned when the railroad went across the lands of Burrell Sauls and Berry Futrell, creating the town of Saulsbury. The demise of the railroads ended once-bustling towns such as Piney Top, Serles, Rogers Springs, Teague, and Vildo.

Merchants of all varieties thrived throughout the county; the old general store was the most popular of all, carrying wares from fabric to farm implements.

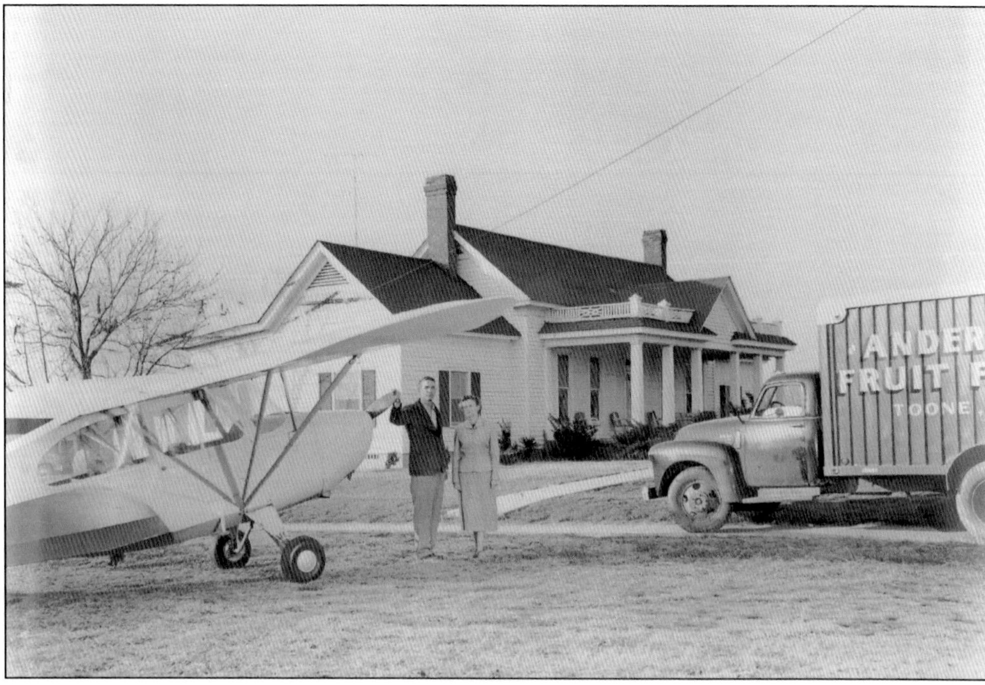

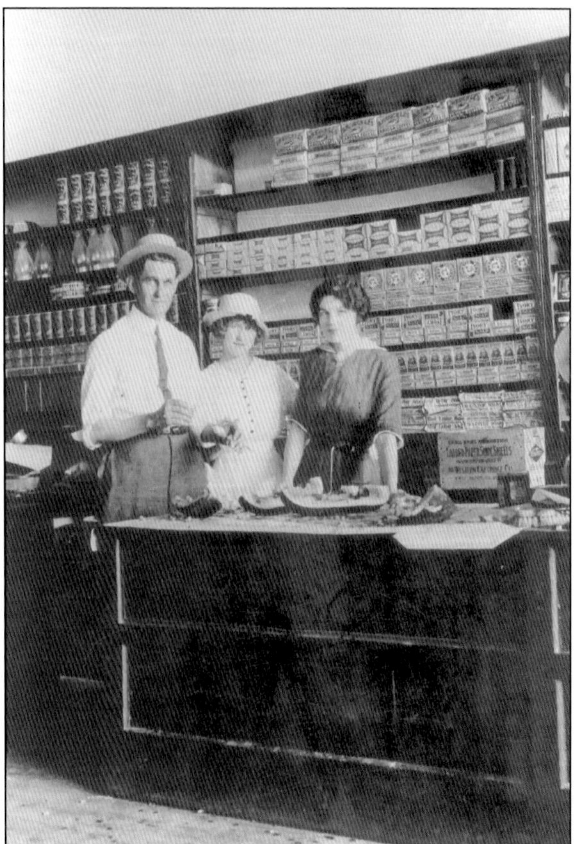

Tom Anderson—"The Flying Farmer" of Cloverport—used his yellow Aeronca two-seater plane to check on his orchard operations in Toone and in Whiteville. Anderson is pictured here with his wife, Martha. (Courtesy Tom Anderson.)

The W.J. Wheeler family operated one of the many general stores in Bolivar. This store was located on Main Street, across from the courthouse. Most general stores offered home deliveries and stocked a variety of items for patrons, including food, fabrics, farm implements, and "ready-made" clothing. (Courtesy Arthur Jr. and Esther Wheeler family.)

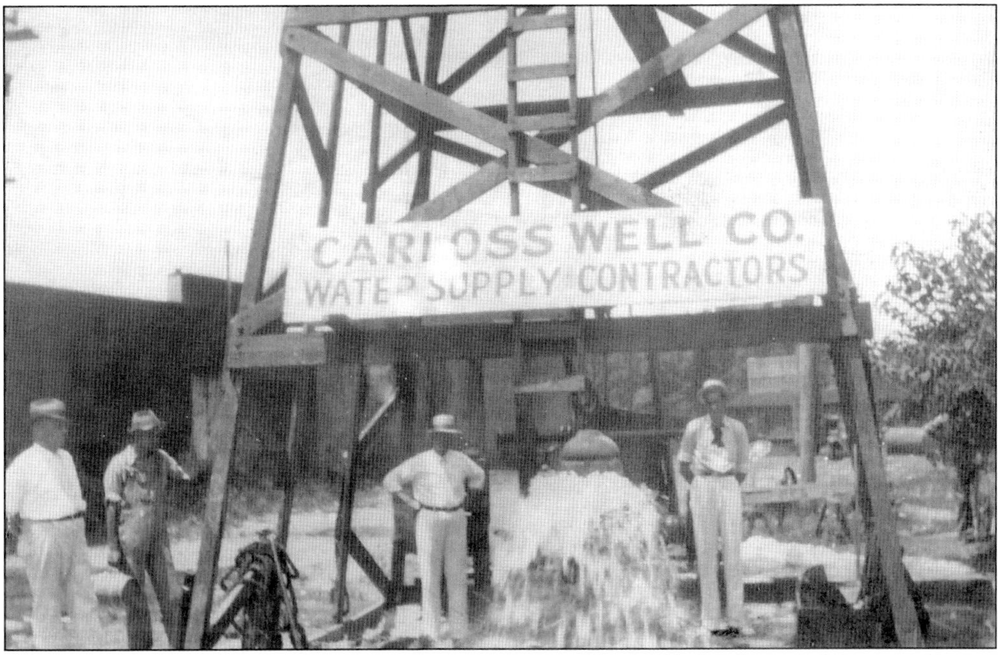

The first well of the new Grand Junction water system was located behind Hess's Garage and began operating in 1935. Pictured with the well are members of the Grand Junction water board: Frank Swift, Jack Mitchell, and James Richardson. (Courtesy Bobby Martindale Memorial Library.)

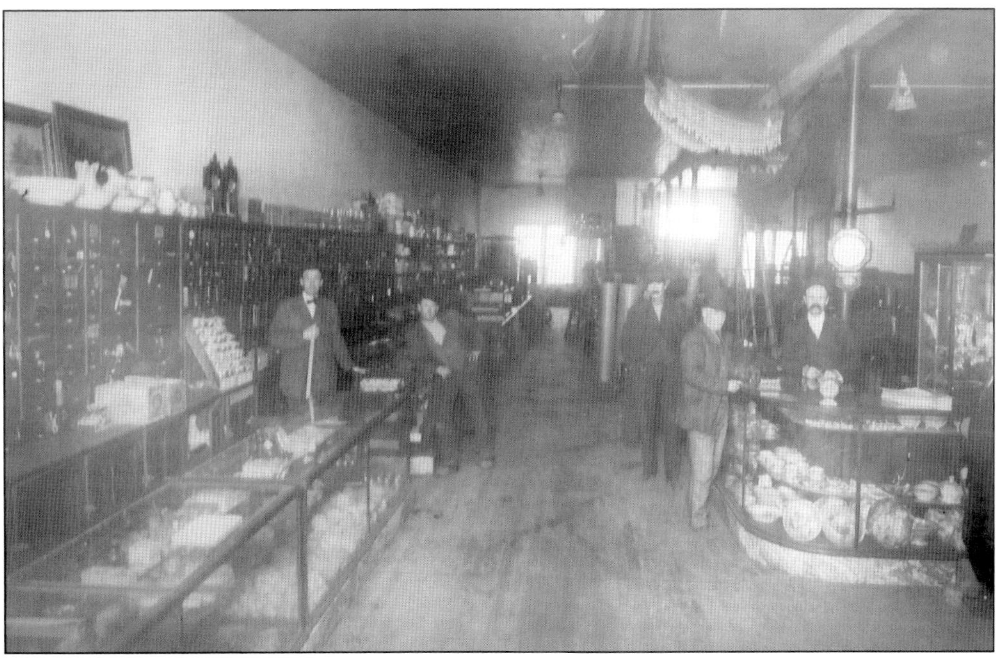

Parker Bros. and Howse Mercantile Store was located at 124 Main Street in Whiteville. Owners William Henry Parker, Jesse T. Parker, and Fred Howse and several customers pose for a photograph in the store. Displays of hardware, tools, and even fine china are visible in the large store. (Courtesy Bettye H. Perry.)

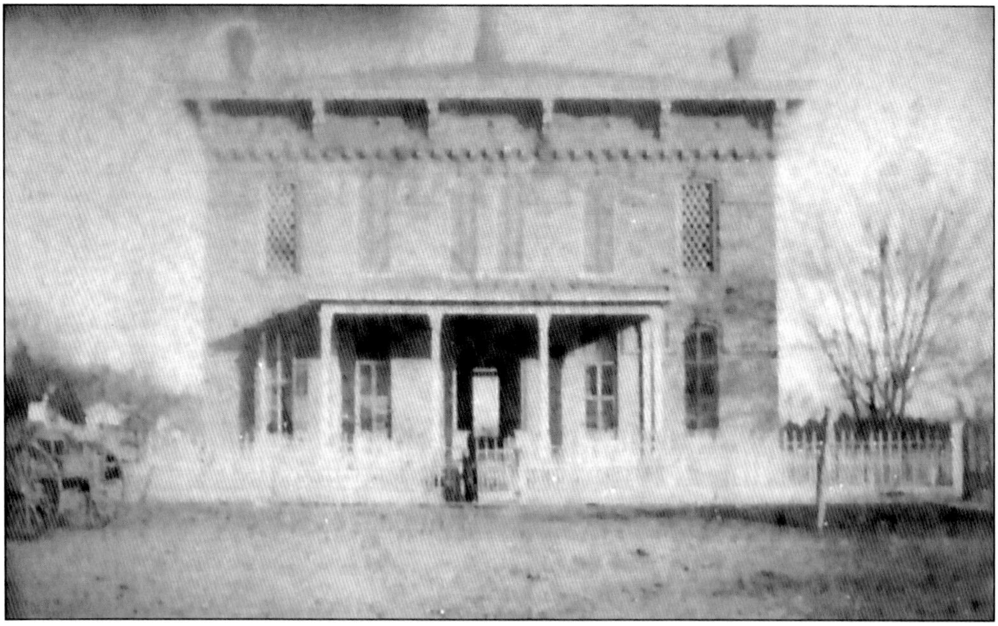

The county's first "jail" in Hatchie Town was a tree near the river where prisoners were chained (weather permitting). In 1824, $40 was allotted to construct a building near the courthouse. A second jail was built about six years later, and a third lasted until an 1876 fire. This photograph is believed to be of the third jail building a few months before that fire. (Courtesy Hardeman County Genealogical Society.)

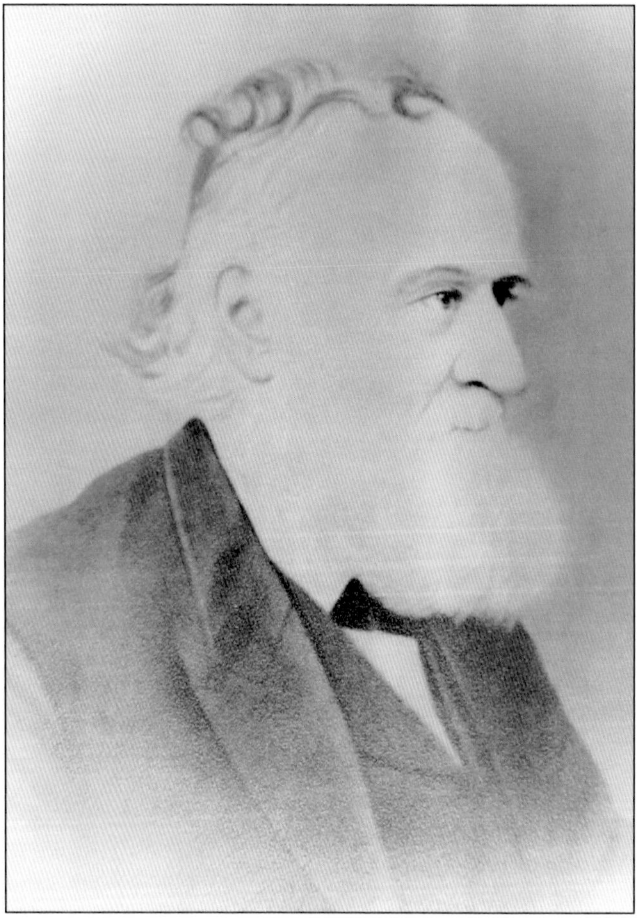

J.C.N. (Julius Caesar Nicholas) Robertson (1792–1880) served as Hardeman County's first sheriff, from 1823 to 1836, and was reelected again in 1840. He and his wife, Margaret Reagan Robertson, moved to Hardeman County in 1823 and became the parents of eight children. As sheriff, Robertson dealt with everything from theft and levying fines to taking care of orphans. (Courtesy Pat Vincent.)

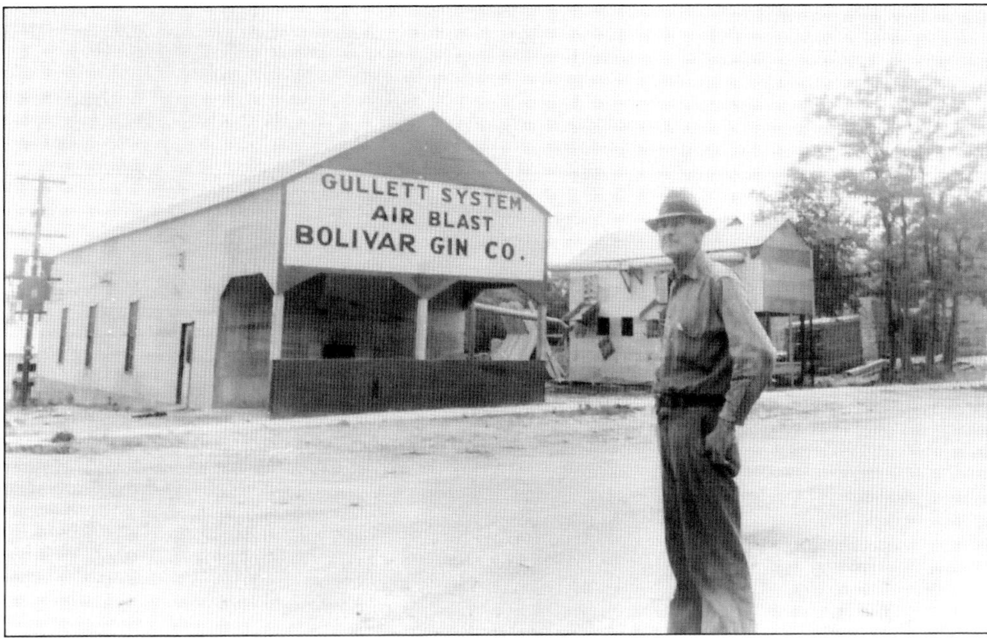

Cotton was the area's main crop for many years, with dozens of gins located across Hardeman County. Schools were always closed for four to six weeks in the fall so that children could help at "cotton-pickin' time." The Bolivar Gin was located on South Main Street and utilized the Gullett System Air Blast method of ginning cotton. Above, Marcus Fulghum is pictured in front of the gin. Below, inside the gin are Roy Jacobs (standing at left) and Theador Joy (front left). (Above, courtesy Hardeman County Genealogical Society; below, courtesy Hardeman County Chamber of Commerce.)

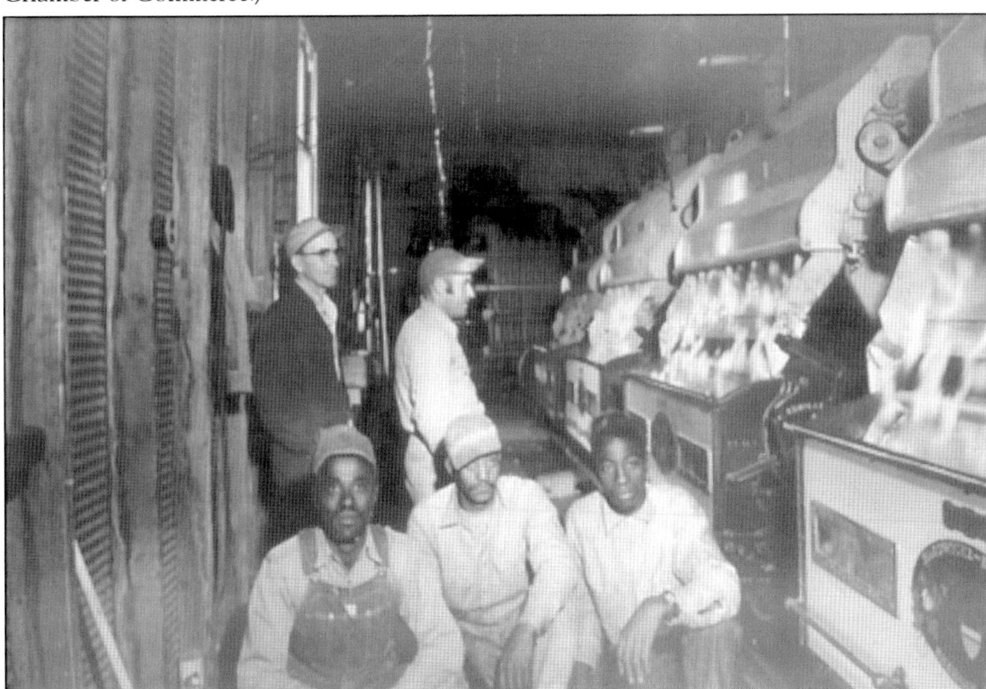

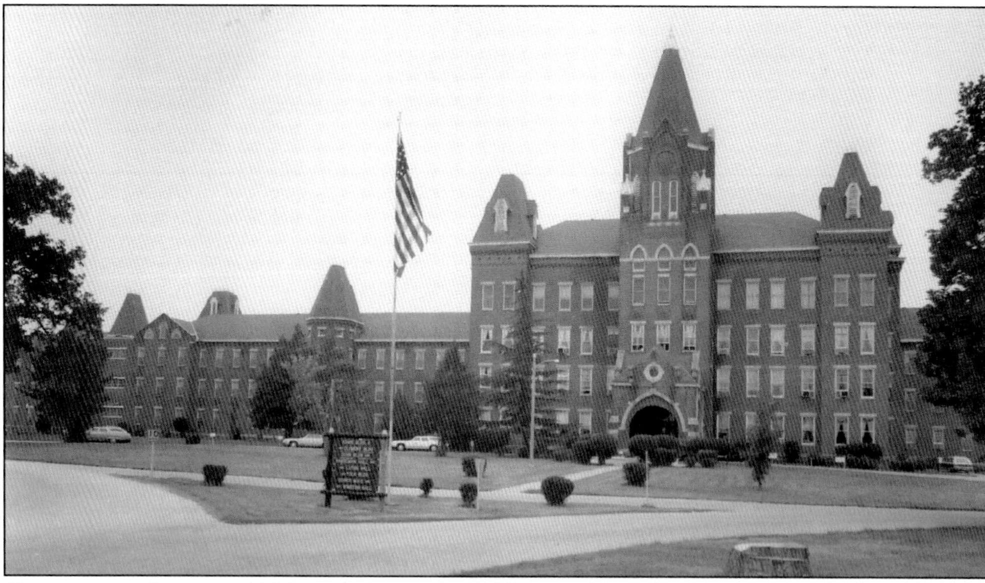

Construction began in 1886 on the state mental hospital in Bolivar, and the doors were opened at the Western Hospital for the Insane at Bolivar on November 22, 1886. The first building constructed was the Administration Building, which housed staff offices, staff apartments, and patient wards. Shown here in the 1970s, the building is still in use by the hospital and currently houses administrative offices. The wings were torn down in 1989 after becoming structurally unstable and unusable. By 1898, the hospital was home to nearly 600 patients and staff (pictured below), and was a self-sufficient community with a large farming operation; clothes and shoes for patients and some staff were made onsite by employees and patients as part of the hospital's work therapy program. (Both, courtesy Western Mental Health Institute.)

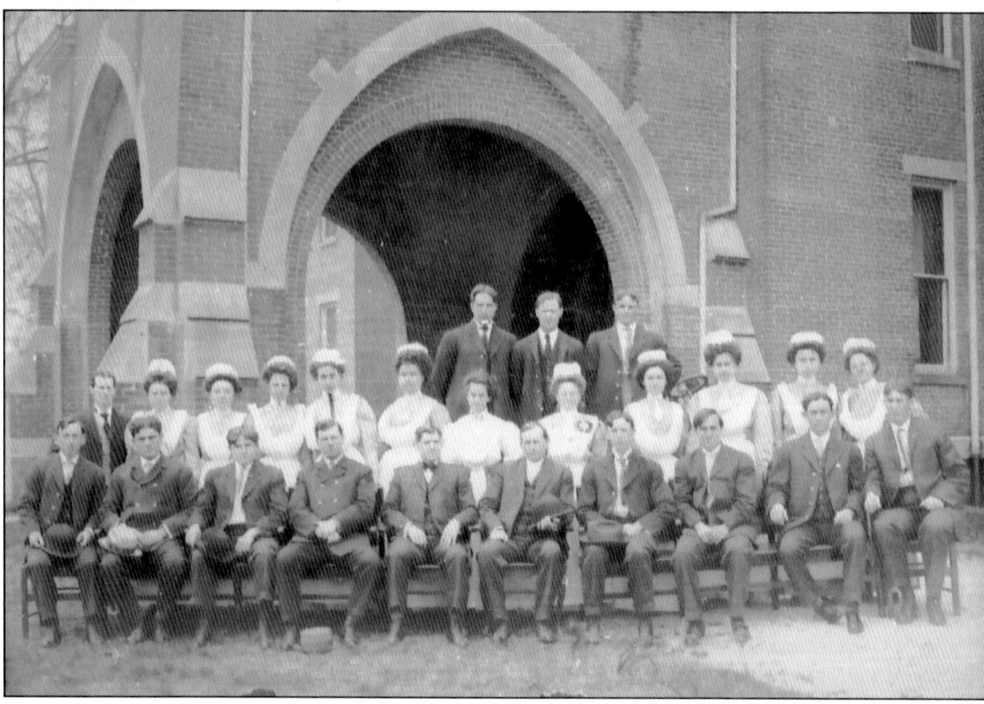

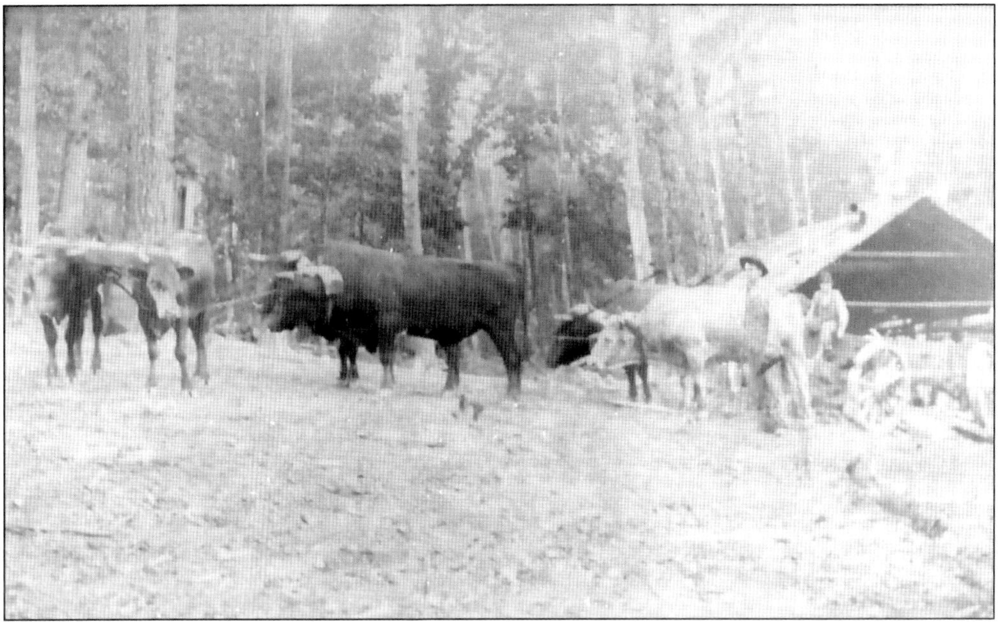

Hardeman County is one of the South's leading producers of hardwoods, and logging has a long history in the area. Many mills became the river ports by which early settlers entered the county, and communities developed around the mills. This mill in the Pine Top community was one of several in the county that provided lumber used in the construction of Western Hospital. (Courtesy Hardeman County Genealogical Society.)

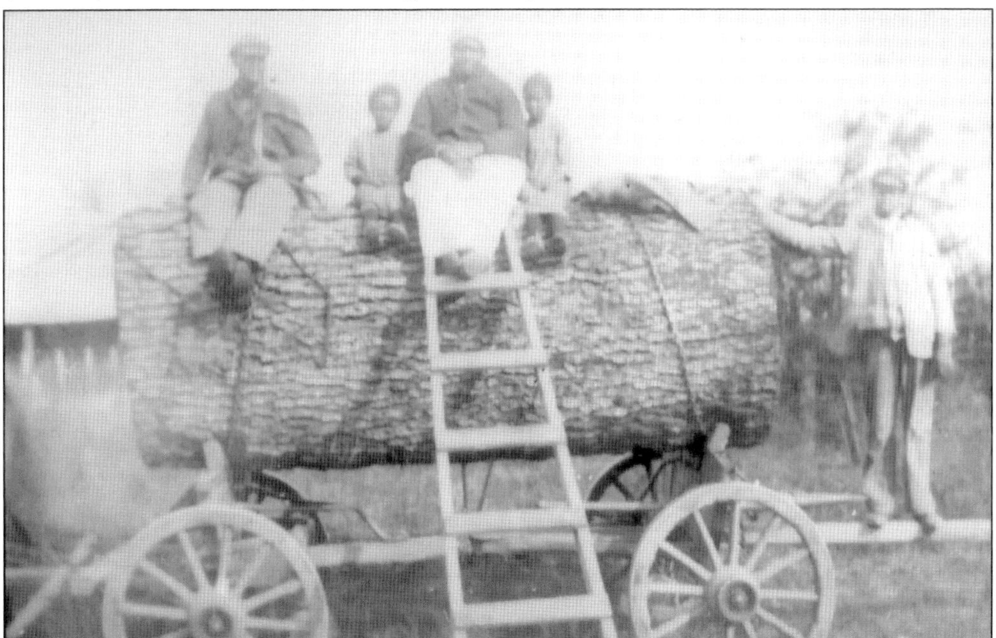

In the late 1880s, logs were frequently "rafted" down the Hatchie River to the Pocahontas mills; each logging camp had a unique mark that ensured that their logs received proper credit when they reached the mills. The very large log shown in this photograph was milled at the J.W. Wardlow Sawmill; the identities of the workers are not known. (Courtesy Esta Lee Lamberth.)

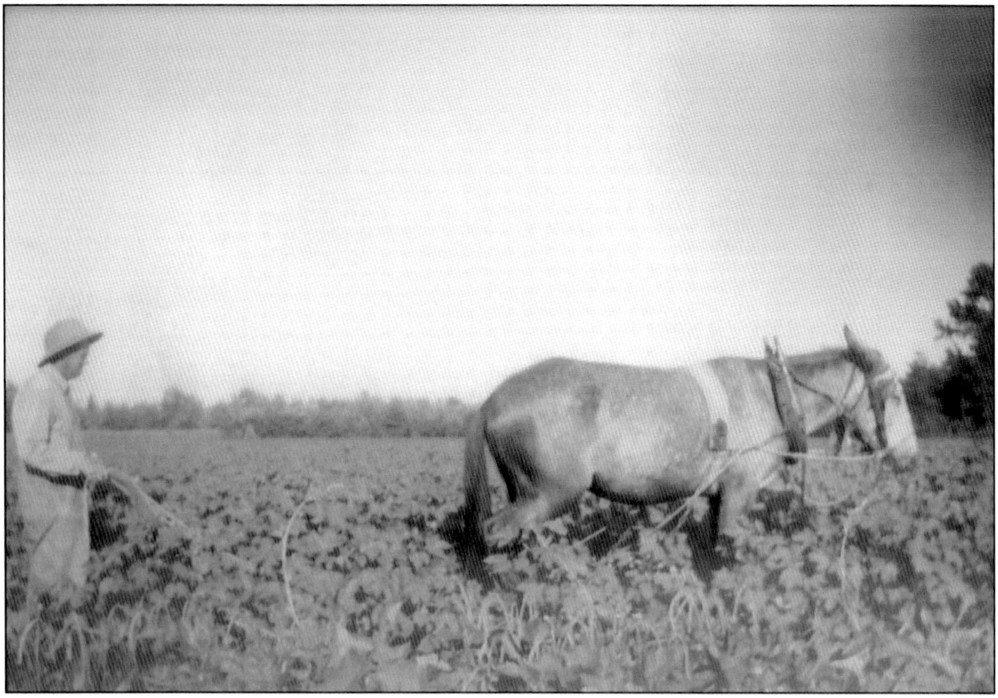

Farming has been a mainstay of the county since the first settlers came to the area. Thousands of county acres are still devoted to agriculture today. Hugh Kiestler (above) worked as a sharecropper in Cloverport, farming acres with a mule-drawn plow. In 1948, at the time of this photograph, he farmed approximately 30 acres this way, as well as tending to cows, chickens, and a vegetable garden. Robert Huddleston (below), shown in Middleton in the late 1930s, also spent many hours working the land with mules. (Above, Lisa C. Coleman; below, courtesy Hardeman County Genealogical Society.)

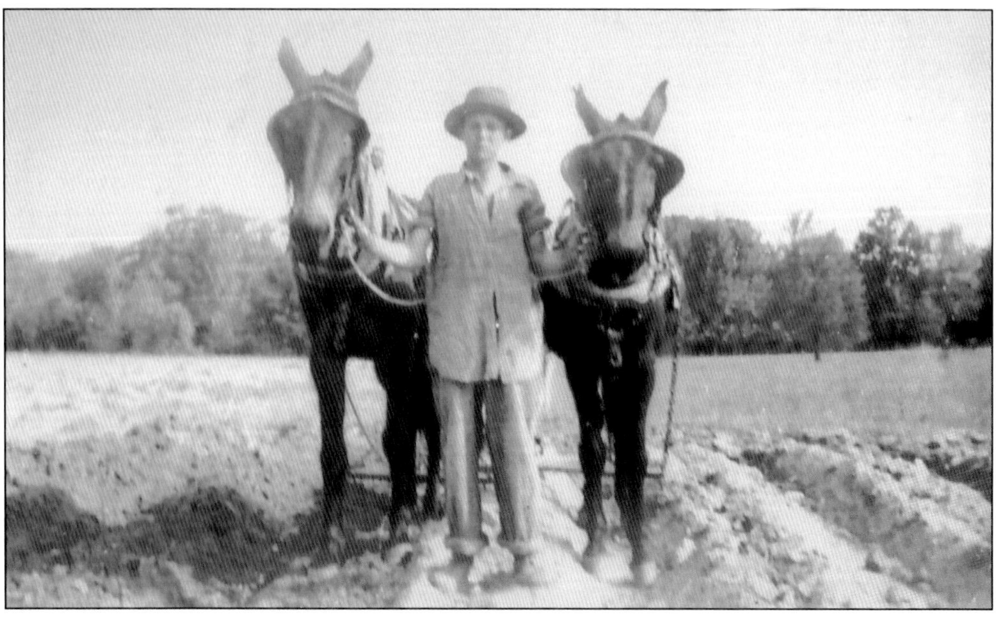

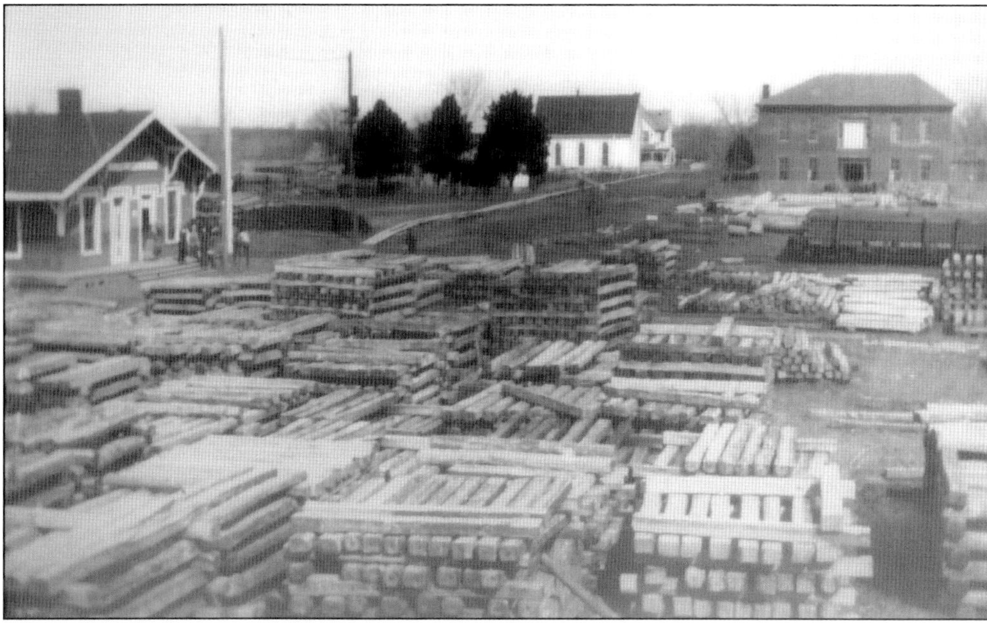

Large stacks of railroad ties, used to repair rail lines, sit in the Pocahontas rail yard around 1910. A train is visible at right; the town's depot is on the left. The two-story structure in the background at right is the Joyner-Carr House. (Courtesy Esta Lee Lamberth.)

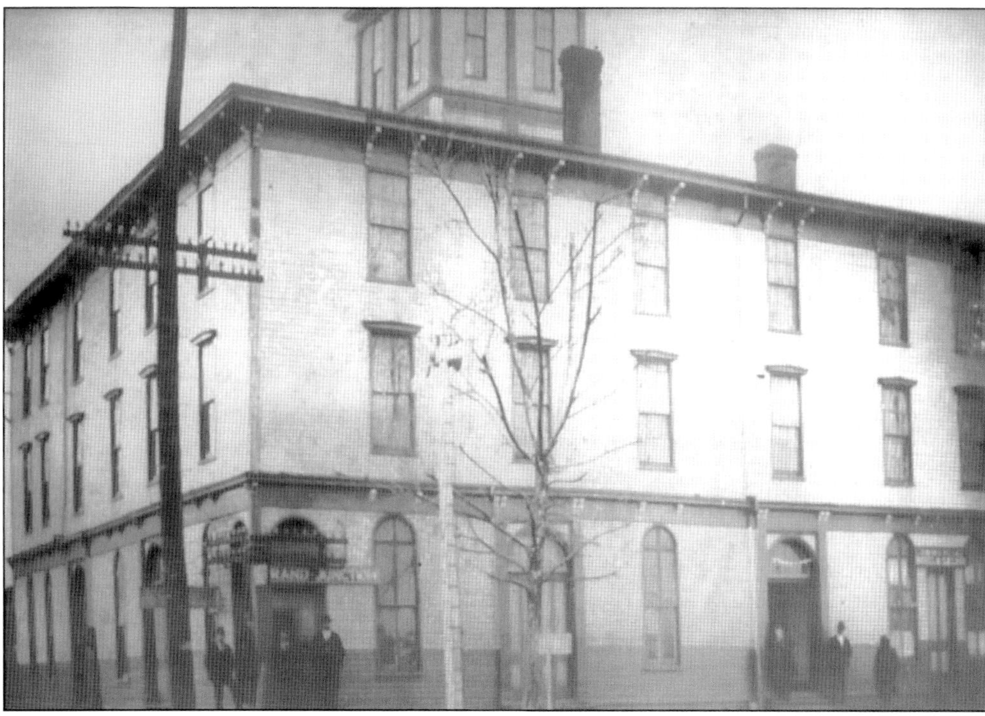

The railroad companies constructed this three-story building, which covered most of a town block, in Grand Junction. Train travelers made regular meal stops at the hotel. First known as the Railroad Hotel, it was renamed the Commercial Hotel around 1902, when Mr. and Mrs. A.A. McLeran were the hotel's proprietors. (Courtesy David Vinyard.)

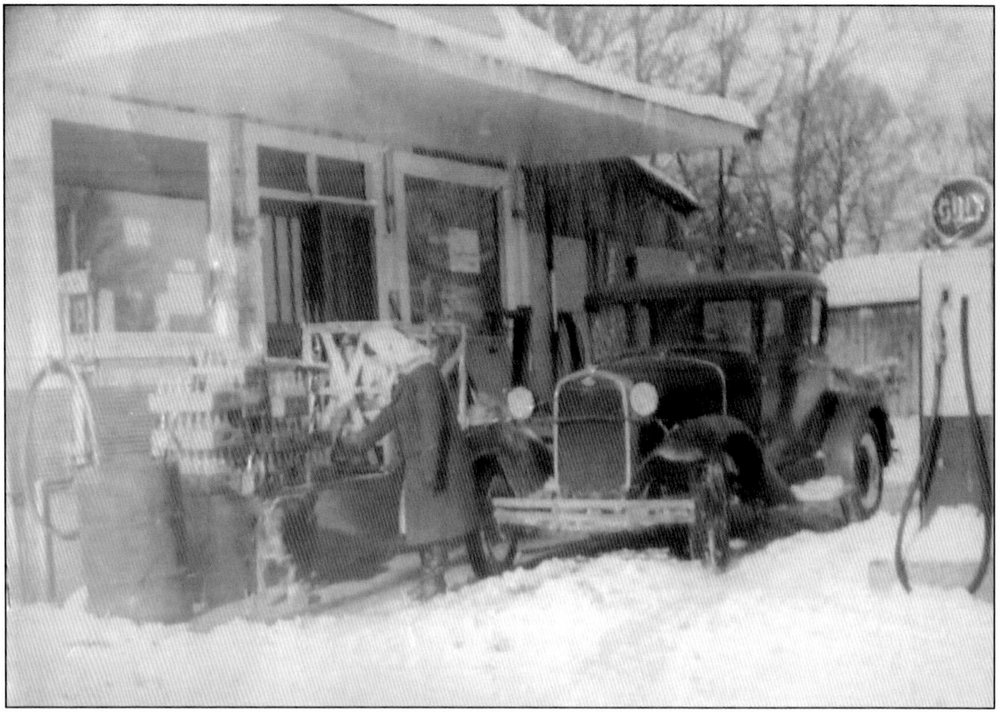

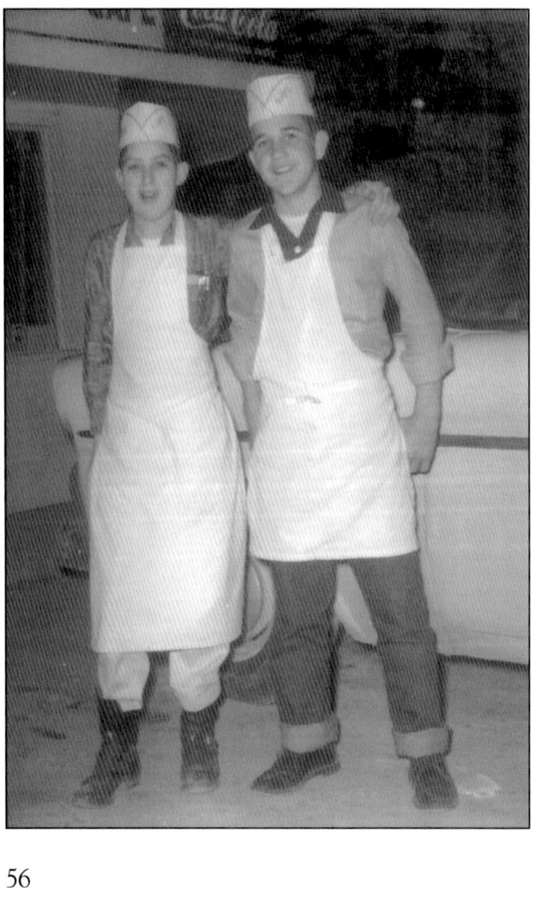

Gooch Store operated in the Hornsby area for many years. First owned by Prentiss Gibson, the store was purchased (and renamed) by Albert and Dottie Gooch in the late 1930s. The store was a gathering place for friends and neighbors for many years, even on a cold day such as the one pictured. (Courtesy Tim Cox.)

By 1959, Henderson Dairy Bar, owned and operated by Lelon Henderson and located at the Middleton Crossroads, was "the" place in town for young people. Vernon Henderson (left) and Don Pulse worked as carhops, delivering orders to patrons. Lelon's three oldest grandchildren—Steve, Reba, and Grady Matthews—also worked as carhops at the dairy bar. (Courtesy Annie Pearl Orman.)

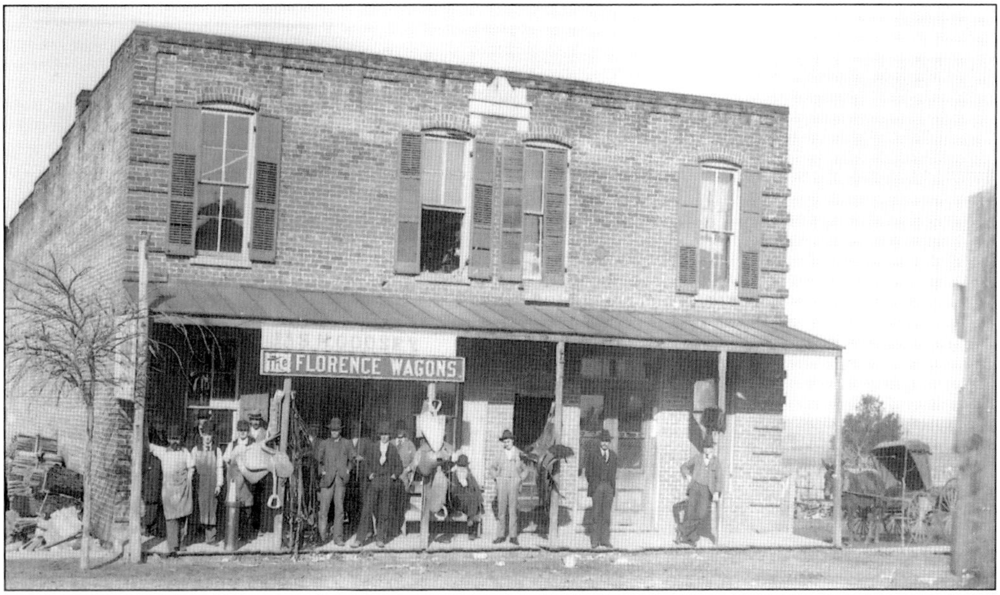

In 1890, this rambling two-story building, constructed by J.T. Low, was located on Main Street in Saulsbury and housed a doctor's office and a large leather goods store. James H. Godsey and several skilled workers made all kinds of harnesses, saddles, and "especially good shoes" (according to one old newspaper ad) in one of the largest leather goods and manufacturing businesses in the area. (Courtesy Saulsbury Community Library.)

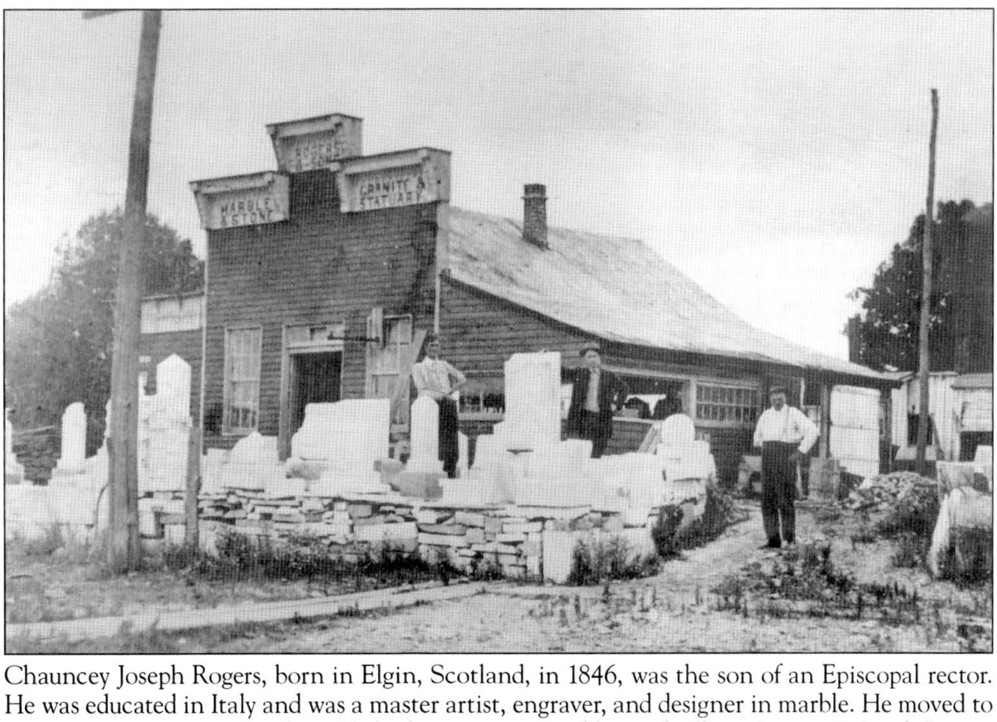

Chauncey Joseph Rogers, born in Elgin, Scotland, in 1846, was the son of an Episcopal rector. He was educated in Italy and was a master artist, engraver, and designer in marble. He moved to Grand Junction in 1879 and established C.J. Rogers Marble Works (later Rogers & Sons). Rogers brought Italian marble-cutters to Grand Junction to train his original workers. (Courtesy Bobby Martindale Memorial Library.)

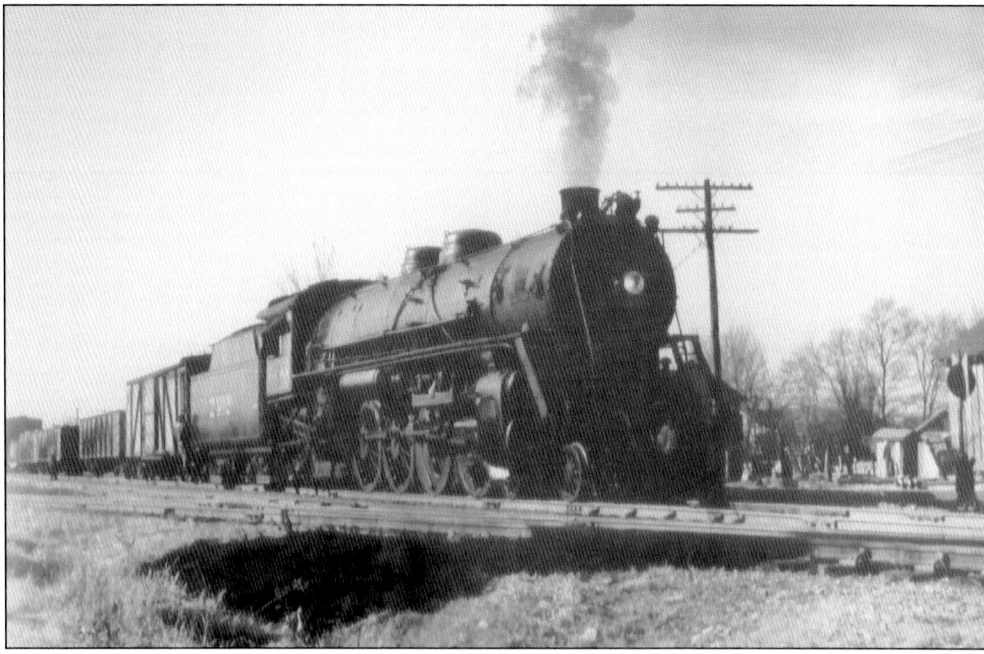

By 1858, the Mississippi Central Railroad was completed from Bolivar to Jackson, Tennessee. Many jobs were added to the town while the railroad flourished, and river trade began to decline at the old Hatchie Town port. This photograph from the 1940s shows the train coming into Bolivar. (Courtesy Hardeman County Chamber of Commerce.)

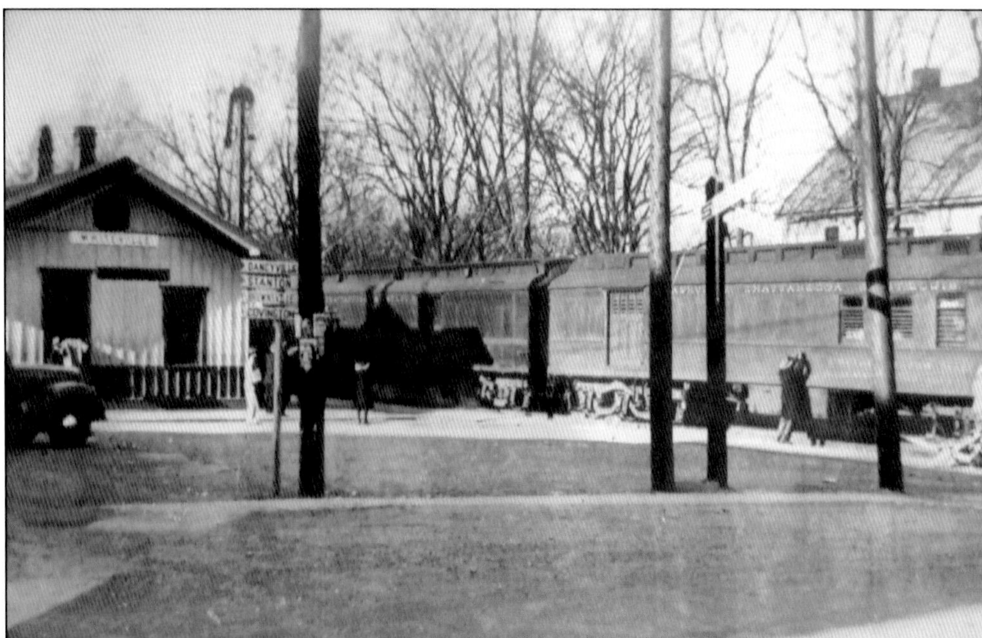

In 1888, the first rail lines came through Whiteville, and the townsite was moved closer to the railroad. The first rail line was the Tennessee Midland, which later became the NC&STL Railroad. The Duncan Hotel (at right) provided meals, at a cost of 25¢ per person, and lodging to passengers traveling through the town. (Courtesy Barbara Blanton and Betty Pepper Fleet.)

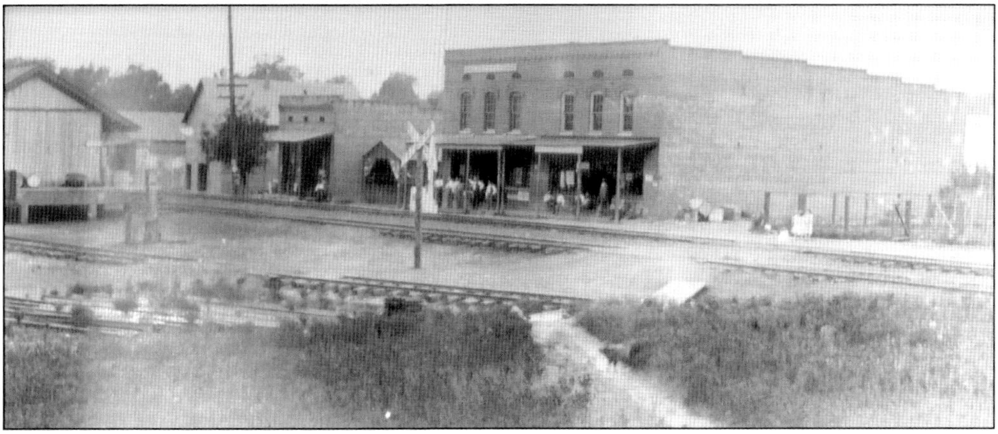

Hickory Valley was an established community in the southwestern part of the county by 1840. Some of its first settlers were Washington Avent, James P. Ferguson, and David McAnulty. Avent is believed to have been the town's first merchant. This c. 1900 street scene of Hickory Valley shows the railroad tracks, which first came through town around 1856. (Courtesy Hardeman County Chamber of Commerce.)

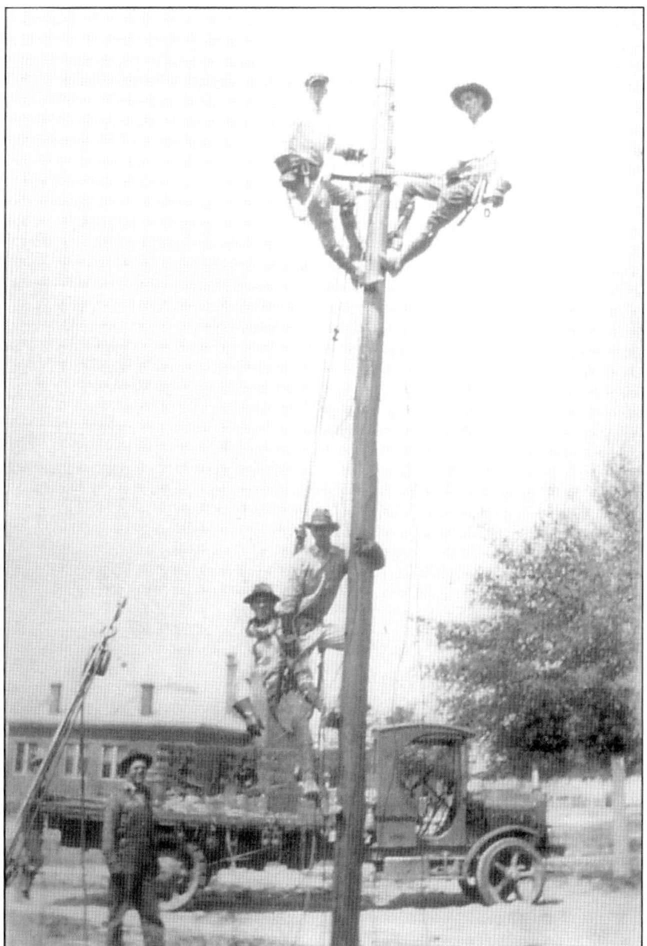

A cable crew poses for a photograph while working near Middleton in the mid-1920s. Claude R. Smith did much of the work for the Progress Telephone Company in its early days. Phone service was about $1 per month, and customers fixed their own phones—the telephone company would send a new battery in the mail to replace an old one. (Courtesy Norma J. West.)

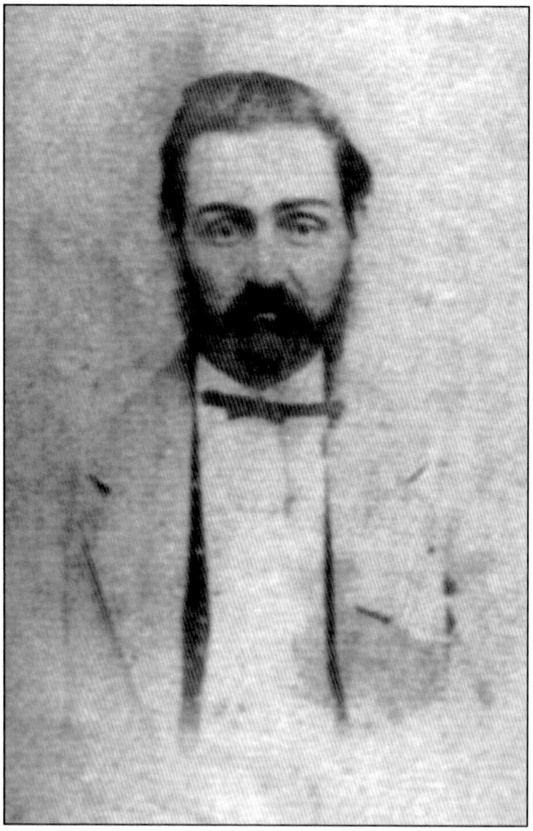

Pleasant Fletcher (P.F.) Wilkinson was born in McNairy County, Tennessee, and served in the 154th Senior Infantry during the Civil War. He moved to Hardeman County after the war and opened his first business in old Crainsville, later establishing a business in Bolivar with his brothers. He died in 1926 at the age of 87 and was remembered in his obituary as "a man of great industry and tireless energy. He was scrupulously honest, a kind and clever neighbor and a good citizen held in the highest esteem by our people." (Both, courtesy John L. Mitchell and Mary Moore.)

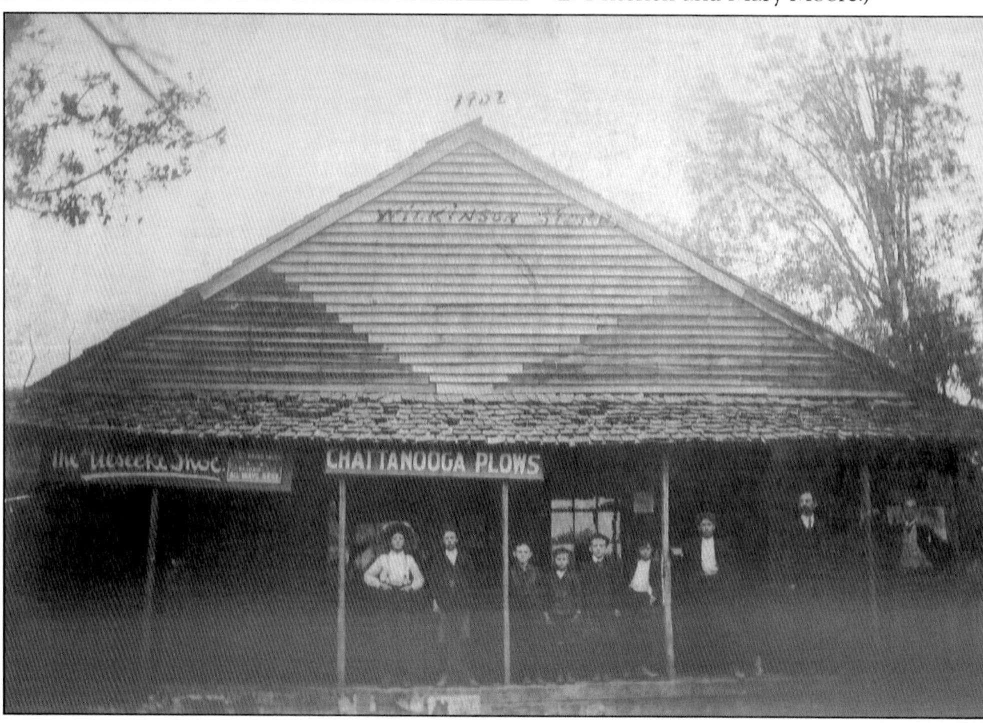

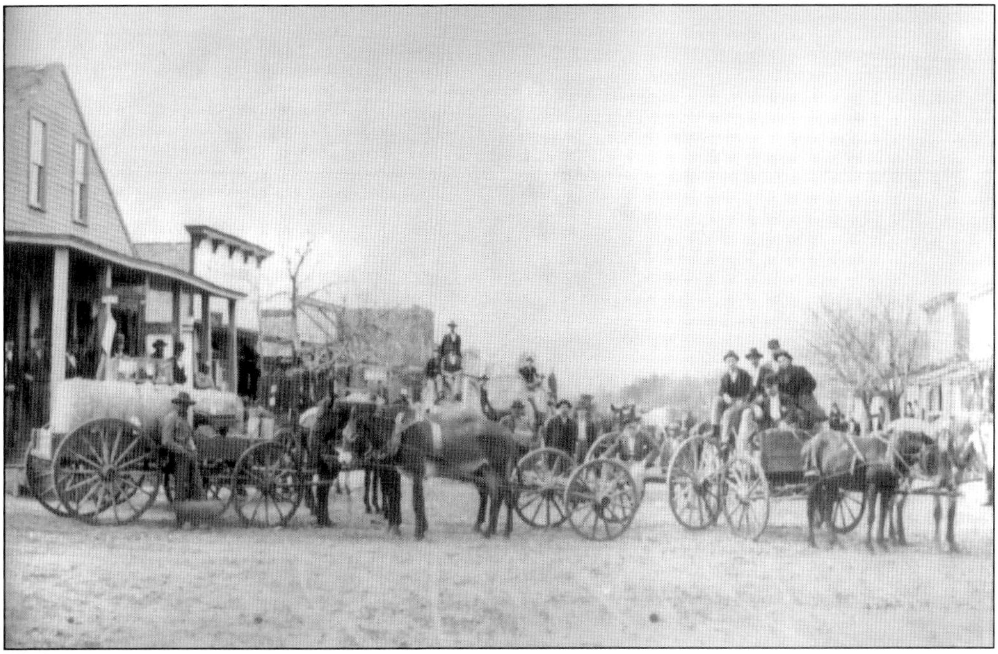

Before the arrival of the railroads, Saulsbury was a leading cotton market for West Tennessee and North Mississippi. Long trains of 15 to 30 wagons would form from as far south as Tupelo, Mississippi, to make the two-to-three-day trip to cotton buyers. So many wagons and farmers came to the area that Esquire Roger S. Clark built a wagon shed to house the vehicles overnight. When cotton was still king in Hardeman County, Whiteville boasted the county's first steam-operated cotton gin. Wagons filled with cotton, as pictured below, were pulled by mule-driven wagons to the gin yard, unloaded, processed, baled, and readied for shipment to market. (Both, courtesy Hardeman County Genealogical Society.)

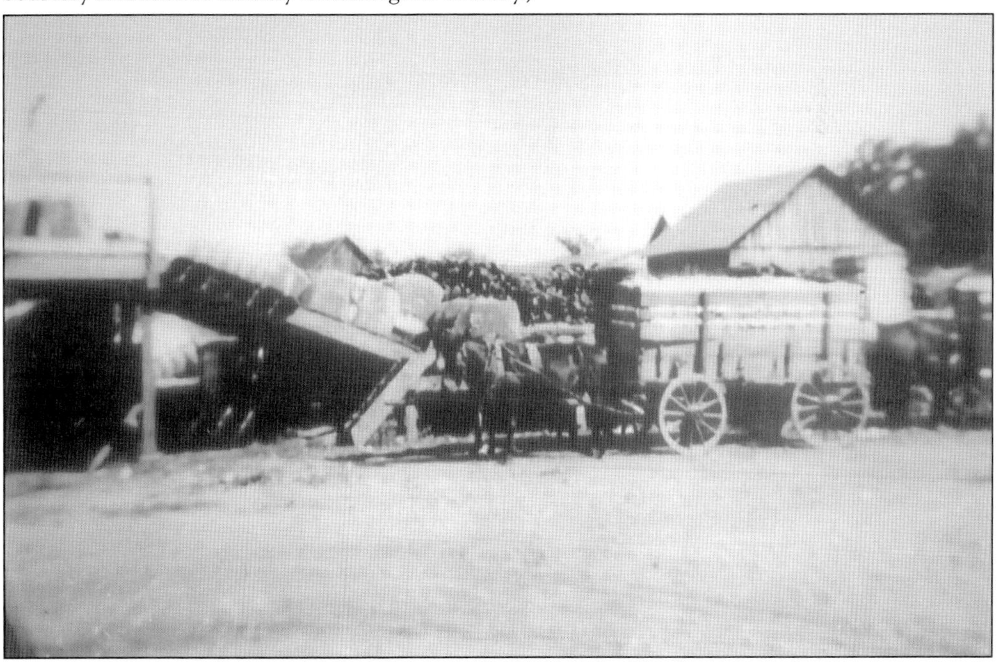

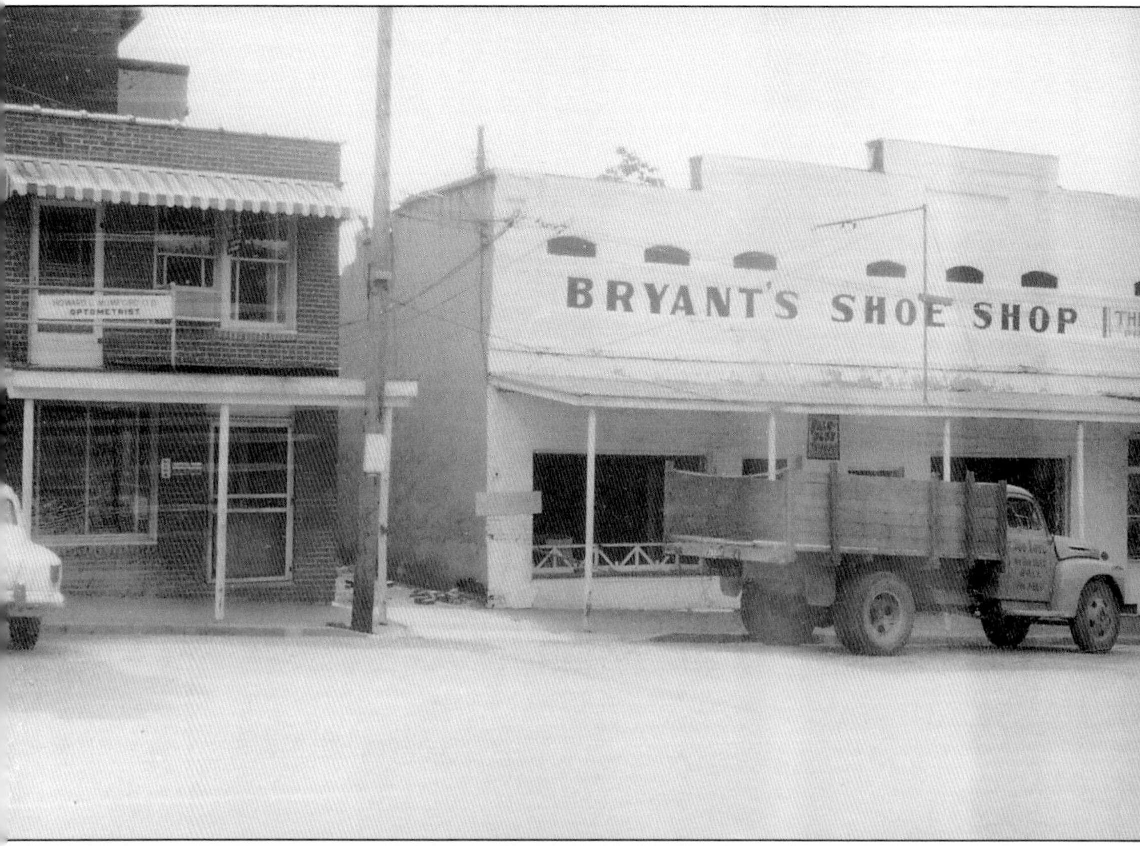

Travis C. Bryant was one of the five children of John Wesley and Pearl Bryant, who operated a shoe shop in Grand Junction from 1922 until about 1925. The shop was relocated to Bolivar, at 109 South Main Street, and renamed J.W. Bryant and Son Shoe Shop. Travis and his wife, Albena Roberta "Bert" Irwin Bryant, continued to operate the shop after his father's death, but were forced to sell it during the Depression. After serving in World War II, Travis came back to Bolivar and opened a shoe shop in the same location, as shown in this photograph. The business expanded quickly and the shop moved to 107 West Market Street, later taking in the building at 109 West Market Street. Many generations of Hardeman County residents have fond memories of purchasing shoes or taking them in for repairs at Bryant's. (Courtesy Karen Brooks Moss.)

Brothers David William and Robert Ashe McAnulty (believed to be the two men in the window) operated the McAnulty Brothers general merchandise store in Hickory Valley. The store bought flour in barrels delivered by the railroad, and sold everything from sewing needles to coffins. D.W. retired in 1916, and the business continued to be operated by his sons Moorman and Ashley. (Courtesy Hardeman County Genealogical Society.)

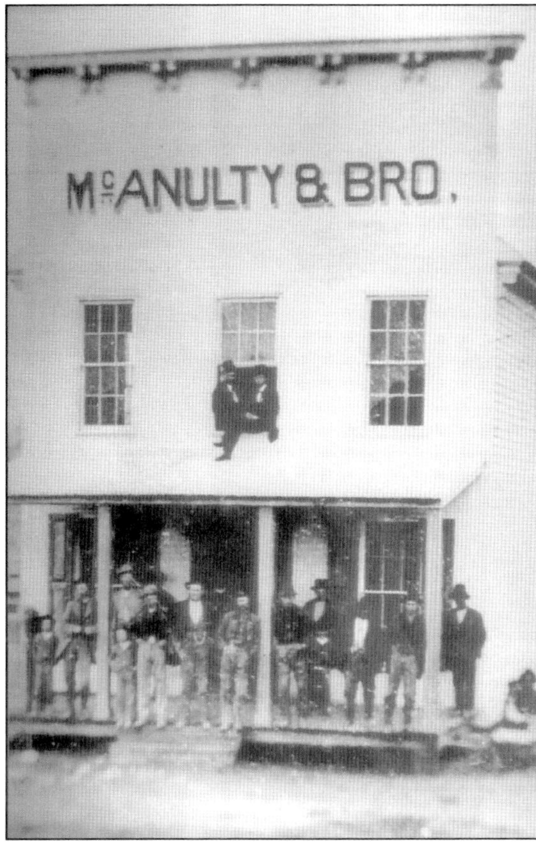

Brothers Tom, Jim, and N.T. (Nathan Thaddeus) Richardson operated family stores in Grand Junction in the early 1900s—one in town and another in the country. "Mr. N.T." (shown below) purchased the store around 1924 and continued to operate it until well past his 100th birthday. Many stories were told around the pot-bellied stove that heated the store. (Courtesy Bobby Martindale Memorial Library.)

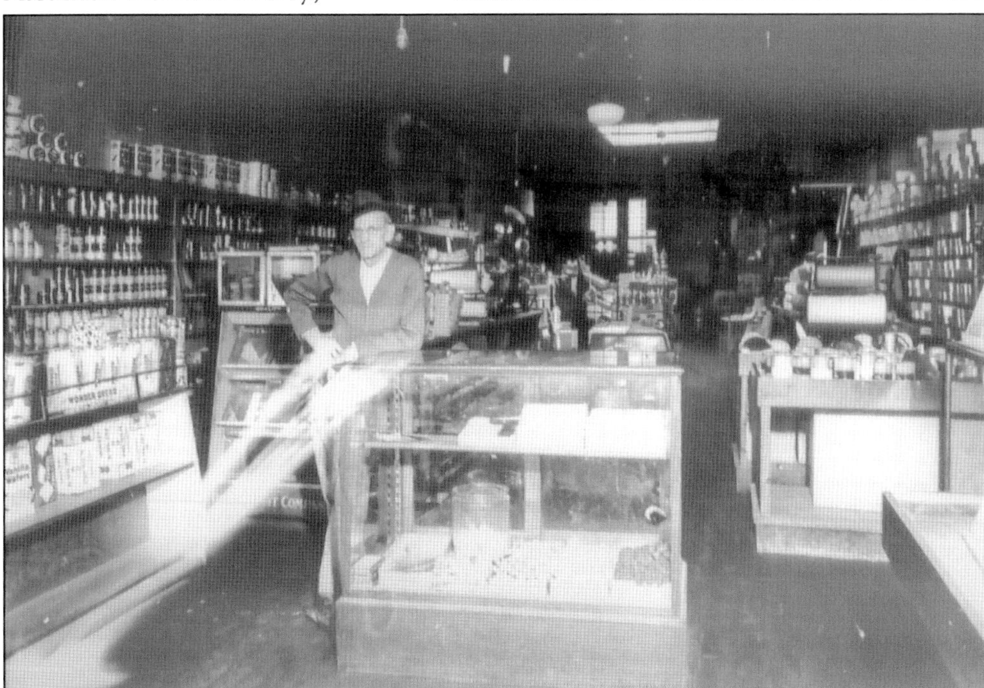

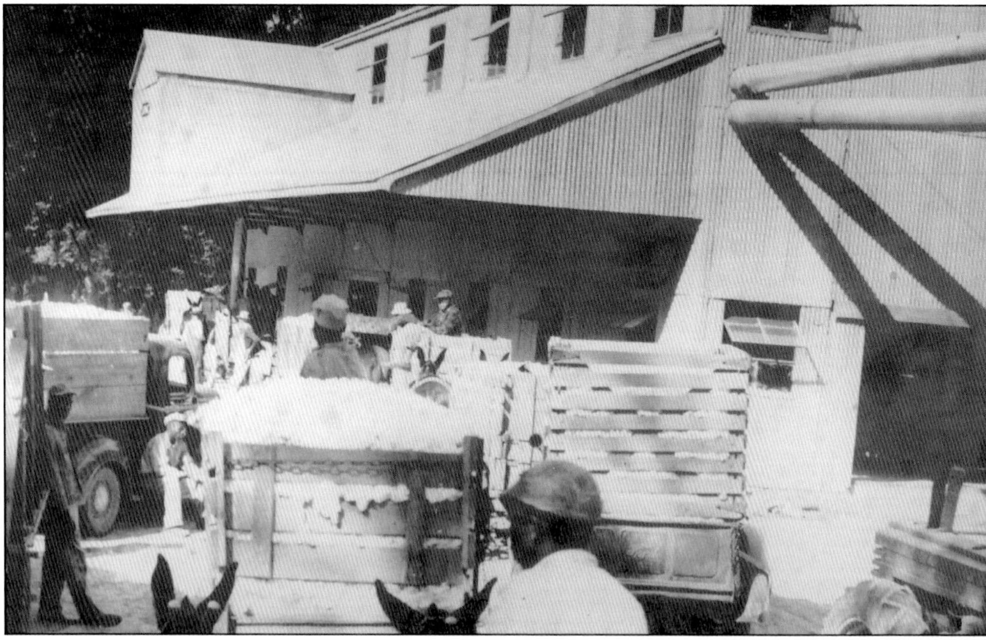

The Grand Junction Cotton Gin was built about 1948 and was operated by Homer Hess. Many thousands of bales of cotton came through the gin from fields in West Tennessee and North Mississippi. The original gin building is still located in Grand Junction, and is currently the location of the Grand Junction Farmer's Market held on Saturdays. (Courtesy Bobby Martindale Memorial Library.)

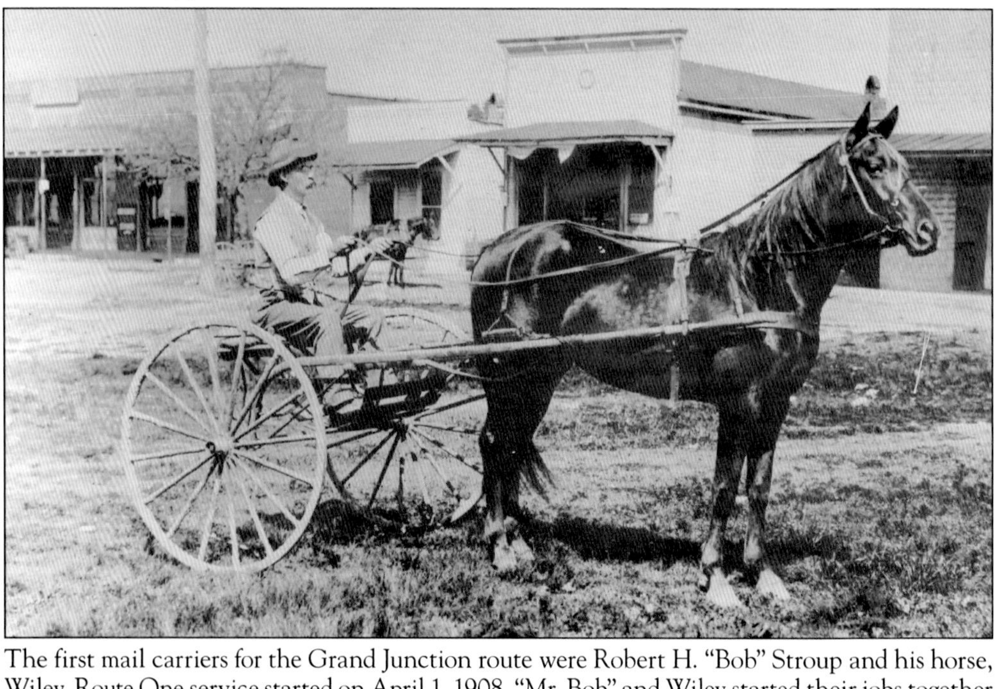

The first mail carriers for the Grand Junction route were Robert H. "Bob" Stroup and his horse, Wiley. Route One service started on April 1, 1908. "Mr. Bob" and Wiley started their jobs together and retired together after many years of service to the people along their daily mail route. (Courtesy Bobby Martindale Memorial Library.)

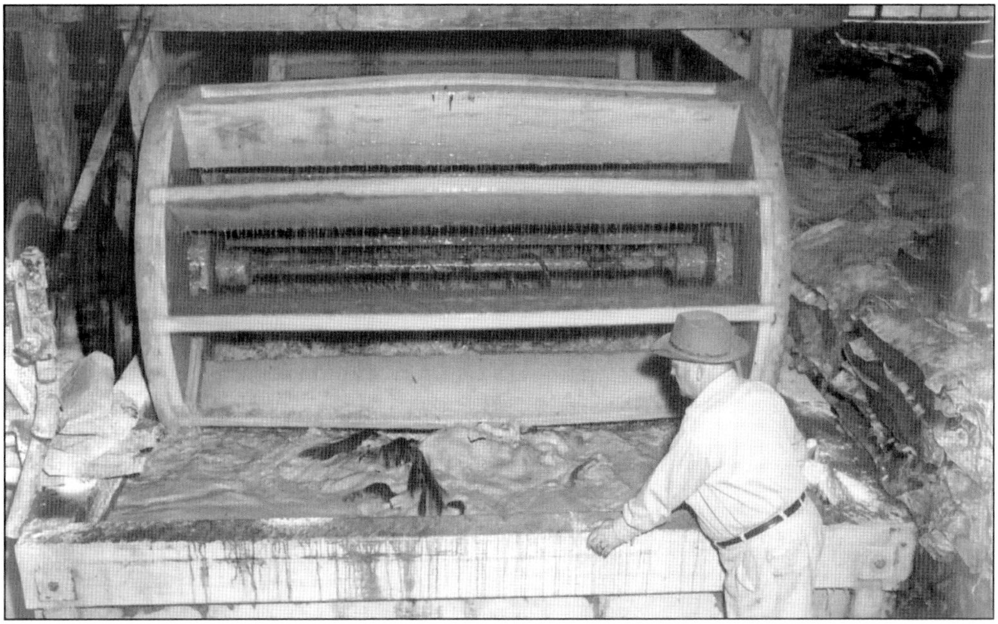

The International Shoe Company began production in Bolivar in early 1948 and recognized "Bolivar's postwar dream of opening an industrial plant in the area." The 1,000 to 2,000 hides tanned per day were used to make upper portions for many well-known shoe companies throughout the United States. Charles "Shorty" Sewell is pictured with the hide-tanning operation in the 1950s. (Courtesy Pat Vincent.)

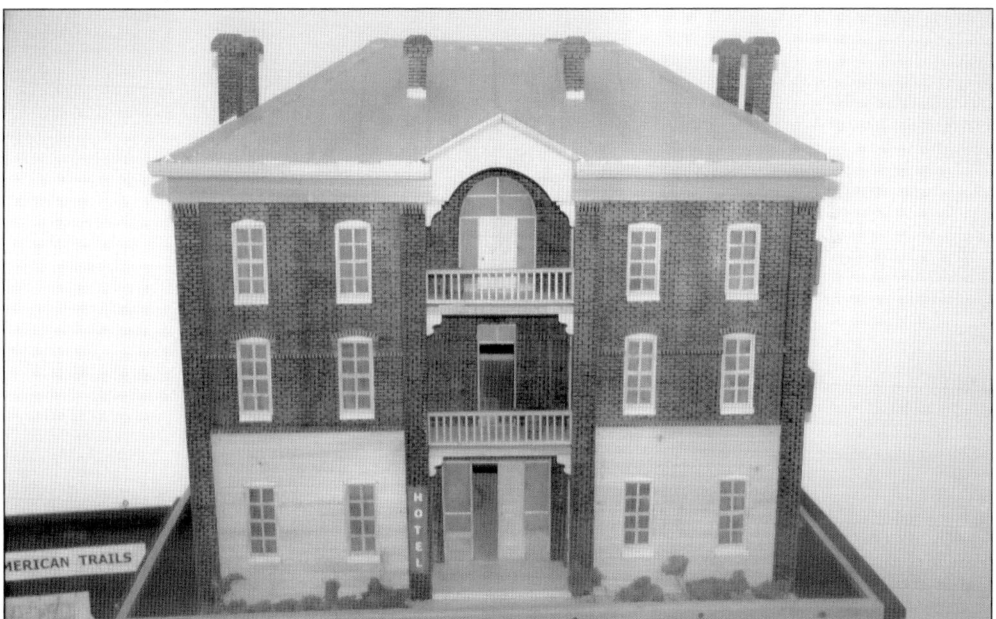

Original stockholders of the old Bolivar Hotel purchased shares in the business for $100 each in August 1872. The three-story structure operated on the court square for many years and was once the tallest building between Memphis and Nashville. This scale model, made by Gordon Smalley, is on display at the Little Courthouse Museum. (Lisa C. Coleman.)

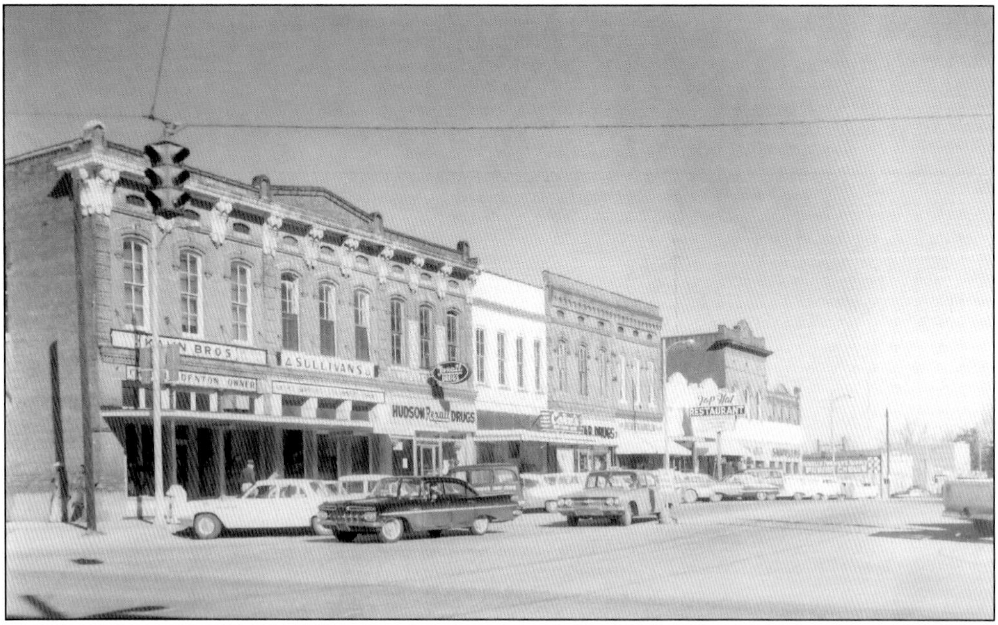

Many early-1960s shoppers in Bolivar remember visiting Kahn Brothers, Sullivan's, Hudson Drugs, and Bolivar Drug Store, and eating at the Top Hat Restaurant. The old Hardeman County Co-Op Building is visible in the distance, at the corner of Main and Jackson Streets. Most businesses closed on Thursdays and opened on Saturdays to accommodate shoppers from more rural areas who came to town on Saturday afternoons. (Lisa C. Coleman.)

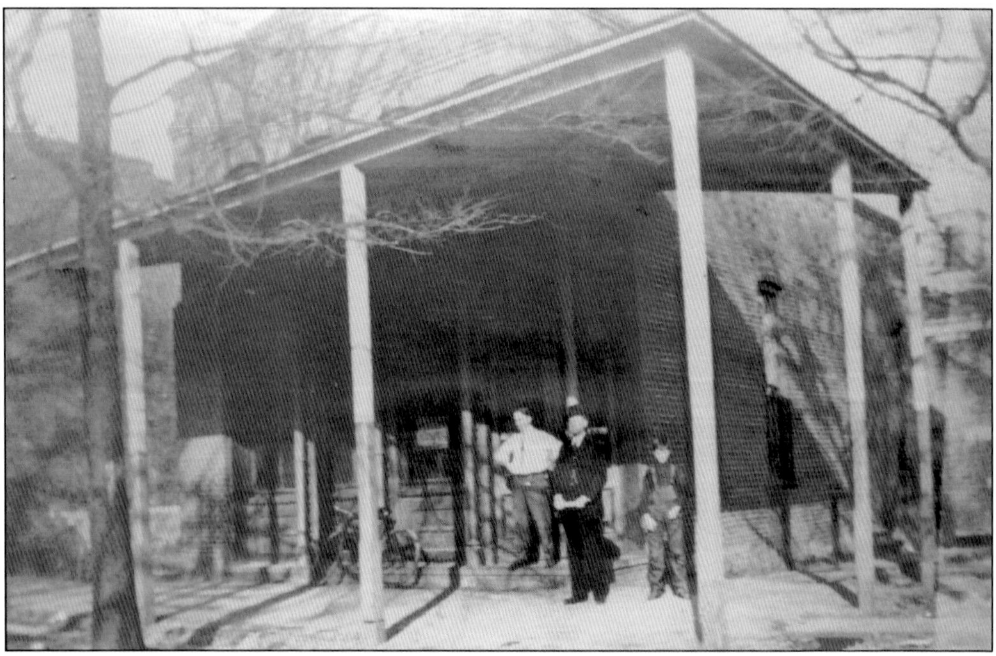

Hardeman County's first known newspaper, the *Bolivar Palladium*, began publishing in 1829. Other papers followed, until the appearance of the *Bolivar Bulletin* in 1865. R.H. Green and Hugh Williams bought the paper in 1888. Its offices and press were located at the corner of Warren and Market Streets for many years. (Courtesy the Arthur Jr. & Esther Wheeler Family.)

Six

The Sporting Life

Hardeman County is or has been home to sports endeavors of all kinds since the first settlers came to the area. Early settlers had contests for everything from horse races to who could catch the largest fish out of the Hatchie, with some astonishingly large catches coming from the river!

As the population grew, sports and athletics became popular activities. Ball teams appeared all over the county—some affiliated with schools, some with the "semi-professional" leagues of their eras. Grand Junction and Vildo boasted popular and successful baseball teams in the early 1900s. For many years, Bolivar's only baseball field was located on the grounds of the Western State Hospital, with a large grandstand for enthusiastic spectators. Basketball and football teams soon followed, and the county has been home to several very successful players and teams. Middleton's Bailey Howell was named a basketball All-American in the mid-1950s, and the Middleton team was ranked first in West Tennessee. Other players from the county who achieved national recognition include Bobby Parks, Willie Kemp, and Wayne Chism. Hardeman County basketball teams have won several state championships, most notably in 2005, when the Bolivar and Middleton boys' teams won state titles in their divisions.

Hunting, which also dates back to the earliest settlers, is another popular aspect of the county's sporting life. Hardeman County is home to the National Bird Dog Museum (in Grand Junction), and the National Championship for Field Trialing Bird Dogs (aka National Field Trial Championship) is held each year on the Ames Plantation.

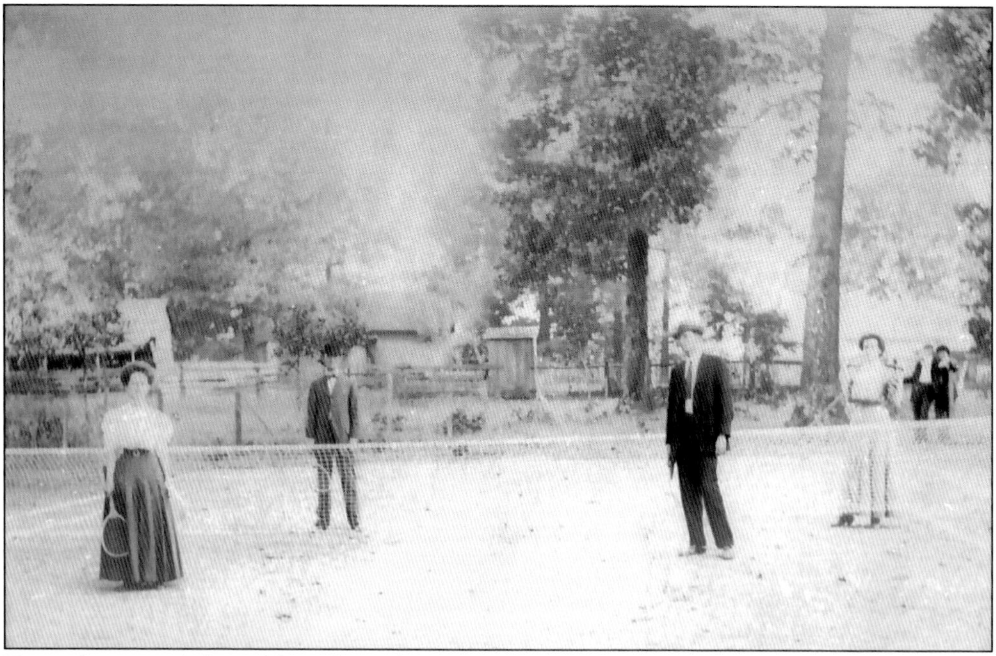

Tennis became a fashionable and popular sport for young ladies and gentlemen in the early 1900s, finding its way to these players in Middleton. Shown at a "town court" on June 16, 1909, are, from left to right, Addie Cox, Tom Moore, unidentified, and Pearl Hudson. (Courtesy Hardeman County Genealogical Society.)

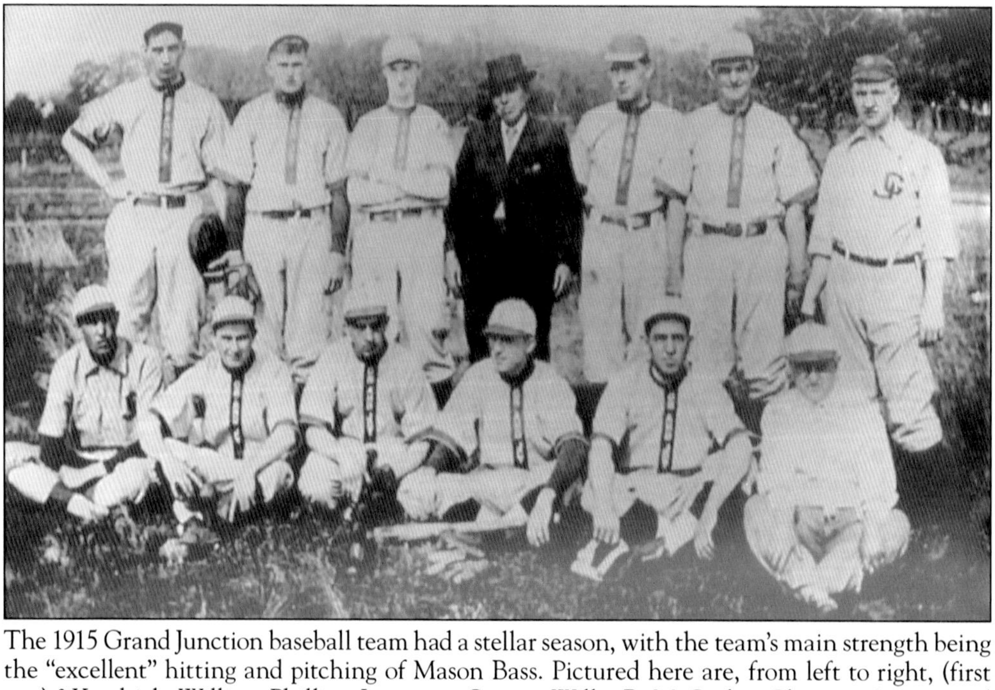

The 1915 Grand Junction baseball team had a stellar season, with the team's main strength being the "excellent" hitting and pitching of Mason Bass. Pictured here are, from left to right, (first row) ? Kendrick, William Phillips, Lawrence Stroup, Willie B. McCarley, Clarence Stroup, and Ike Ewing; (second row) Ed Gibbs, Mason Bass, Jim Grant, manager C.M. Hunt, Bruce Tipler, Lloyd Stroup, and J.E. "Ted" Gee. (Courtesy David Vinyard.)

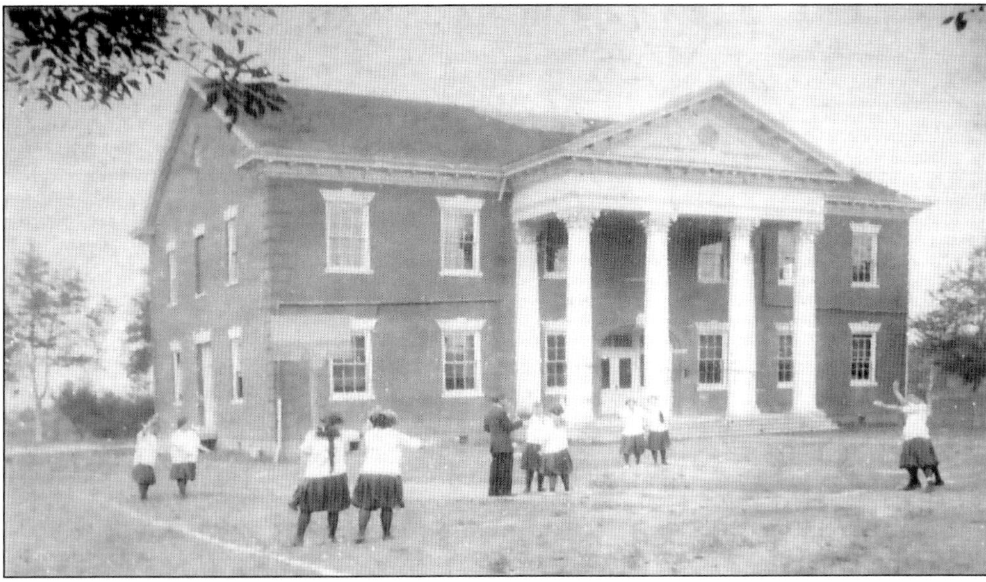

Organized sports teams for girls increased in popularity around the early 1900s. The 1915 Bolivar Central High School girls' basketball team is pictured practicing in front of the school. Lucy Smith and Eleanor Ferguson are two of the players shown on the grass court; other players are unidentified. The young ladies are wearing the team uniforms of the time—loose blousy tops, skirts, and dark tights. (Courtesy Hardeman County Genealogical Society.)

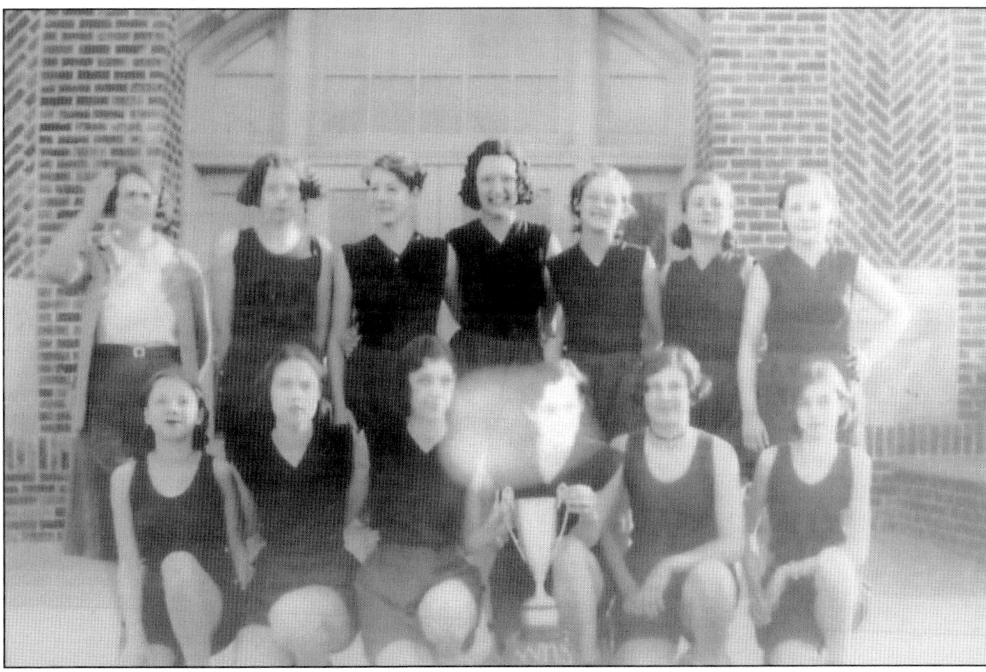

Pictured in 1932 is the first basketball team at the "new" Whiteville High School. The team members are, from left to right, (first row) Maxine Woods, Rachael Buchanan, Venita Hazelwood, Evelyn Deen, Poly Holmes, and Gwendolyn Hazelwood; (second row) unidentified, Ellen Coffman, Virginia Mitchell, Frances Coffman, Margaret Jo Mitchell, Opal Woods, and Marie Rogers. (Courtesy Bettye H. Perry.)

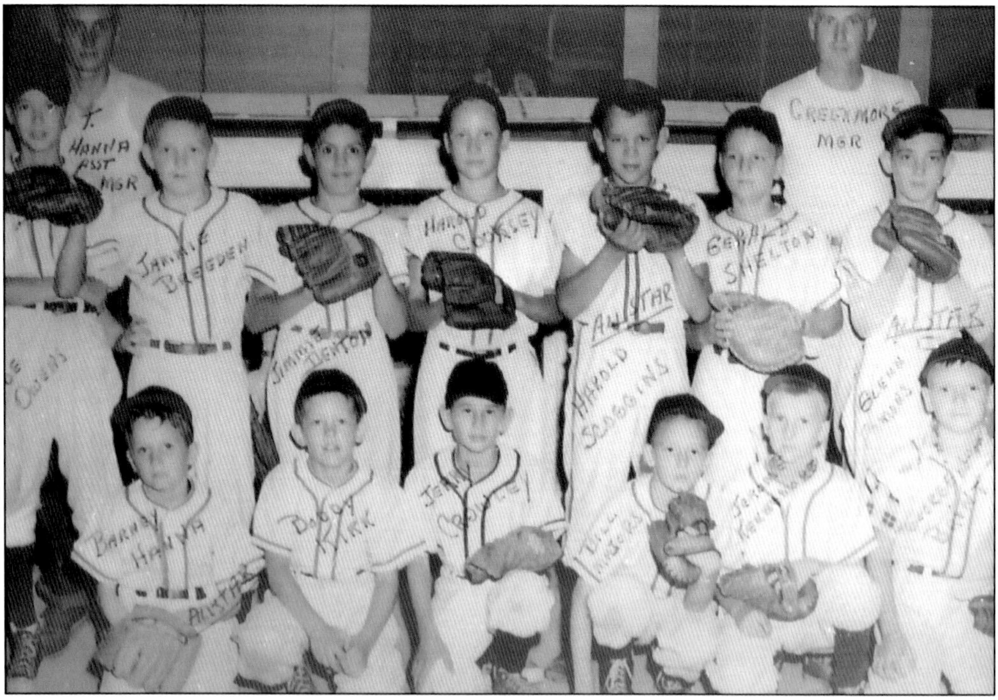

Little League arrived in Bolivar in the 1950s, beginning with four teams. Pictured above is the Rotary team; they are, from left to right, (first row) Barney Hanna, Bobby Kirk, Jerry Crowely, Bill Majors, Jerome Kennamore, and George Wayne Brint; (second row) Joe Owens, Jamie Breeden, Jimmie Denton, Harold Cooksey, Harold Scoggins, Gerald Shelton, and Glenn ?. Assistant manager Terry Hanna (left) and manager Marion Creekmore Sr. stand behind the team. The VFW team photograph below includes, from left to right, (first row) Bill Cates, Larry Creekmore, Ted Clifft, Bill Moss, Johnnie Doyle, and Terry Bomar; (second row) manager Robert S. Owens, Tommy Stallings, Greg Polk, Jerry Alphin, Jimmy Cupples, Don Clifft, Jimmy Bankston, and assistant manager Marion Creekmore Jr. (Both, courtesy Hardeman County Genealogical Society.)

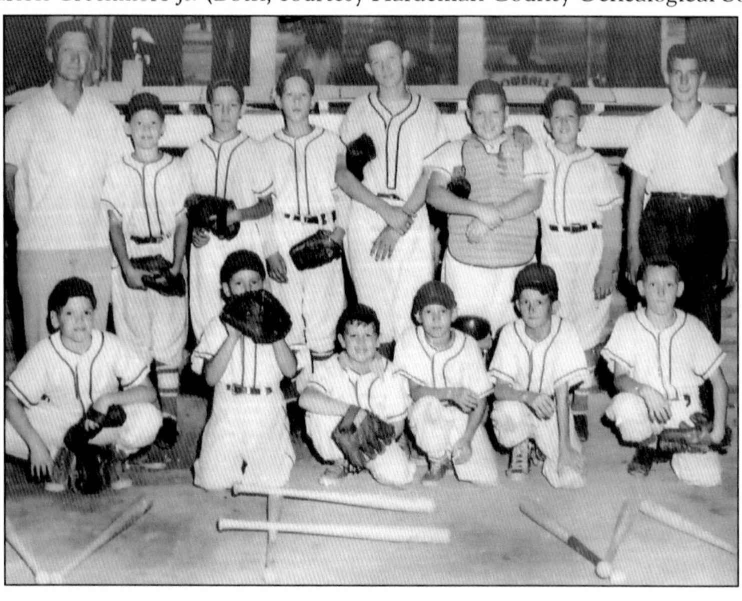

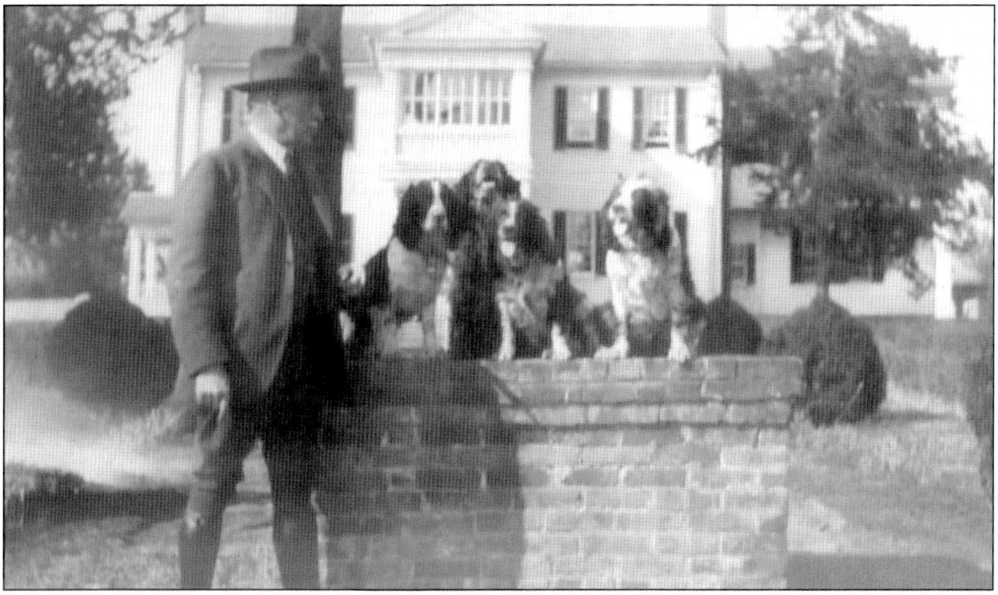

The home of Hobart and Julia Ames, purchased about 1901, eventually became the permanent home of the National Championship for Field Trialing Bird Dogs. Hobart Ames, an avid sportsman, is pictured about 1940 at the manor house entrance with a brace of English Springer Spaniels, a flushing breed the Ames were quite fond of, although they are best known for association with the pointing dog breeds. (Courtesy National Bird Dog Museum.)

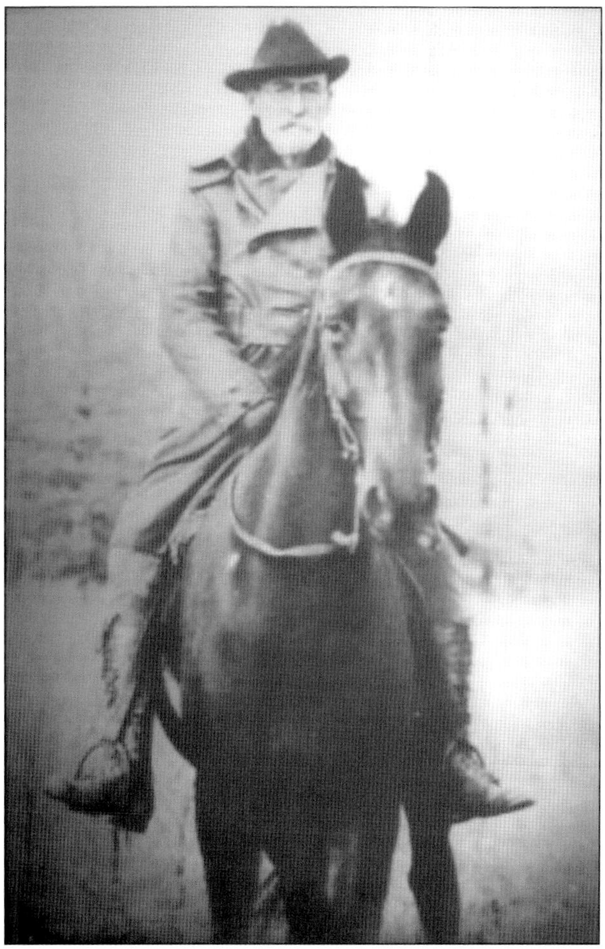

James Monroe "Jim" Avent from Hickory Valley, pictured around 1898, ran a hunting lodge and a popular summer retreat at Rogers Springs called "The Rustic Inn." Best known as a bird-dog trainer and field trial competitor, his dogs won the National Field Trial Championship eight times, beginning with the 1896 inaugural event. He also kept foxhounds and was nicknamed "The Fox of Hickory Valley." (Courtesy National Bird Dog Museum.)

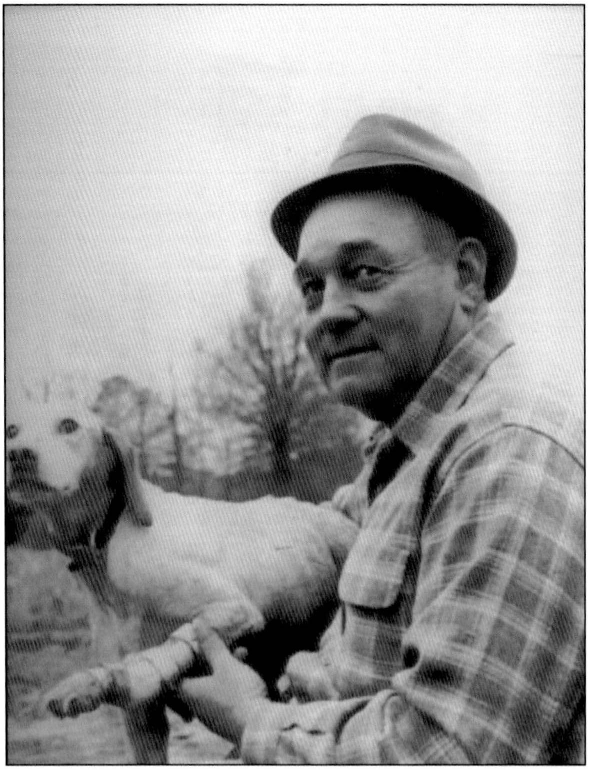

Dick Goddard Sr., of Grand Junction, is pictured in 1960 with an English Pointer female named "Lady Ames." Goddard, originally from Georgia, was an assistant manager who joined the University of Tennessee-Ames Plantation staff in 1956. He had a special affinity for bird dogs. The plantation is one of the University of Tennessee's ag research and education centers. (Courtesy National Bird Dog Museum.)

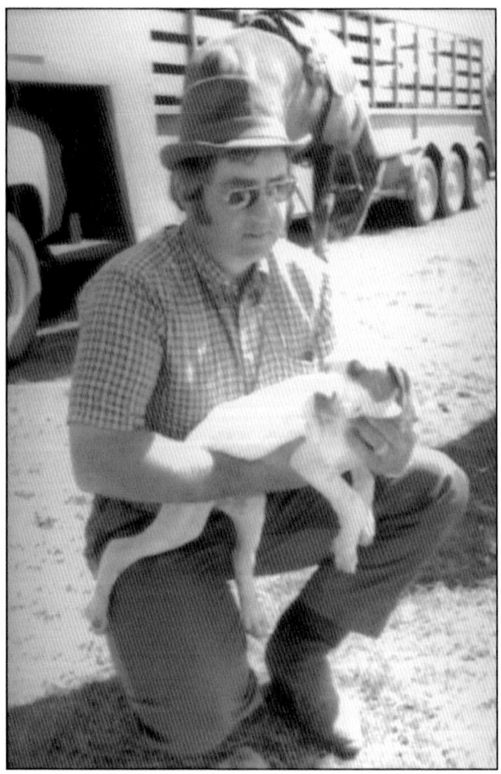

John Rex Gates, of Bolivar, had a stellar career as a trainer of winning field trial bird dogs and is pictured with an English Pointer puppy in the mid-1960s. Gates was elected to the Field Trial Hall of Fame in 1978. Both dogs and people are eligible for nomination to the Hall of Fame. (Courtesy National Bird Dog Museum.)

In this c. 1950 image, Vaiden Jenkins, of Saulsbury/Grand Junction, releases a brace of English Setters. Jenkins was a professional trainer of competition bird dogs. Though he never won, his career included at least one appearance in the National Field Trial Championship, when he handled a dog named "Stylish Mr. Joe" in 1935. (Courtesy National Bird Dog Museum.)

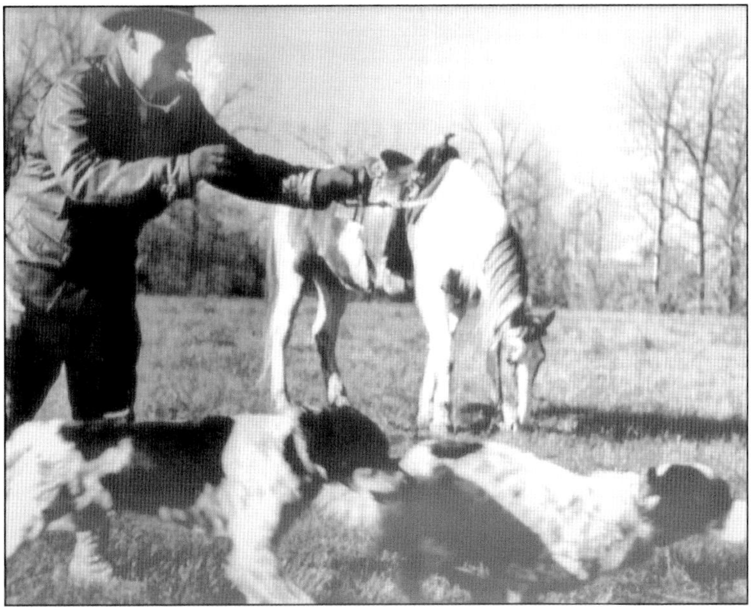

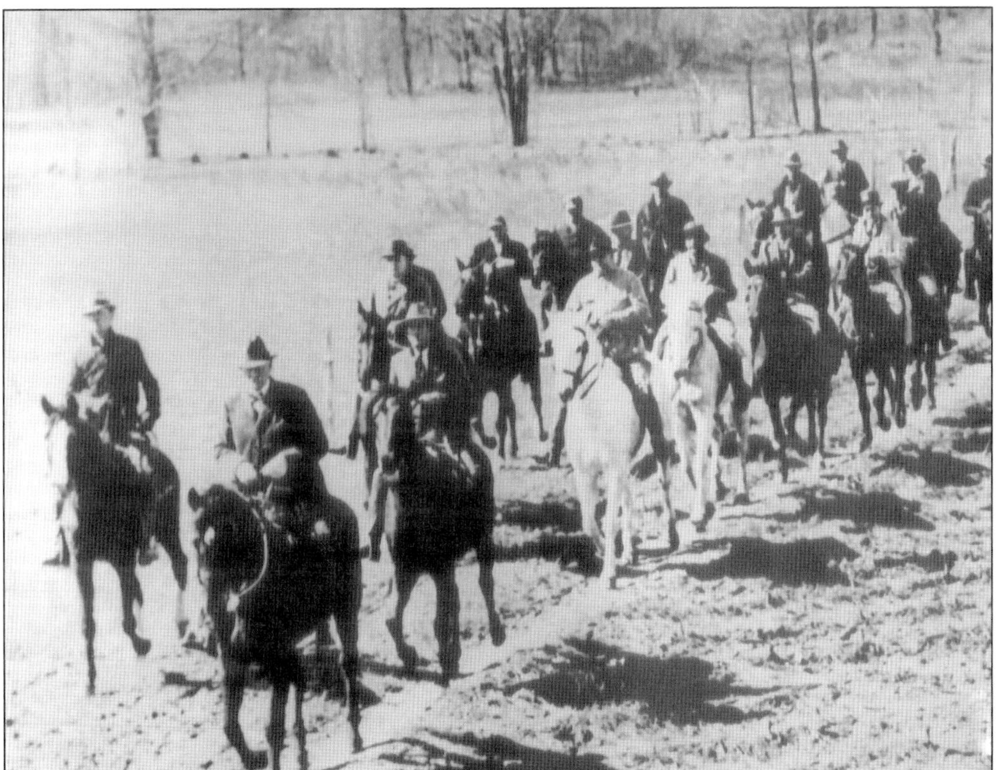

The National Field Trial Championship was first organized and run in 1896 near West Point, Mississippi, moved to Rogers Springs and Grand Junction, and found a permanent home on the Ames Plantation in 1915. Each February, entrants come from across the United States and Canada to compete. This gallery, during one brace at the 1937 championship, shows Hobart Ames riding at the head of the line. (Courtesy Hardeman County Chamber of Commerce.)

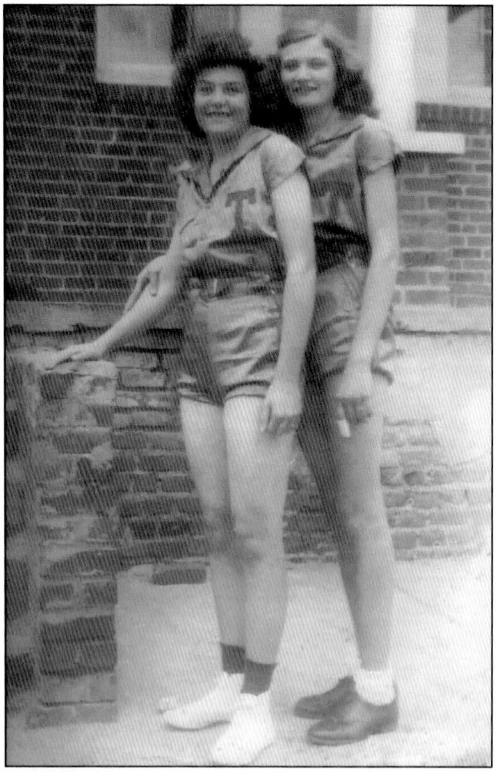

Freddie Kiestler (Coleman), left, and Bernice Overton (Daniel), right, played for the Toone School girls' basketball team in the late 1940s. On one memorable occasion, the team visited another school and the host team locked all of the Toone players in the locker room before the game! (Lisa C. Coleman.)

The Allen White School, in Whiteville, boasted championship boys' (in 1938) and girls' basketball teams; the girls' team won the 1940 and 1941 National Negro Basketball Tournaments, held in Tuskegee, Alabama. The members of the 1941 championship team pictured here are, from left to right, (first row) Georgia McKinnie, Elizabeth Jones, Addir Bell Williams, and Helen Brown; (second row) Ida Tynes, Helen Shepherd, Emma D. Herron, Matha Woods, Beatrice Woods, and Marie Brady. (Courtesy Evelyn C. Robertson Jr.)

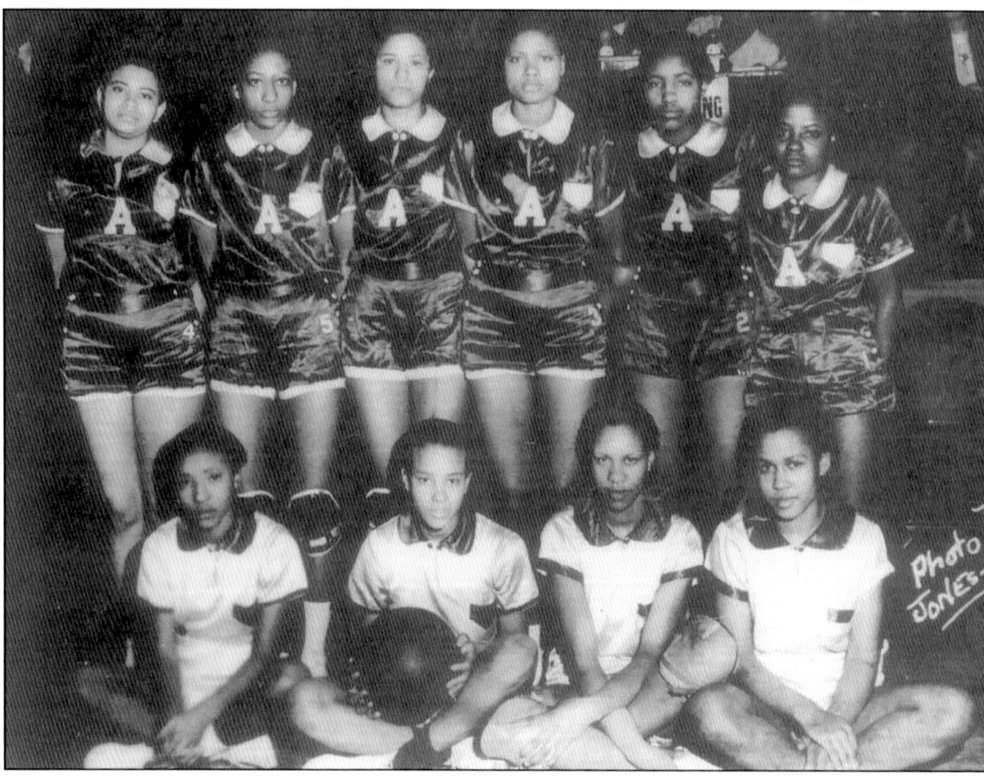

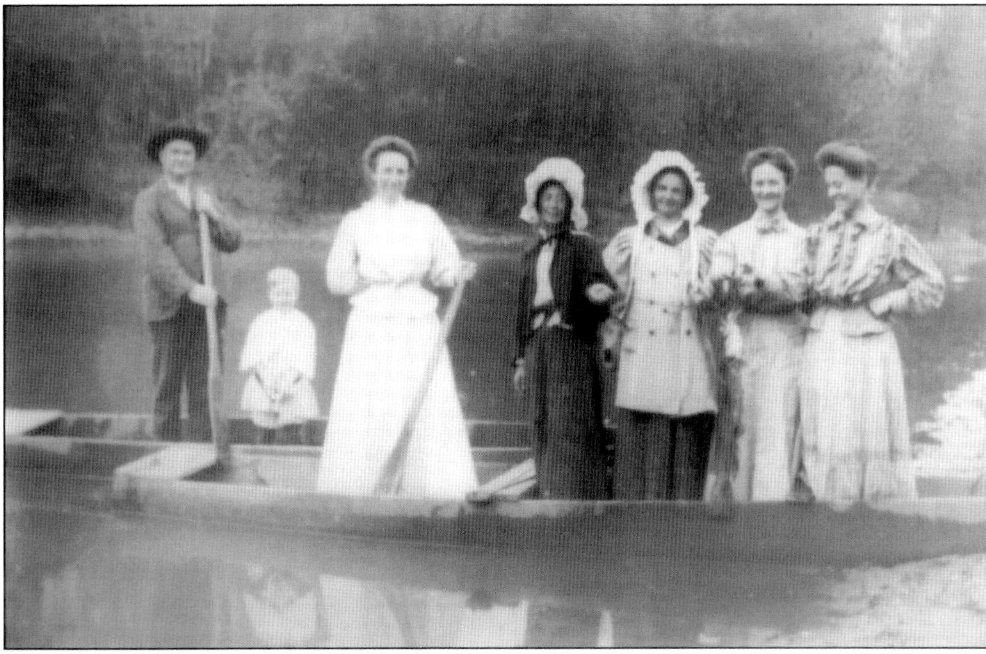

Fishing was very popular along the Hatchie River and was a pastime enjoyed by all ages. Young William Charley Joyner is shown at left with his parents (to his left and right) and unidentified family friends after a day of fishing on the river. William Joyner later served as a mail carrier in the Pocahontas area for many years. (Courtesy Esta Lee Lamberth.)

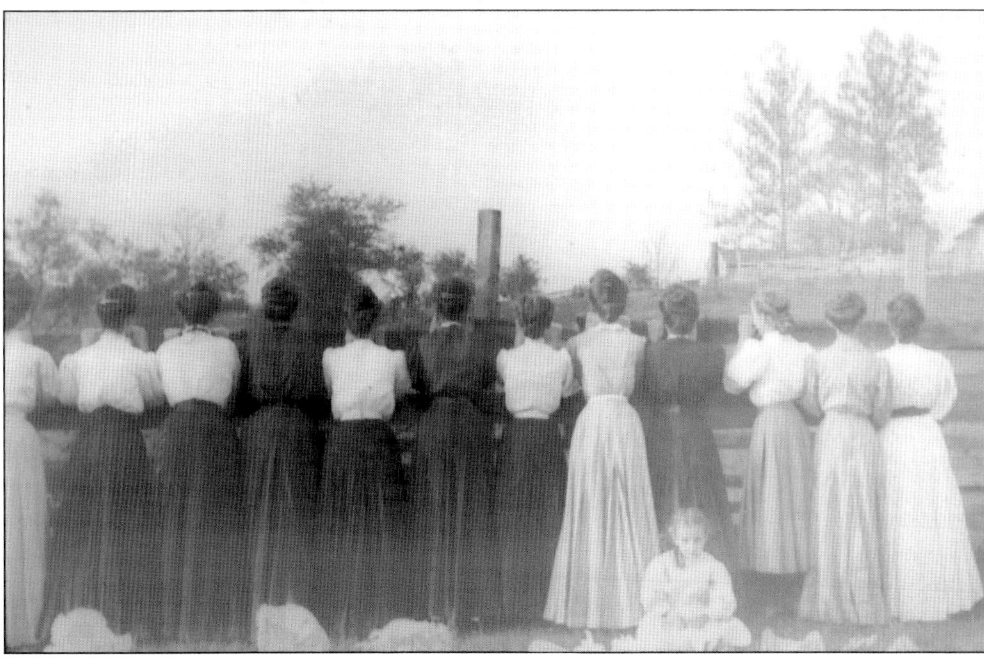

In the early 1900s, the owner of the livery stable at Pocahontas made a racetrack beside the stable and held horse races. Gentlemen spectators could sit or stand trackside to watch the races, but women, like the ones pictured here, had to watch from behind a fence. (Courtesy Esta Lee Lamberth.)

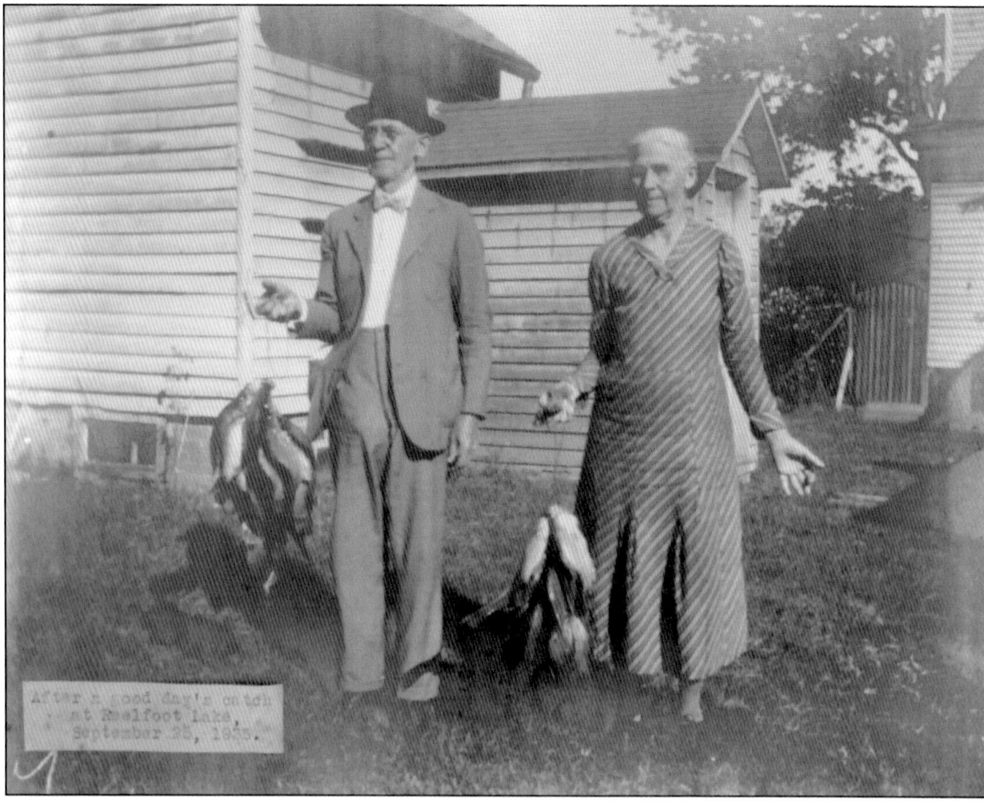

Dr. B.V. Hudson was a well-loved and respected pharmacist in Hardeman County. He and his wife, Maggie (Coleman), were married on November 8, 1887, and both enjoyed outdoor pursuits. Dr. Hudson is remembered as an "ardent sportsman" who enjoyed hunting, fishing, trapshooting, baseball, and many other sports. He and Mrs. Hudson are pictured above on September 25, 1935, with what they called "a good day's catch" after fishing at Reelfoot Lake. Below, a photograph from November 19, 1924, shows Dr. Hudson and his son-in-law, A.B. Young, after returning from a successful duck hunt at Reelfoot Lake. (Both, courtesy Gary Fish.)

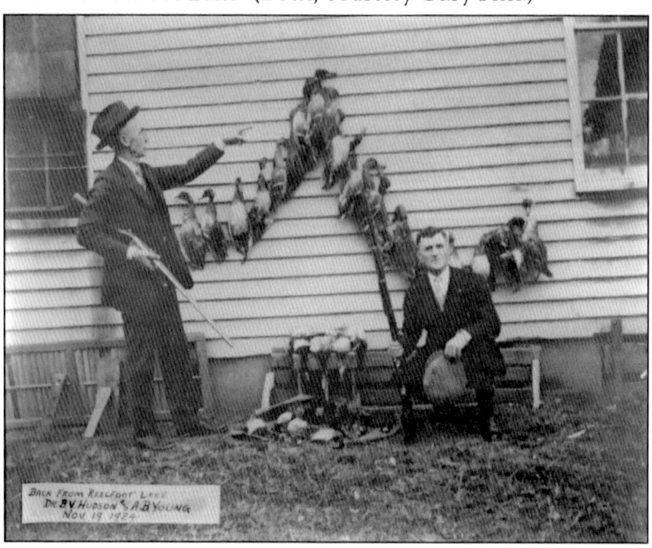

Seven

Music Makers

The earliest musical sounds made in the county no doubt came from the indigenous Chickasaw tribes who inhabited the area for hundreds of years. Many of the early white settlers hailed from North Carolina, Virginia, and East Tennessee, and brought their instruments and the music of their ancestors with them to the Tennessee frontier, making "new music" in the young county. Their voices and songs could be heard as they worked, rocked their babies, celebrated, mourned, and worshipped.

Early newspaper accounts mention singings and various musical programs in all parts of the county, usually associated with school programs or church services. In the years after the Civil War, "musicales" became a popular pastime, usually held at a home for a small group of family and friends. Local bands and musicians performed for groups, special events, and local politicians traveling through the area. Music instructors patiently taught students each year and showcased the young talents in recitals and programs. Later, school bands added notes to pep rallies, parades, and ballgames.

In 2007, the Hardeman County Music Commission was formed to continue the county's musical traditions. Hundreds gather each Friday night on the court square from April through October for "Music on the Square," open-mike nights are held on the square on Tuesday evenings, and Saturday nights are reserved for gospel music. Throughout the year, festivals all over the county feature local musical talent of all ages. The Hardeman County Music Festival and Hatchie Hollow Hog Fest began in 2008 and quickly became a very popular event, with attendance of over 8,000 during the October 2010 event.

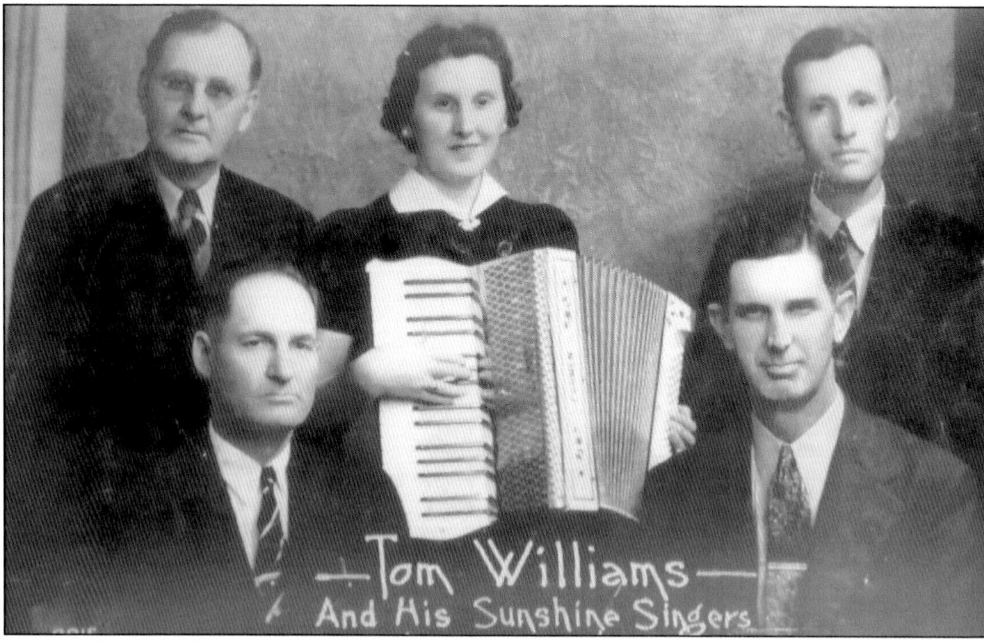

Tom Williams & his Sunshine Singers, pictured above, were a popular musical group from Middleton (one member was from Henderson, Tennessee). The group performed all over West Tennessee and North Mississippi and later appeared for many years on a 1940s radio program that was broadcast from Jackson, Tennessee. Pictured in a 1940s photograph are, from left to right, (first row) Ike Street and Walter E. Howell; (second row) "Uncle" Tom Williams, Lillian Howell, and Carl Alford. The c. 1917 photograph below shows Burley Howell (left) and a young Walter Howell playing music on the accordion and fiddle. (Both, courtesy Gail Mills.)

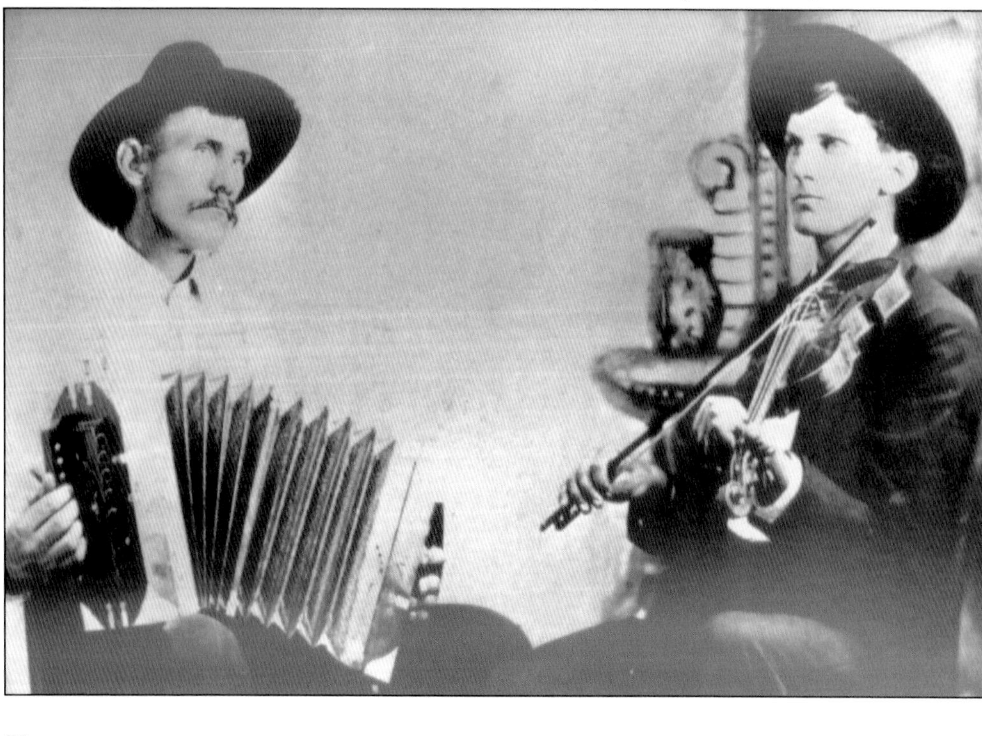

Bertha Sipes Vaughan (right) was born and raised in Hardeman County and has loved music from an early age. A member of the Slim Rhodes weekly television and radio shows in Memphis, she also performed with the band at area shows. Music has remained an important part of Vaughan's life, and in the early 1980s she was one of the original organizers of the county's *Hee Haw!* show, an annual fundraiser for the American Cancer Society. Early shows (below) had Vaughan as the musical director and Don Shackelford (bottom right, facing the stage) as writer, producer, and director. (Both, courtesy Ed and Loretta Doles, Country Cabin Music Museum.)

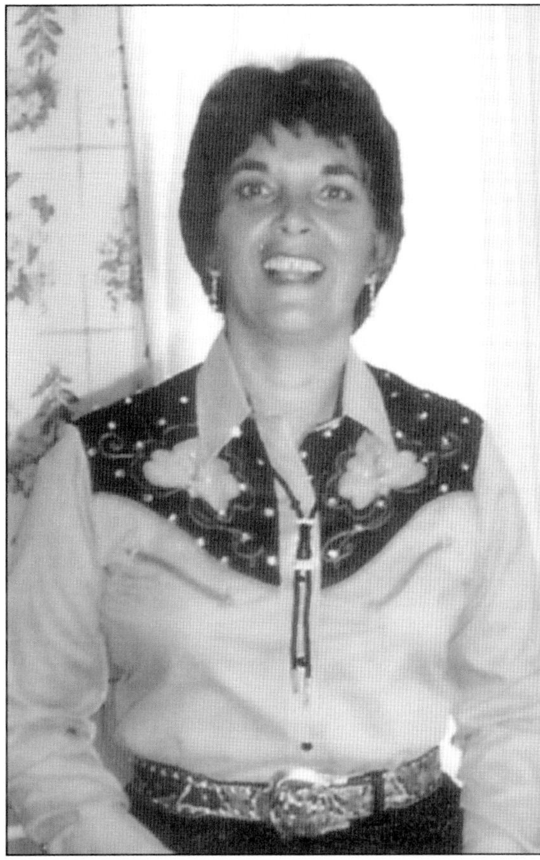

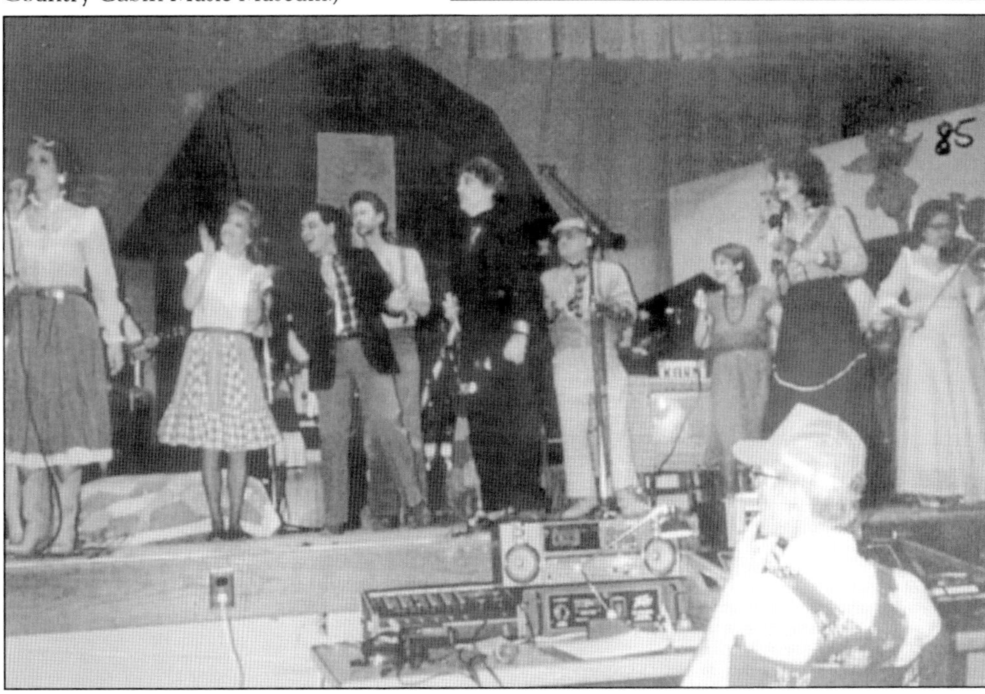

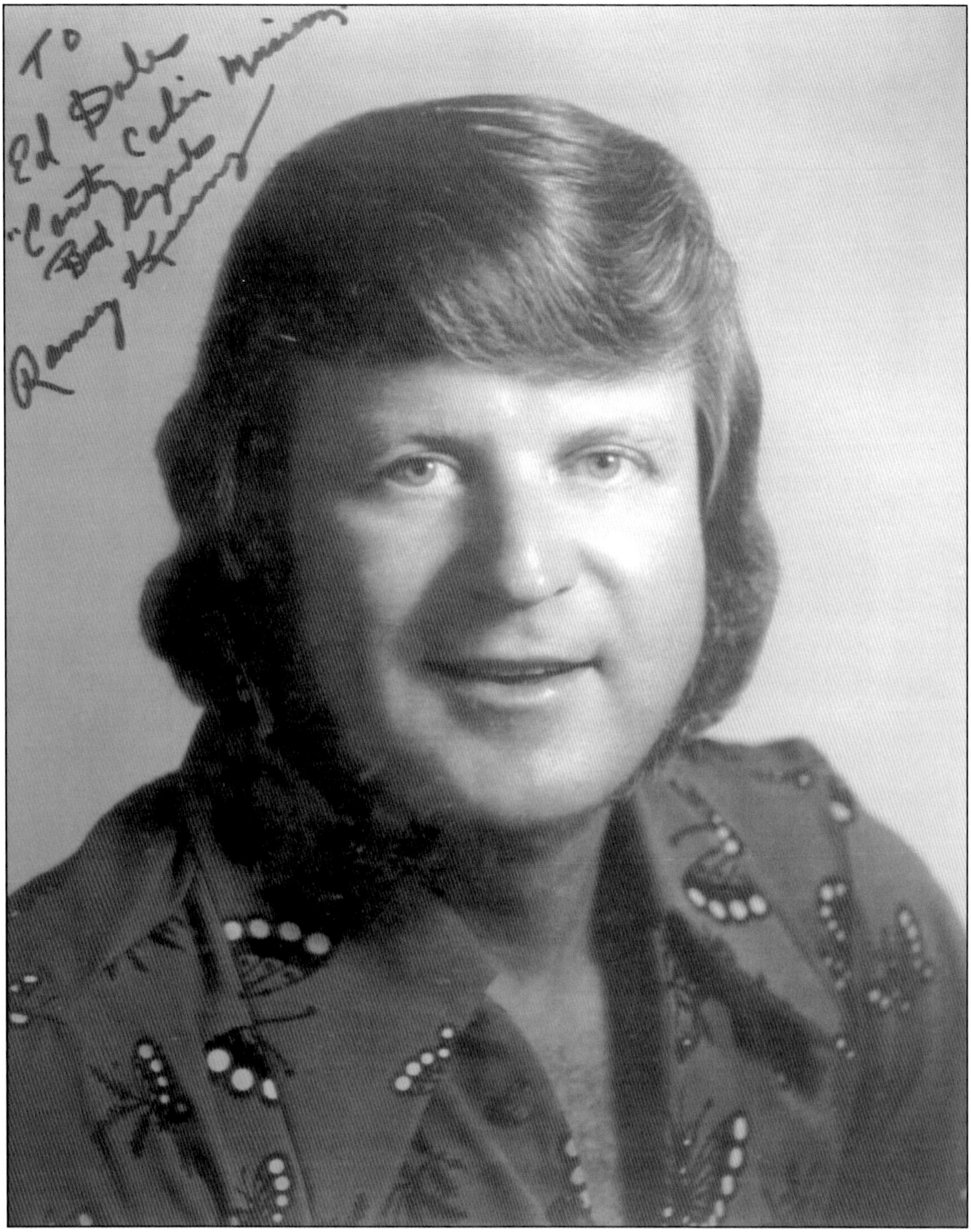

Bolivar native Ramsey Kearney began playing music on WDXI in Jackson as the "Dixie Farmboy" and later hosted his own program for several years; Carl Perkins was an early guest on one of his shows. Kearney continued to work in the music industry, eventually going to Nashville, where he found success working as a songwriter for the Acuff-Rose Publishing Company. He has been a singer, writer, producer, and arranger and is the owner of Nashco Music Service. (Courtesy Ed and Loretta Doles, Country Cabin Music Museum.)

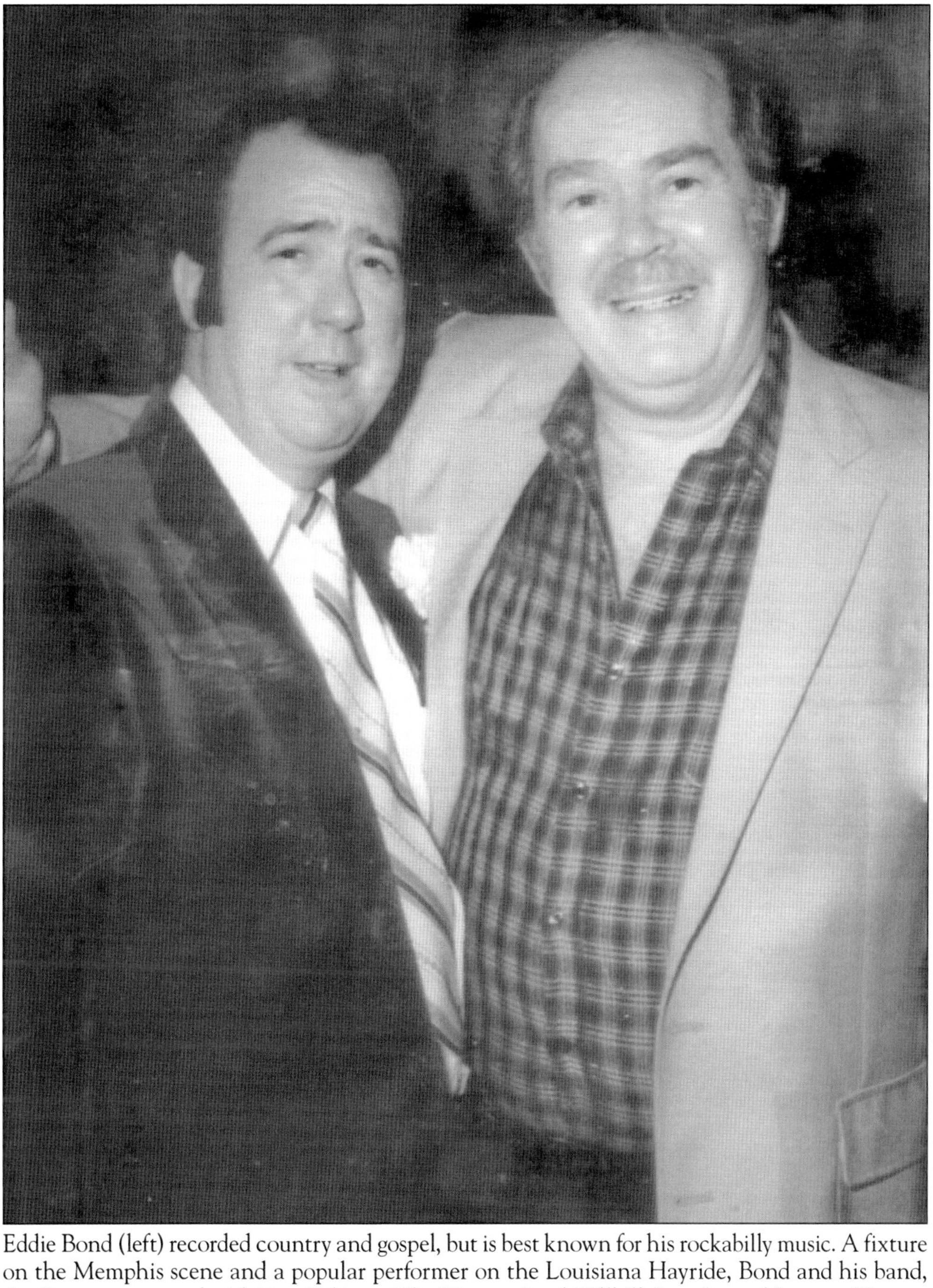

Eddie Bond (left) recorded country and gospel, but is best known for his rockabilly music. A fixture on the Memphis scene and a popular performer on the Louisiana Hayride, Bond and his band, the Stompers, toured with Roy Orbison. The "Brown-Eyed Hillbilly" performed for over 50 years in venues across the United States and also had a large European fan base. He is shown with Jim Sanderson, a Hardeman County native who played music for many years, including a stint as a steel guitar player for Jerry Lee Lewis in the late 1950s. Sanderson later became an attorney, but continued to be involved in music for his entire life. (Courtesy Ed and Loretta Doles, Country Cabin Music Museum.)

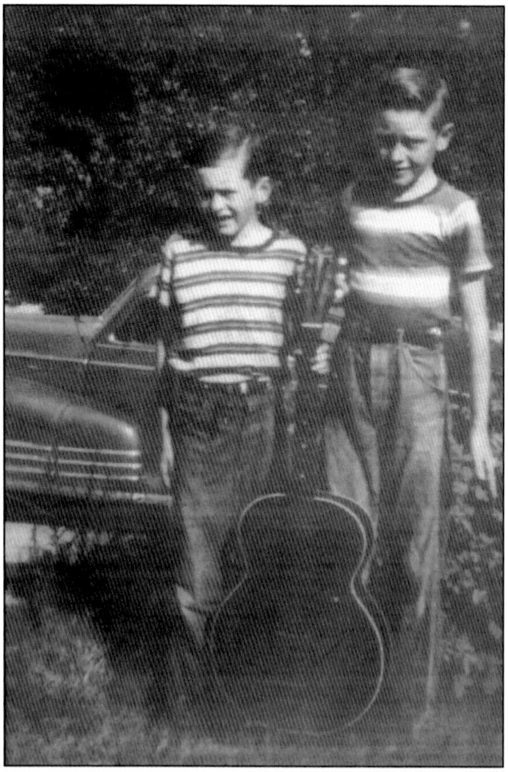

Ed Doles (pictured at left with his brother, Willard), born and raised in Hardeman County, developed an early love of music. In the 1960s, he was one of the members of Gladys Griffen and The Dixie Playboys, and Doles and his high school sweetheart, Laura Loretta Sheehy (pictured below with Ed) married about the same time. A chance friendship with rockabilly legend Eddie Bond later encouraged them to open the Country Cabin Records & Museum in Hornsby. The museum includes photographs, records, costumes, instruments, and even a replica of the 1950s-era control room at Memphis radio station WHBQ—the station that first broadcast rock 'n' roll to the world. (Both courtesy Ed and Loretta Doles, Country Cabin Music Museum.)

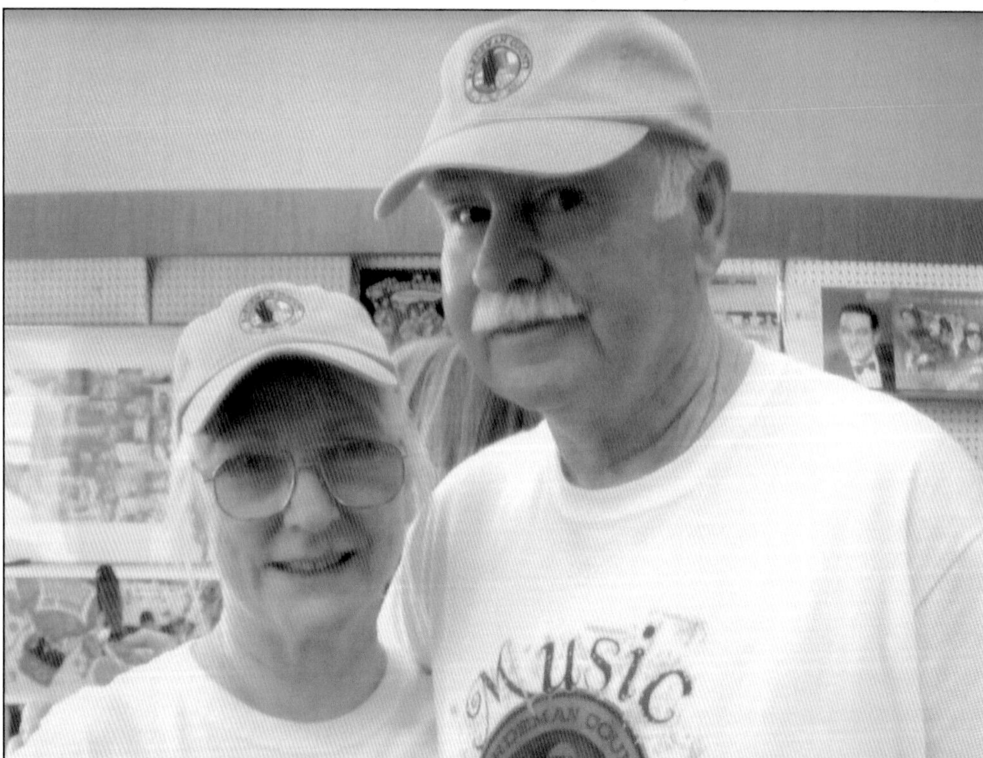

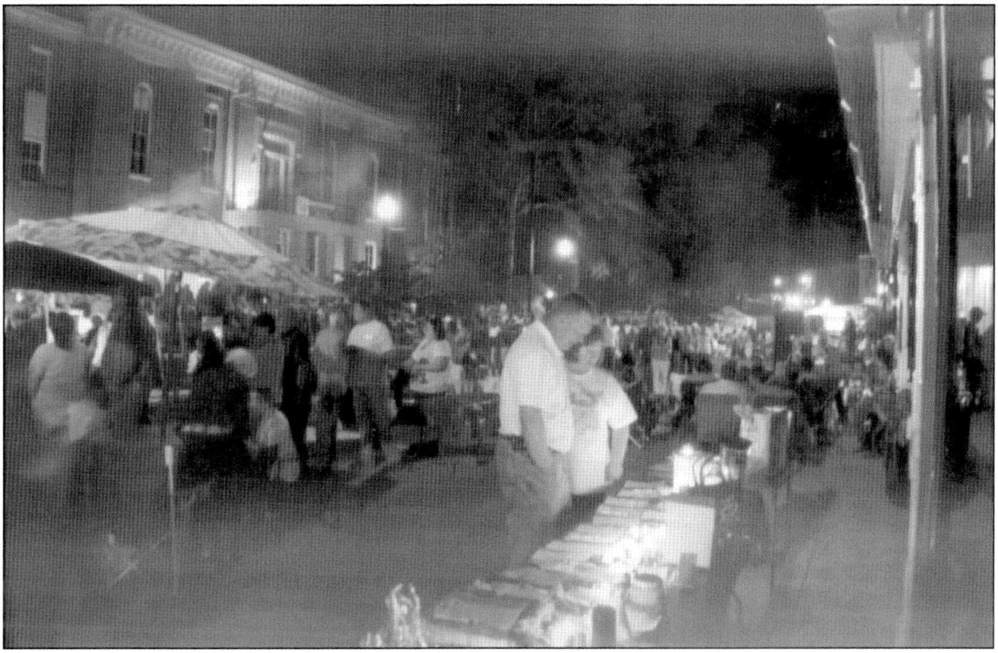

Friday nights are music nights at the courthouse square in Bolivar. "Music on the Square" is held every Friday night from May through October and features musicians from the county and its surrounding area. The kickoff event for Music on the Square is the annual Relay for Life event. (Lisa C. Coleman.)

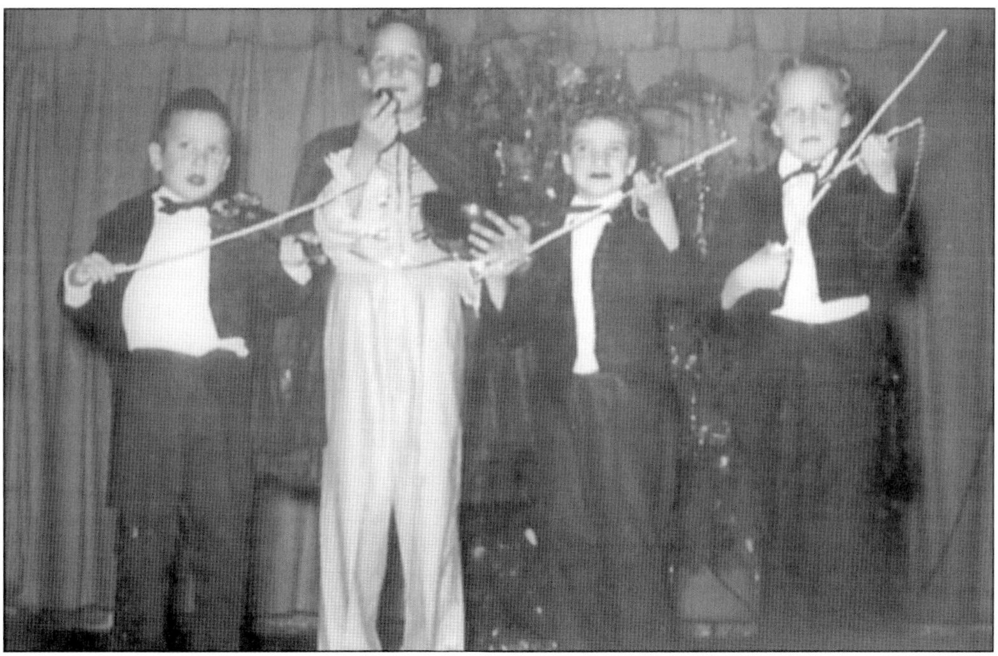

Musical programs are always popular events for schools, and this group of youngsters at Grand Junction School enjoys the holiday play and musical during the 1954–1955 school year. Portraying "Old King Cole and His Fiddlers Three" are, from left to right, David Stewart, Kenneth Daniels, Lynn Ray, and Billie Maclin. (Courtesy Jane Maclin Moore.)

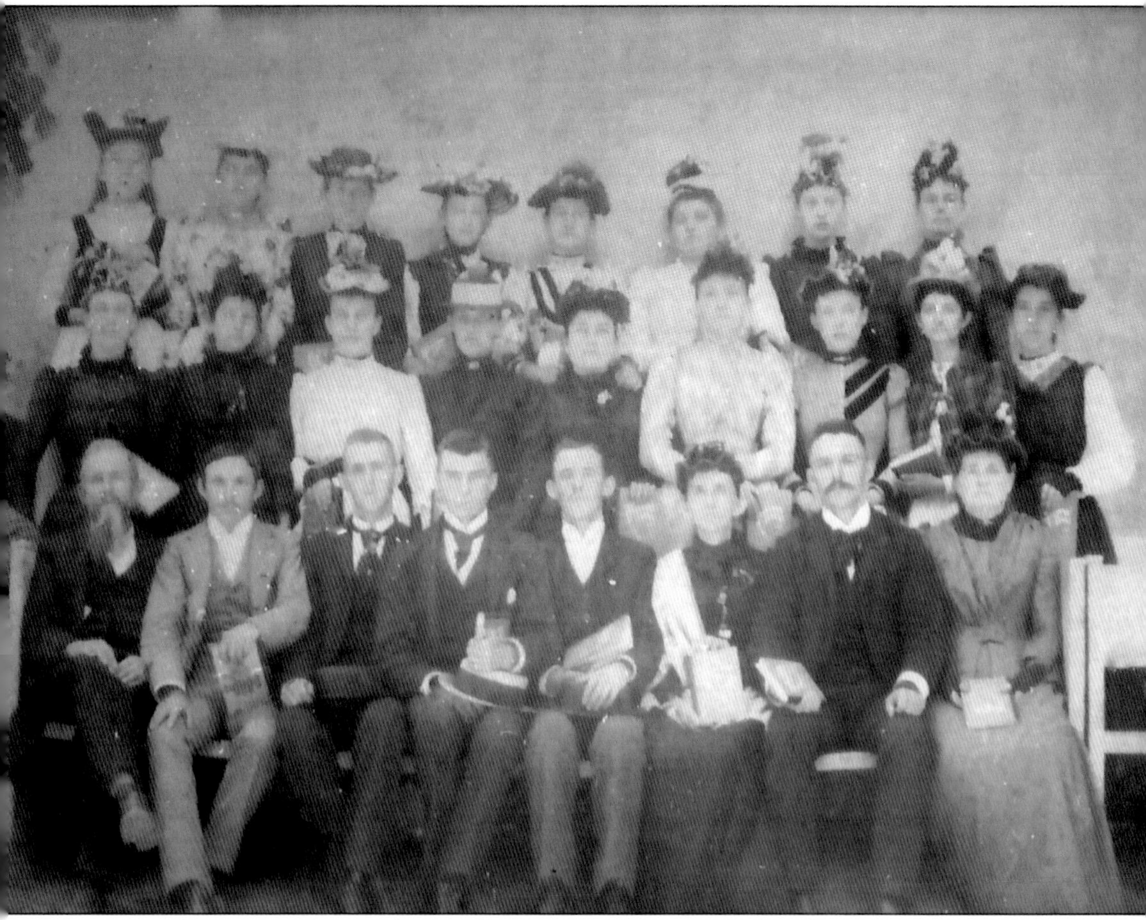

Around 1843, David Wood began efforts to establish a Methodist church meetinghouse in the Shinault Community (near present-day Hickory Valley) by asking friends and neighbors to donate whatever they could—nails, logs, labor, or money; one man, Boling Branch, agreed to donate 50 pounds of nails. Contributions for the church came from New Castle, Middleburg, and Van Buren. Trustees for the church, named the Bush Meeting House, were William A. Mask, T.P. McLarty, John M. Richardson, Henry Williams, and David Woods. The Bush Meeting House and later the Bush Campground enjoyed a large membership, and meetings at the campground each summer were eagerly anticipated. This choir from 1899 added music to the services that were held that summer. Seated fifth from left is David McAnulty; the others are unidentified. (Courtesy Hardeman County Genealogical Society.)

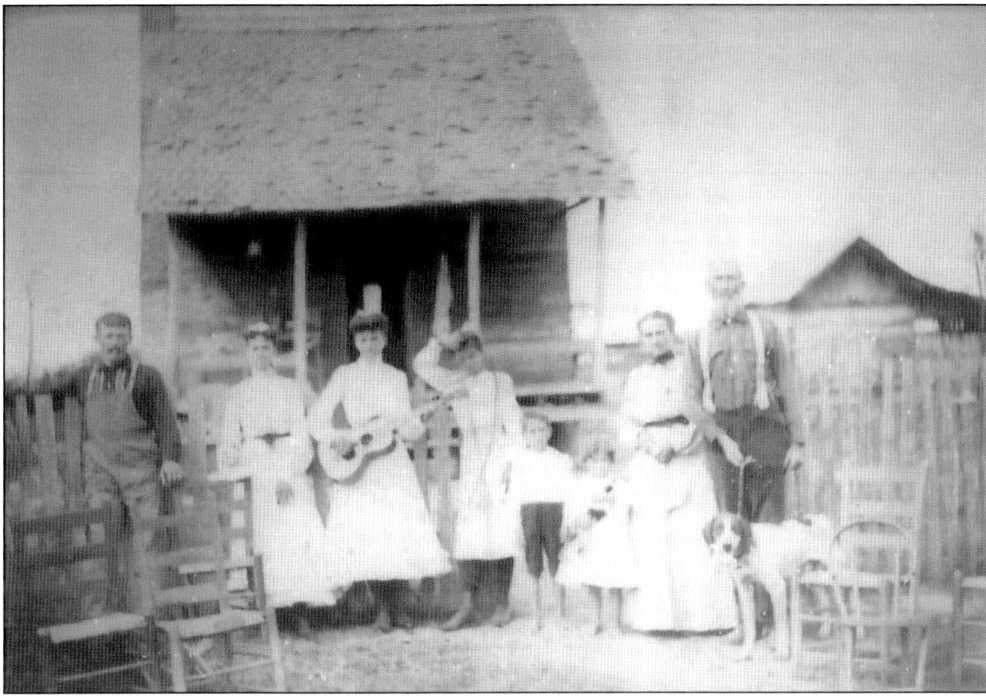

Pitser Miller Smalley and Maria Adeline "Addie" Achord married on February 5, 1874, and became the parents of nine children. Smalley and Achord are pictured here around 1910 with their children at their home near Middleburg. Singing, playing, and enjoying music together as a family are, from left to right, Jack Clark, Bettie Mae, Ada, Minnie Lee, Jesse, Elsie, Addie, and Pitser. (Courtesy Pat Vincent.)

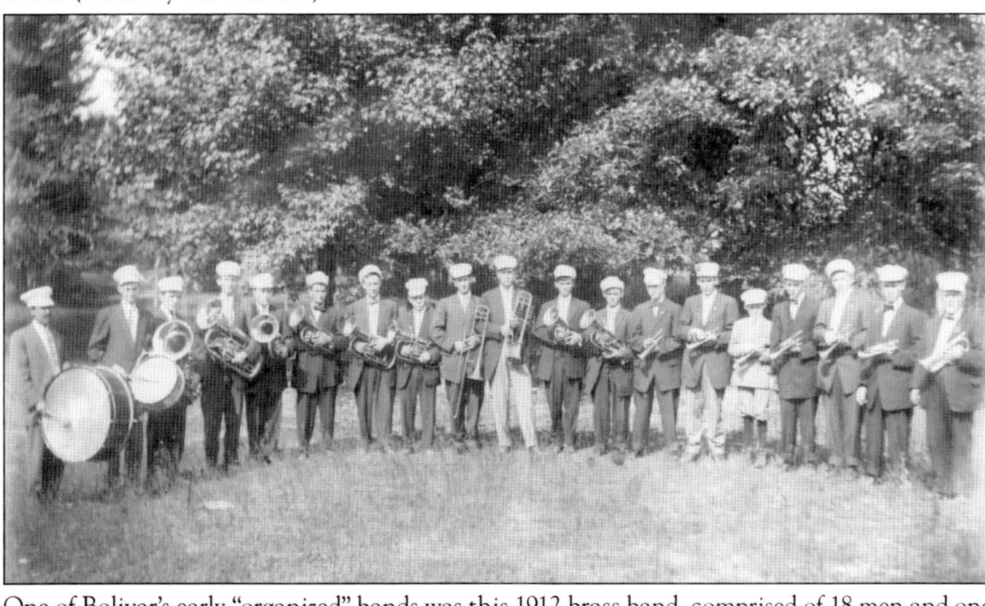

One of Bolivar's early "organized" bands was this 1912 brass band, comprised of 18 men and one young boy, under the direction of Professor Firth. The trombone player on the right is Alan Pruett, who later became a Tennessee State Supreme Court justice. Next to Pruett is Austin Baker; the other band members are unidentified. (Courtesy Hardeman County Genealogical Society.)

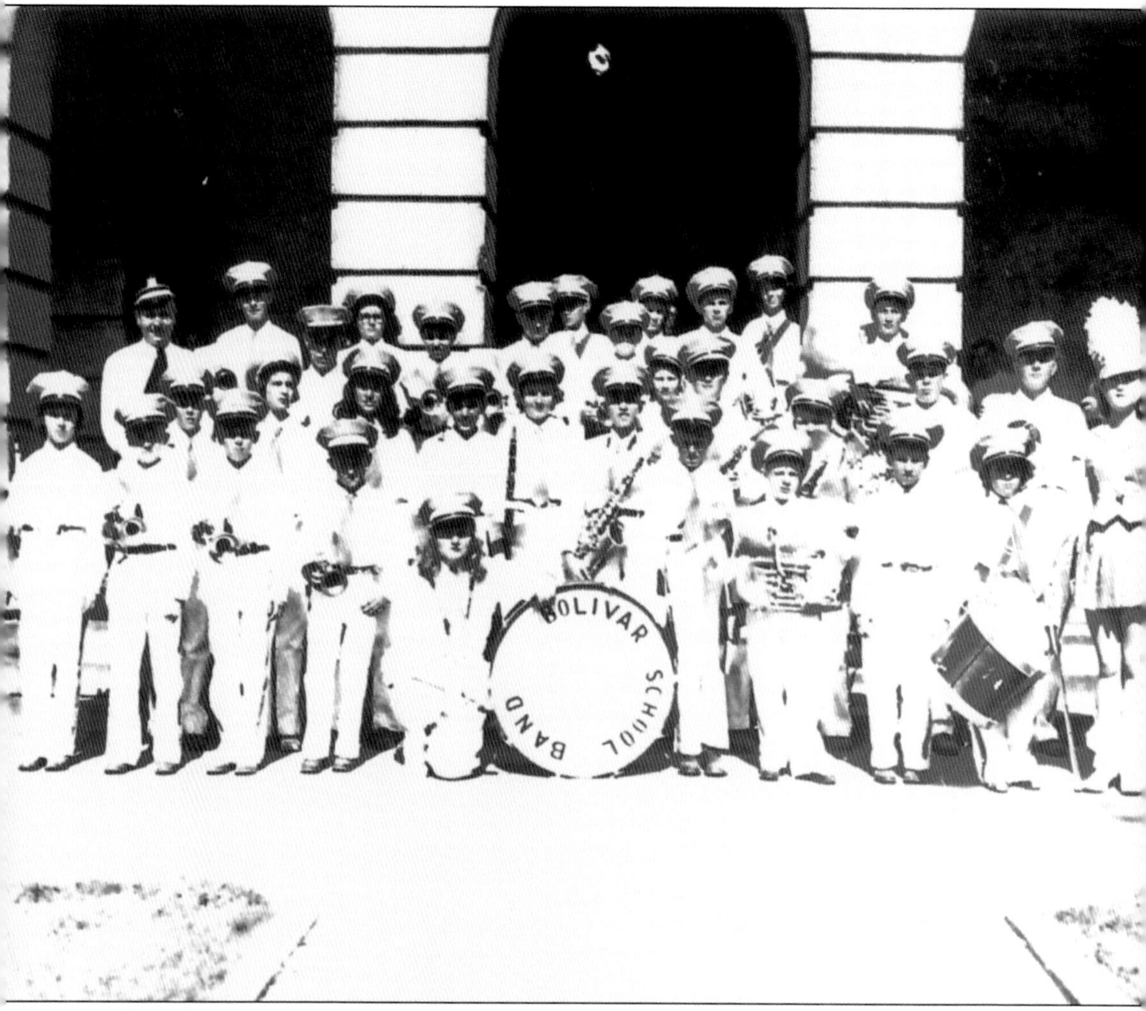

When the Bolivar Central High School Band was first organized, it was not part of the school curriculum. Tony Wald and his wife came from Jackson to Bolivar in the early 1940s to organize the band. Parents made early band uniforms—the pom-poms on the hats were made of tissue paper and had to be replaced whenever the hats got wet. Wald continued as the first band director when the band was made part of the school curriculum; he is also credited with writing the school's alma mater. In this picture, one of the early bands stands in front of the courthouse. (Courtesy Hardeman County Genealogical Society.)

Eight

IN UNIFORM

Hardeman County has sent many of its sons and daughters into the armed service, in all branches of active duty, reserves, and National Guard. Several early settlers in the area were veterans of the Revolutionary War, and Hardeman Countians have been defending freedom in every war or military action since then, with many currently serving overseas and stateside. Others have donned uniforms of other kinds—as police officers, firefighters, emergency and rescue personnel—all willingly serving their fellow man.

The county's—and the country's—history is often divided into the years before and after the Civil War. There were many battles and skirmishes around the county during the war years; Hardeman County was valuable to both sides for two very important reasons—the river and the railroads. Middleburg was the site of a large skirmish on August 19, 1862. The Union Army occupied Bolivar from 1862 until May 7, 1864. There were many camps, with thousands of soldiers on both sides, all over the county. Many familiar names came through the county during the war—Grant, Sherman, McPherson, Sturgis, Wallace, Forrest, Neely; some made their headquarters in the grand old homes in the county, and some came through under cloak of darkness.

Whether they serve in peacetime or in combat, Hardeman County is proud of all of its men and women who serve and protect.

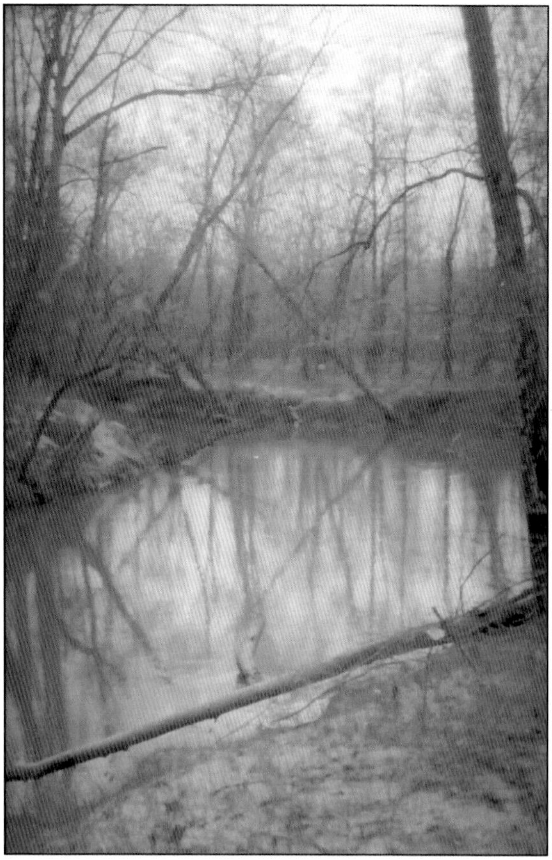

The second largest Civil War battle in Tennessee—the Battle of Davis Bridge—was fought on October 5, 1862, two miles south of Pocahontas on the Hatchie River (left). Over 20,000 Union and Confederate troops were involved in the battle. Through the tireless efforts of local historians Herbert Wood and Rex Brotherton, hundreds of acres of the battlefield have been purchased, and the site became the county's first national park, as a part of the Shiloh National Military Park system, in 2010. Shown below from left to right are Shiloh National Park superintendent Woody Harrell, Brotherton, and Wood, as they make the official land donation to the national park system. The battlefield is often referred to as one of the most pristine Civil War sites in the United States. (Left, Lisa C. Coleman; below, courtesy Darrell Teubner, the *County Journal*.)

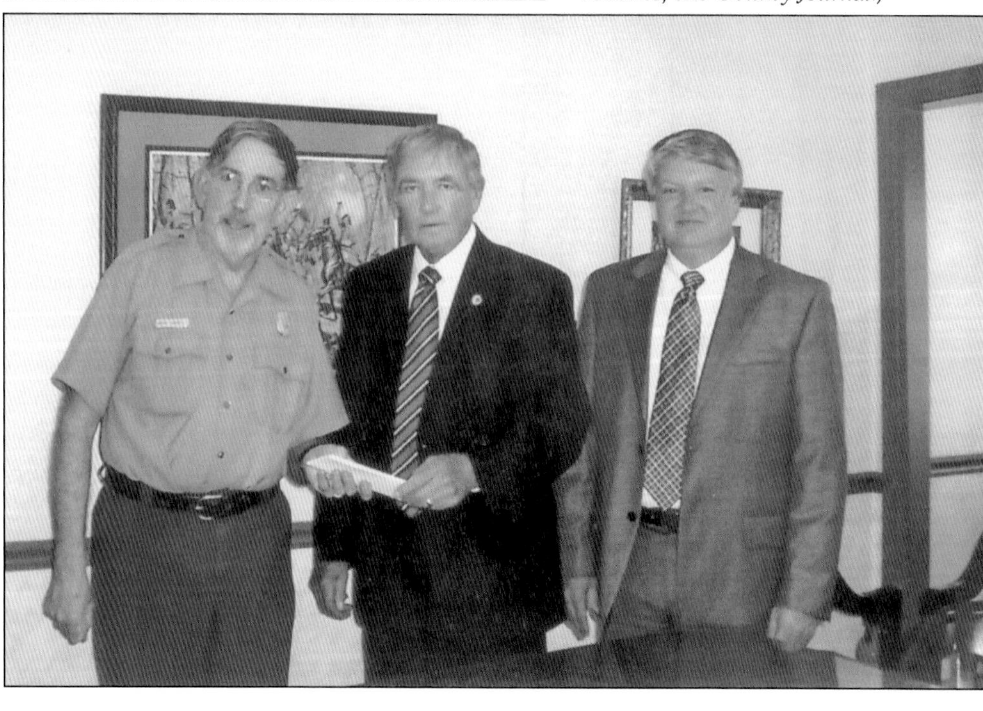

William Louis (W.L.) Edwards, born and raised in Cloverport, served in the US Army in World War II and with the Tennessee National Guard 278th Infantry in Korea. He worked for Provident Life & Accident in Chattanooga and later earned his law degree. At age 64, he began his "second" career as an attorney specializing in estate planning. (Lisa C. Coleman.)

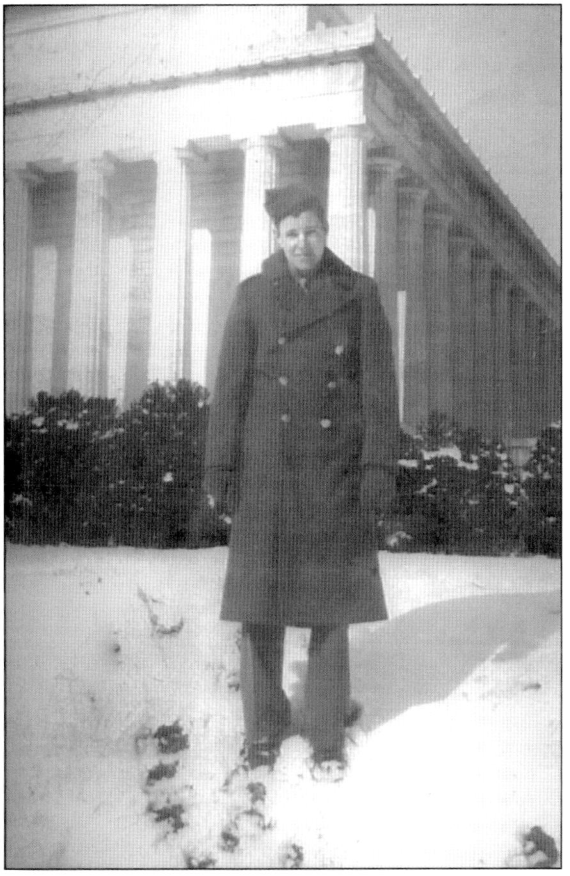

Almost 2,000 Hardeman Countians served the United States during World War II, with 40 giving the ultimate sacrifice for home and country. As groups left for distant shores, they had photographs made on the steps of the Hardeman County Courthouse in Bolivar; these are known as "going away" photographs. (Courtesy Pat Vincent.)

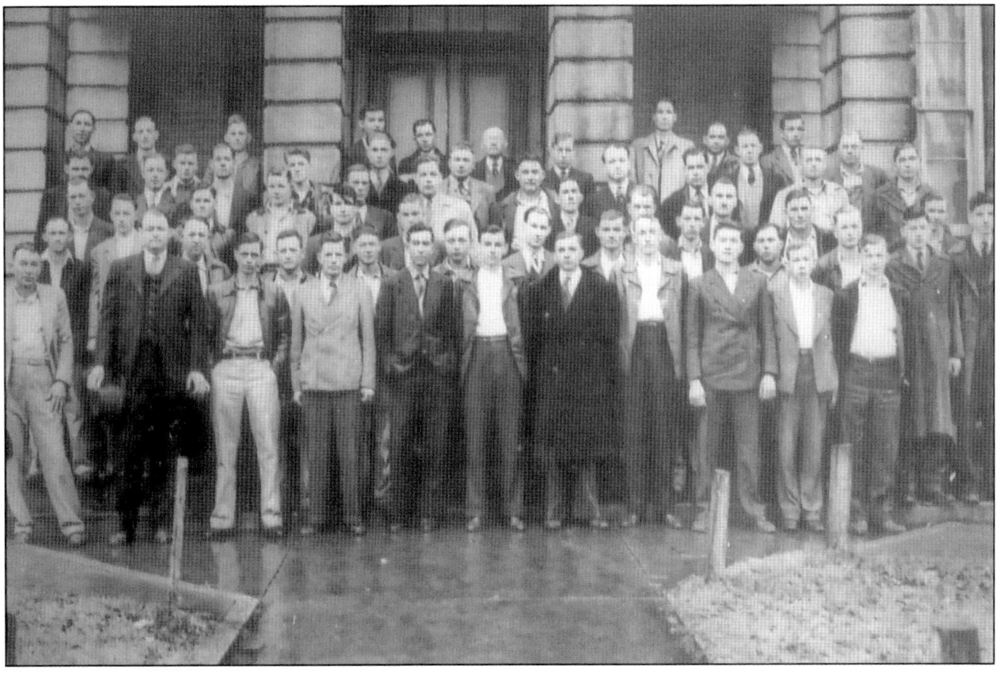

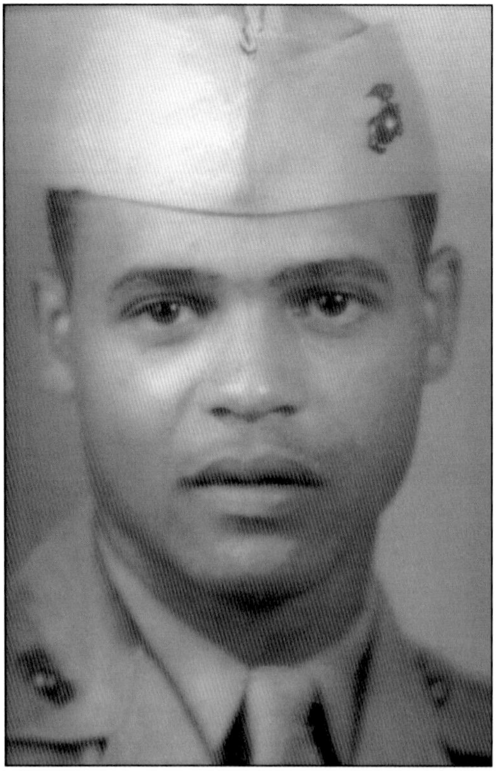

Jeff E. McKinnie Jr. served in the US Marine Corps during World War II and, during basic training, met a lifelong friend in Odell Horton, who later became a judge in Shelby County. After the war, McKinnie returned to Hardeman County and followed in his father's footsteps, teaching for the Hardeman County school system for 38 years. (Courtesy Audrey McKinnie.)

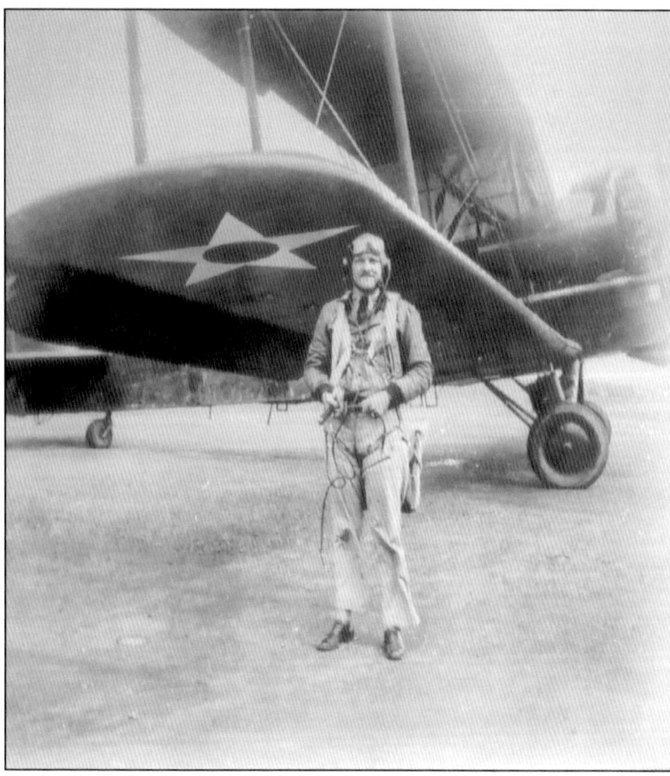

Joseph Alexander McAnulty served in the Army Air Force in 1931, commissioned as a second lieutenant, and returned to Bolivar, but was called back to active duty seven months before Pearl Harbor. He was assigned to Langley Field as assistant base operations officer and spent two years in Delhi, India, as a liaison officer between the Air Traffic Control and the 10th Air Force, commissioned as a major. (Courtesy Louise McAnulty Manhein.)

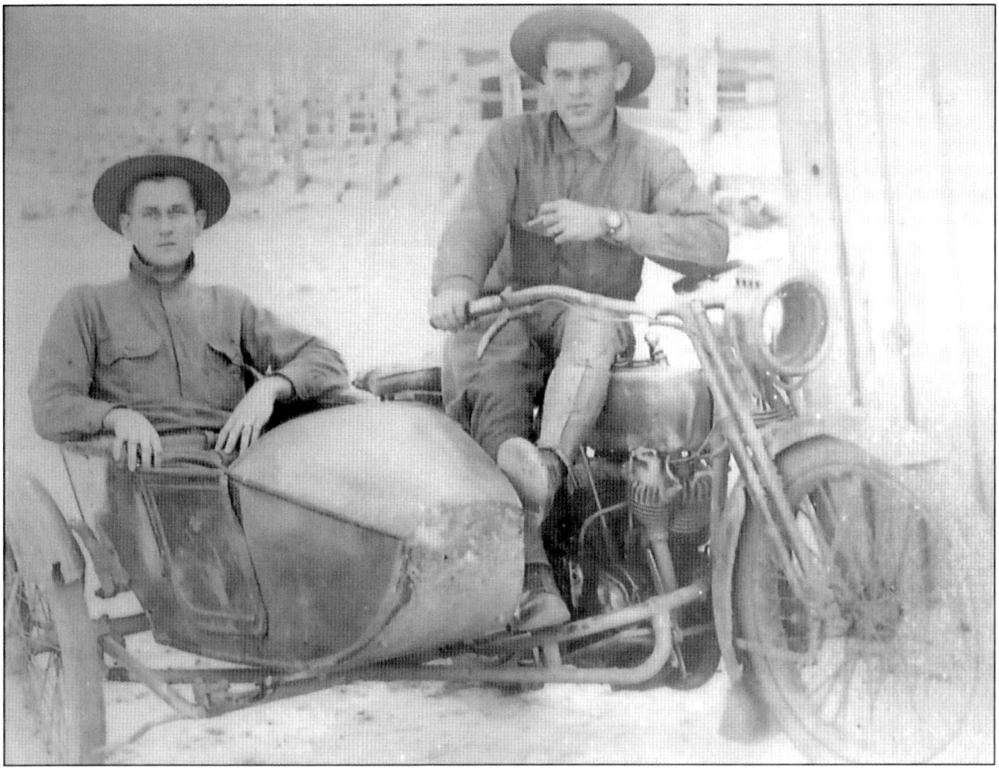

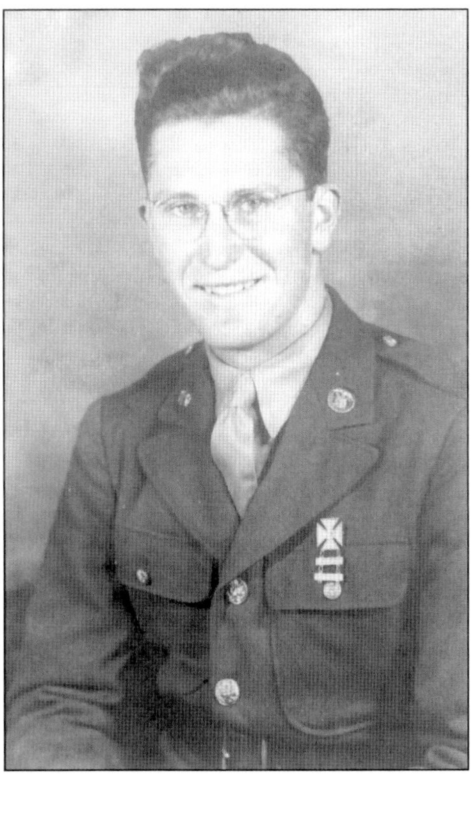

Samuel Arthur Wheeler Sr. (above, left), born in 1887, served in World War I in the 320th US Field Artillery, and is shown around 1917 with Harden Wilkerson. After the war, he married Mary Reynolds Wheeler and became a merchant. His son, Samuel Arthur Wheeler Jr. (left), served in the Army during World War II. After being involved in combat in the European theater, he returned home and worked for Shackelford Funeral Directors; in 2000, he was recognized by the Tennessee Funeral Directors Association for 50 years in the funeral service. He and his wife, Esther (Siler) Wheeler, later operated Bolivar Florist. (Both, courtesy Arthur Jr. and Esther Wheeler family.)

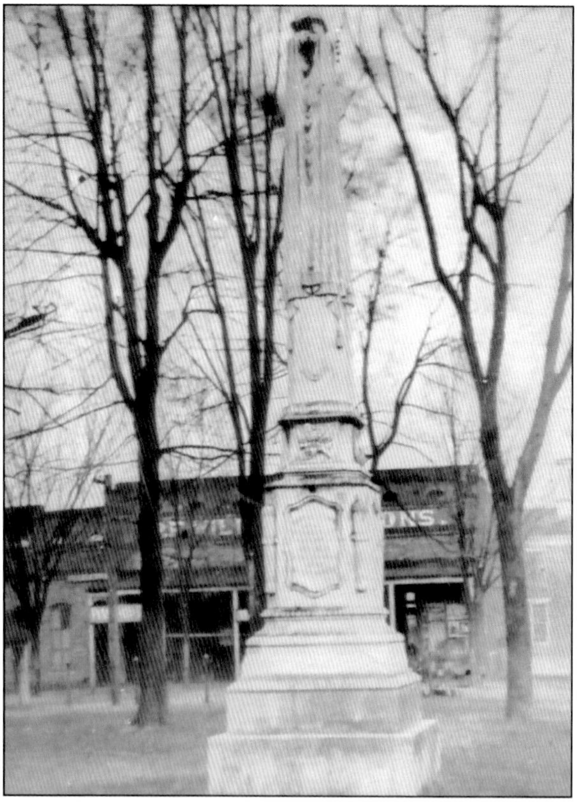

A Monumental Association was formed after the Civil War, and citizens donated over $1,800 for a monument. The monument, dedicated in 1873, was said to be the first such public structure dedicated in the South, and it remains a fixture on the courthouse lawn today. Confederate veteran reunions were held in the county for many years; the group below, from about 1890, met in Bolivar that year to reminisce and remember their shared experiences. Unfortunately, none of the men in the photograph are identified, but all are believed to be from Hardeman County. (Both, courtesy Hardeman County Genealogical Society.)

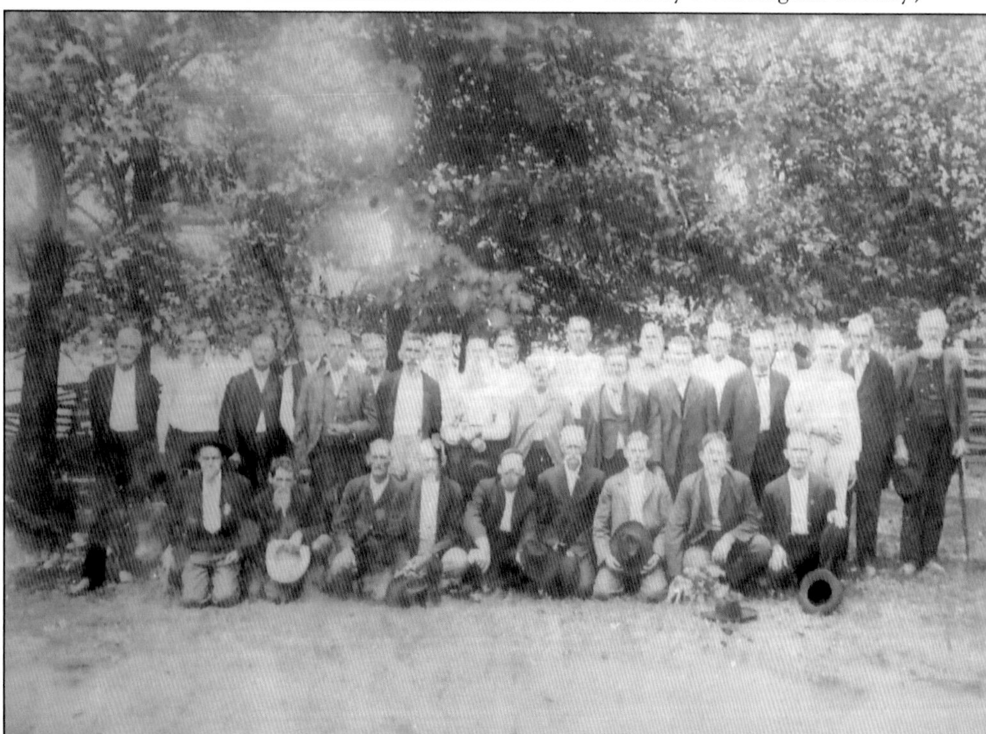

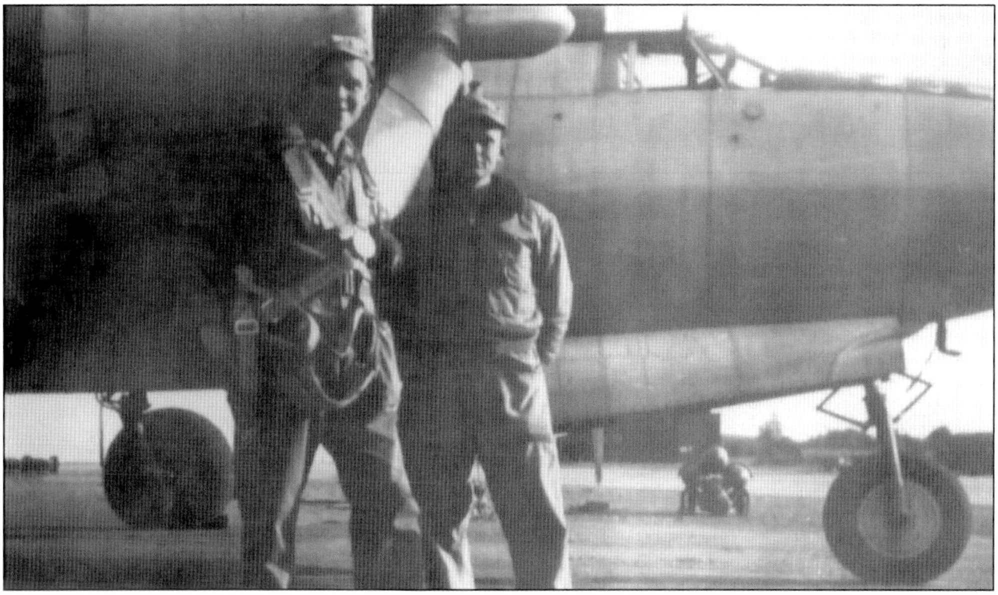

Vernon Cox (right) served in the Army Air Corps during World War II and graduated from the parent radio school of the Air Forces Technical Train Command in 1943. T.Sgt. Cox was a radio gunner on B-26 bombers and was stationed in England during the war, eventually flying in 66 missions in Europe. (Courtesy Tim Cox.)

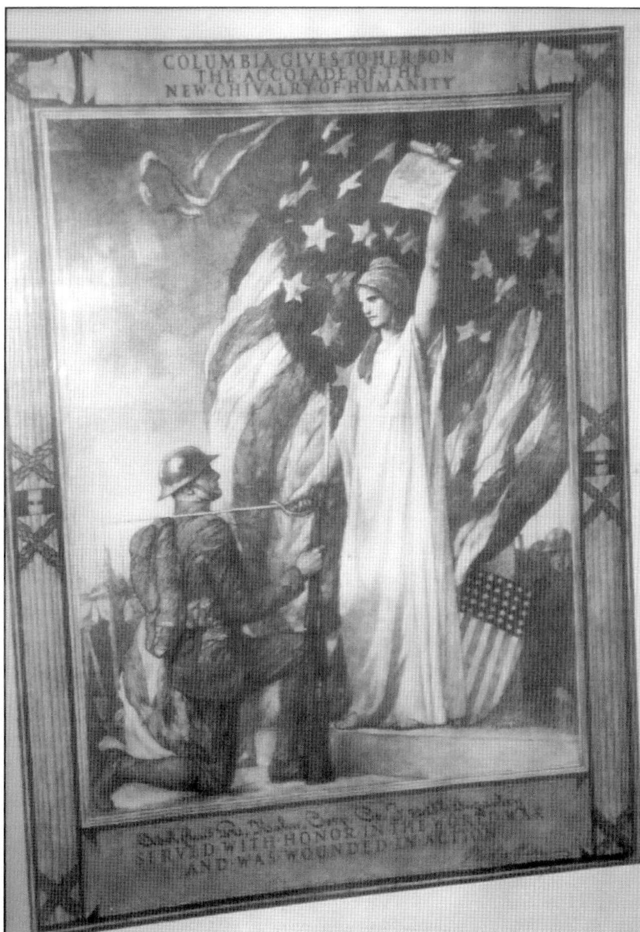

This certificate is entitled, "Columbia Gives to Her Son the Accolade of the New Chivalry of Humanity." The bottom portion of the certificate reads, "Adolphus R. Kahn, Corp. C. F. 327th Infantry, Served with Honor and in the World War and was Wounded in Action." The certificate was signed by Pres. Woodrow Wilson. (Courtesy Ken Kowen.)

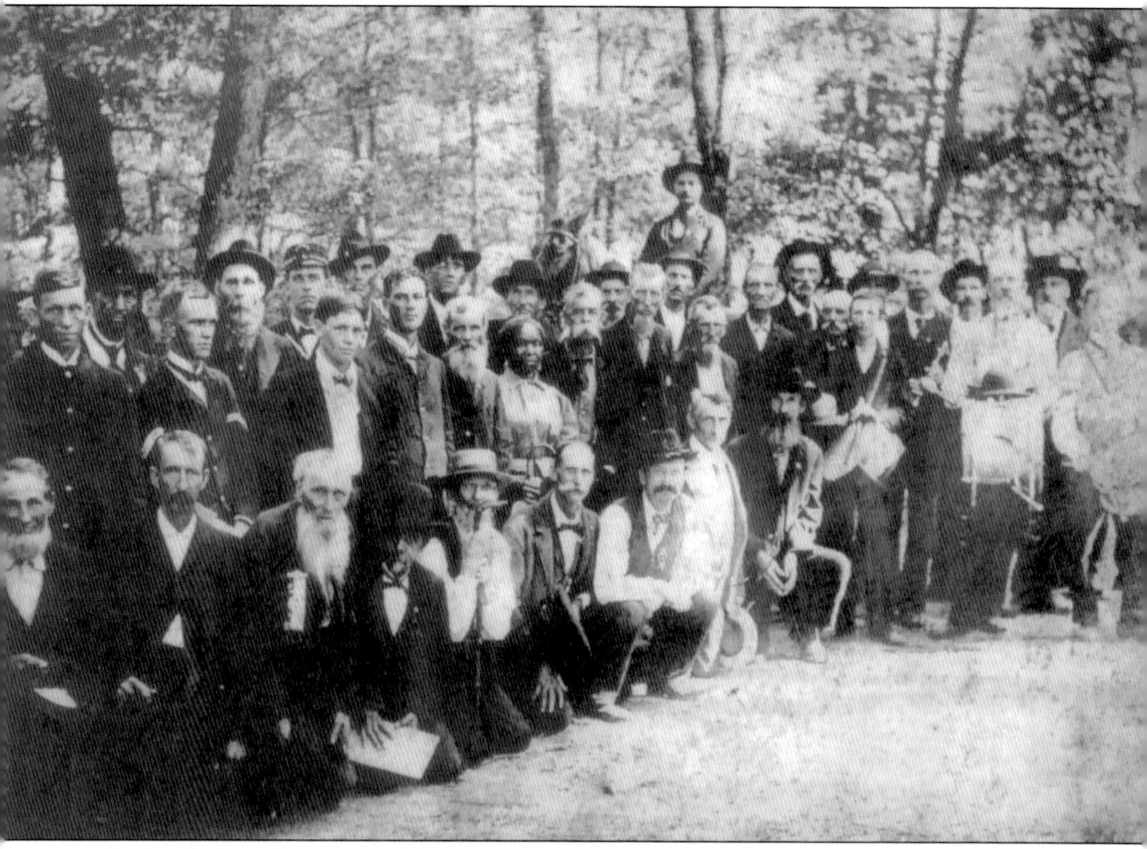

A close look at the center of this 1898 reunion photograph of veterans of the 23rd Regiment, Union Army Indiana Volunteers, shows Lucy Higgs Nichols, born a slave in Mississippi and sold to an owner in Hardeman County as a young girl. Nichols and her child escaped in 1862 and went to the 23rd Indiana camp near Bolivar. She nursed the sick, cooked and washed for the officers, and traveled with the regiment before mustering out in Indianapolis at the end of the war. "Aunt Lucy," as she was affectionately known by "her soldiers," was made an honorary member of the Grand Army of the Republic in 1892 and was awarded a military pension by a special act of Congress signed by President McKinley. She died in 1915 and was buried with full military honors. (Courtesy Curtis and Pam Peters and Vic Megenity.)

Nine

Family, Faces, and Places

The word "home" brings many powerful memories to mind, each unique to the owner. Many people have called the area known as Hardeman County their home. From the Chickasaws to the early pioneers, the merchants, the teachers, the farmers, the preachers, and the scores of people who built the county and its towns and villages, as well as each resident living in the county today, each one had a part in shaping these places.

Celebrations and remembrances, musicals and plays, school days and workdays, and every sort of day—some commonplace and others once-in-a-lifetime—weave the fabric of the people and places of Hardeman County.

Be it ever so humble, there is no place like home . . . in Hardeman County.

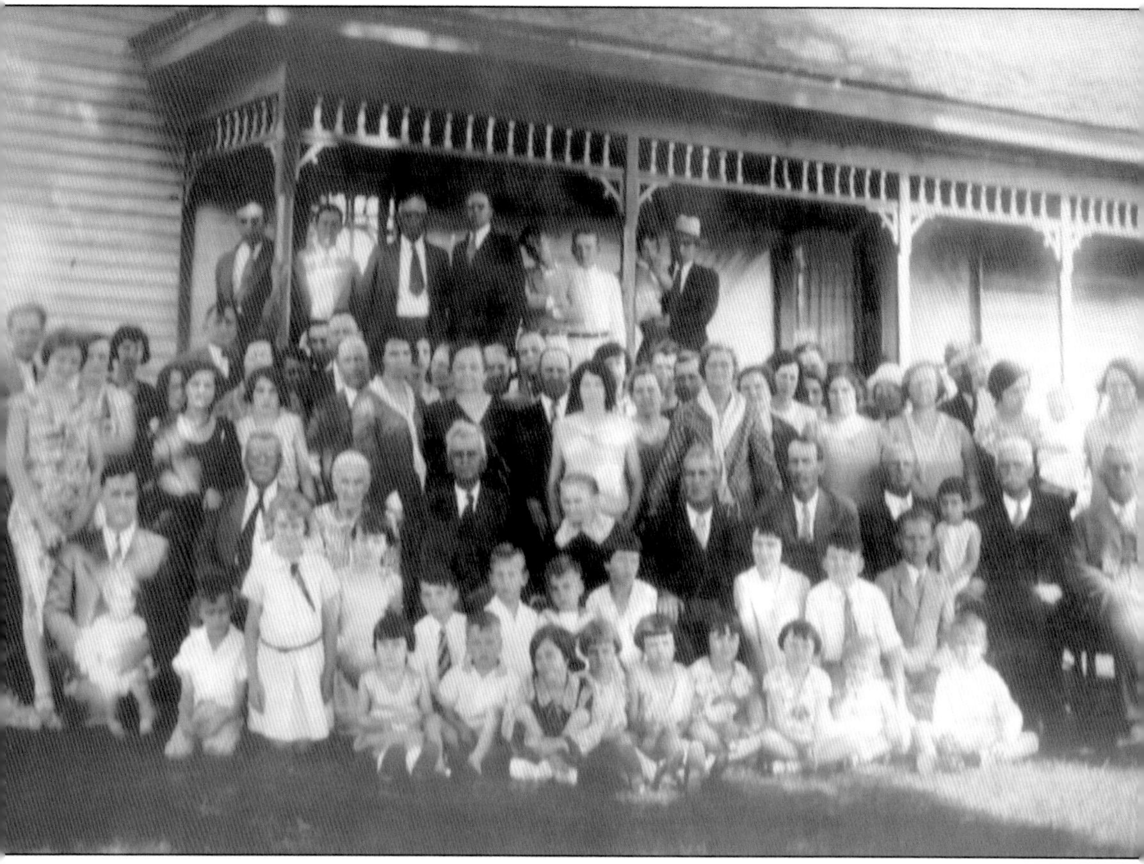

Many members of the Stroup and Taylor families made their homes in and around the Grand Junction area. A number of them traveled to Ashland, Mississippi, in 1930 to a family reunion at the home of L. Pink Stroup. Identified in this photograph from the event are James Murray Taylor Jr. (the fifth child in the second row), along with siblings Bert Stroup, Molly Stroup, Kimery Stroup, Sid Stroup, Betty Stroup, Will Stroup, L. Pink Stroup, James H. Stroup (holding Mattie Lee Stroup), Daniel Stroup, and Robert H. Stroup (in the third row). Standing on the porch are, from left to right, Lawrence Stroup, two unidentified, Charlie Kidd, two unidentified, and Dewey Hudspeth. (Courtesy James Murray Taylor Jr.)

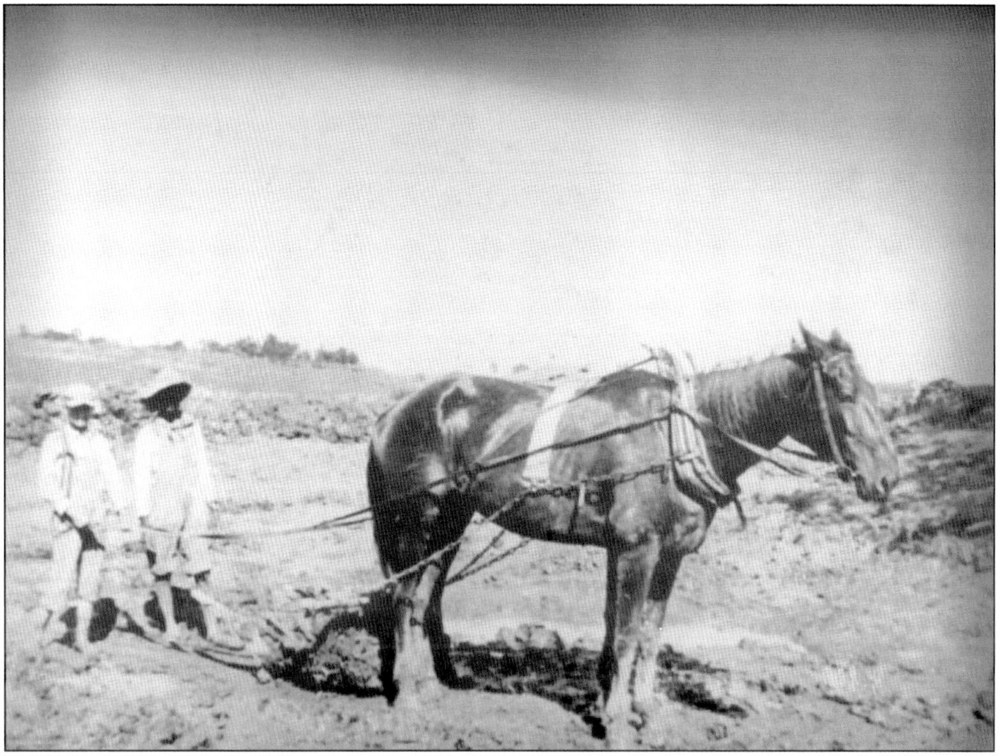

Always chores to do! These two young boys are cleaning silt from a pond near their home in Grand Junction. This chore was done when the water in the pond was at its lowest point. Pictured in the c. 1917 image are Brooks Stroup (left), age 13, and an unidentified friend. (Courtesy Bobby Martindale Memorial Library.)

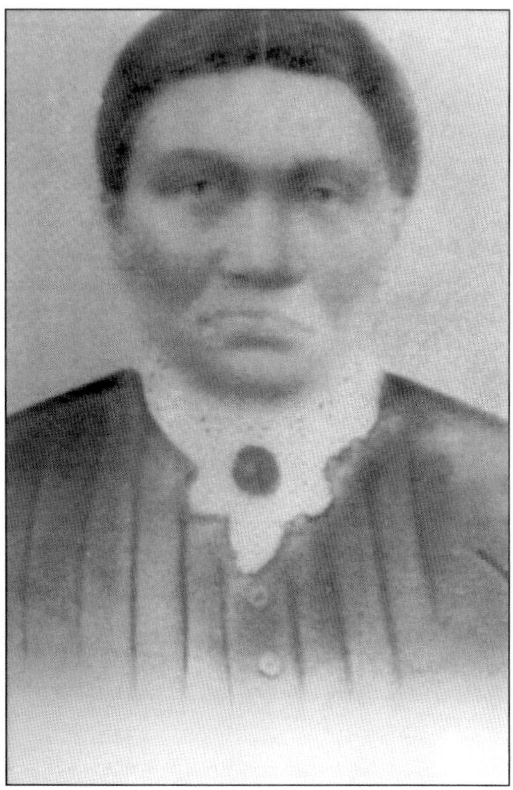

Emeline Prewitt Morgan (1844–1926) is buried at Bolivar. This picture was probably taken about 1890 or earlier. She was born, raised, and lived all of her life in Hardeman County and was the mother-in-law of Joseph Combs. She is the maternal great-grandmother of Hattye Thomas Yarbrough. (Courtesy Hardeman County Multicultural Museum.)

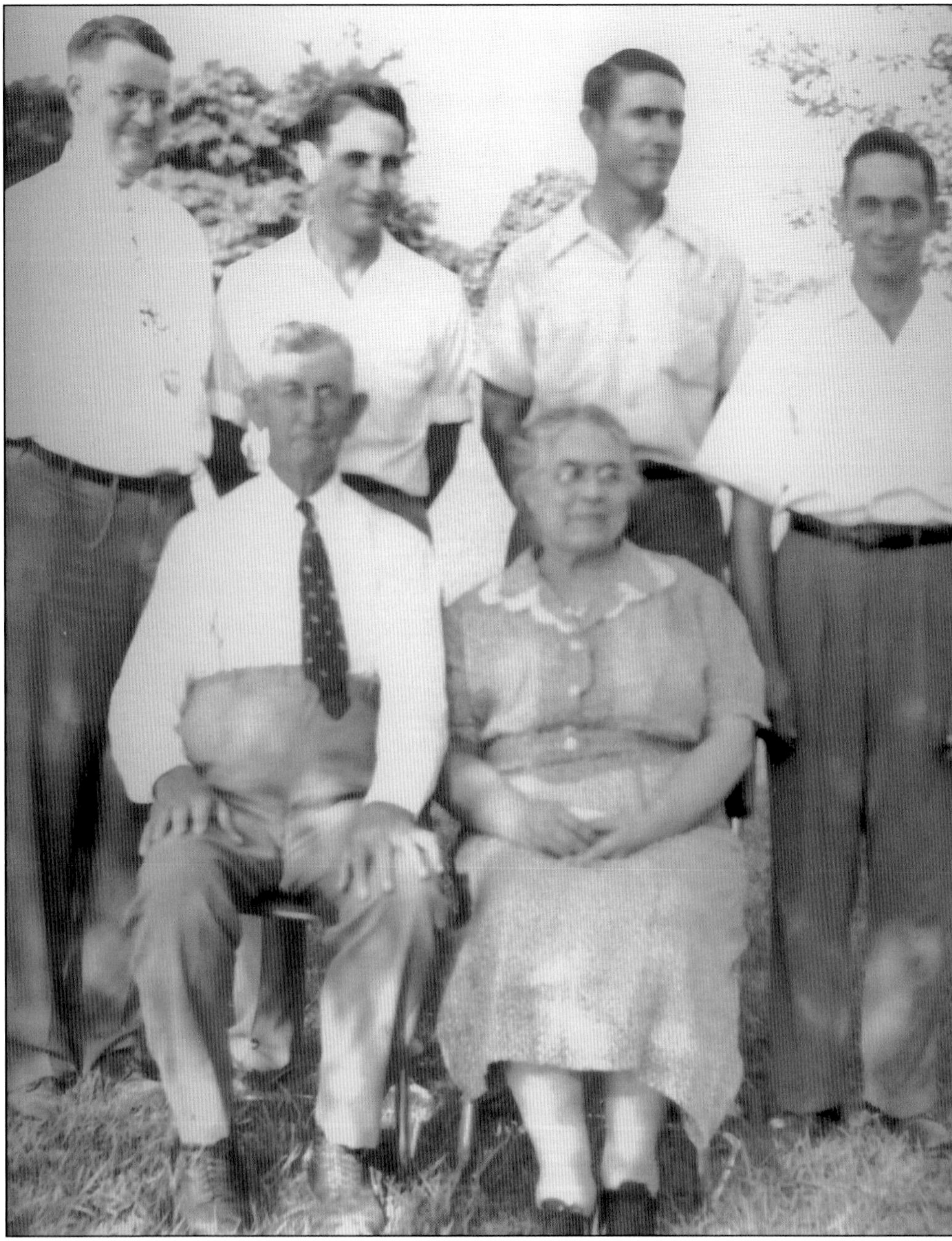

The Anderson family of Cloverport has been involved in farming for several generations and continues to farm in the area today. This undated photograph shows John Calvin Anderson and Ivy Haynes Anderson (seated) with their sons. The sons are, from left to right, John V. Anderson Sr., a farmer and merchant who brought mechanized farming to the area and founded Anderson Tractor Company; James Luther Anderson, who graduated from and worked for the University of Tennessee and School of Agriculture, retiring as an assistant to the president; Thomas Anderson, known as the "Flying Farmer," who planted the first apple orchards in the area; and Daniel Clifton Anderson, a farmer and merchant who operated Anderson's Store in Cloverport for many years. (Courtesy John V. & Susan Anderson.)

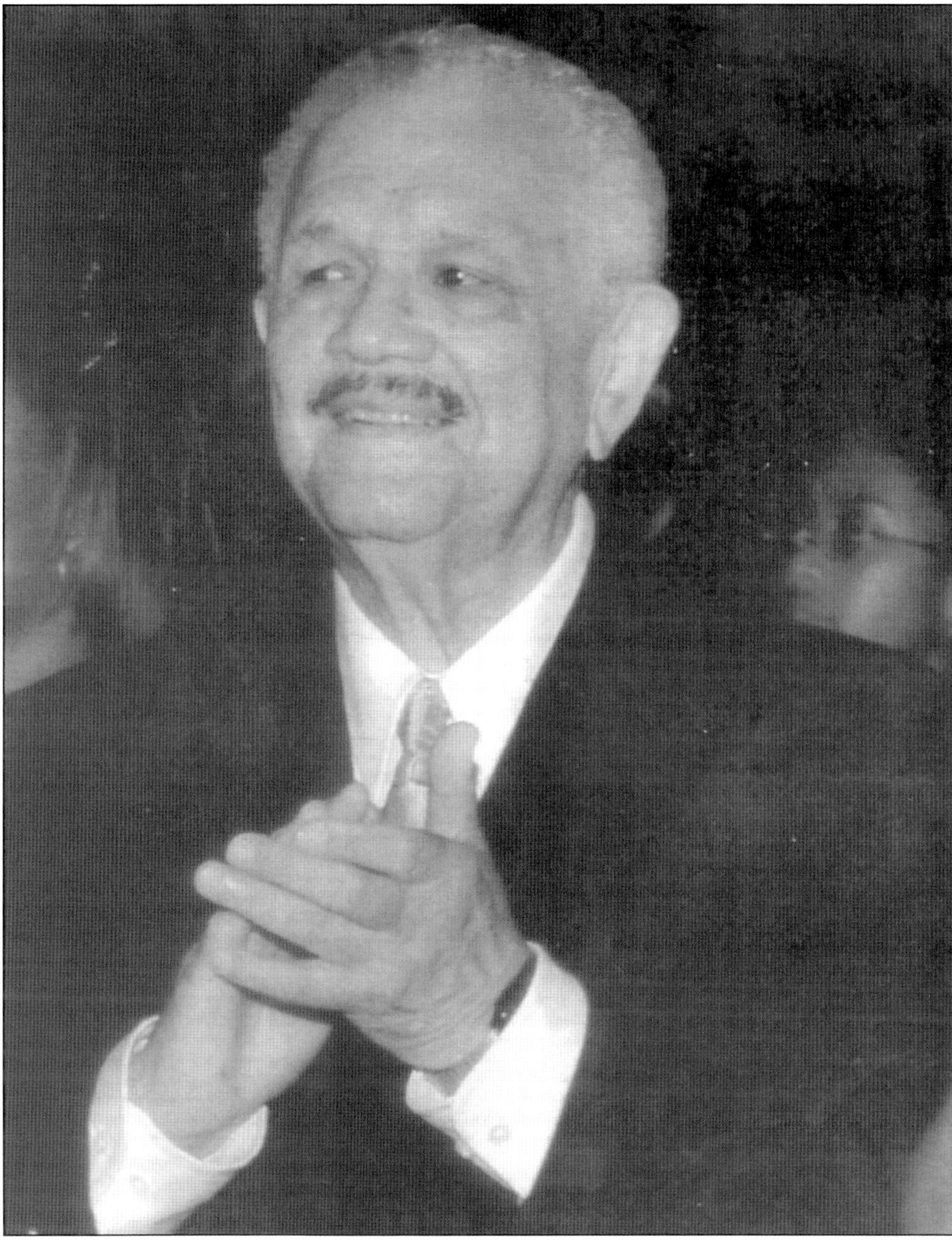

Vernon Jarrett was born in 1921 in Saulsbury, Tennessee, attended Knoxville College on a football scholarship, and wrote for the college newspaper. After serving in the Navy, he moved to Chicago in 1949 and wrote for the *Chicago Defender*, the *Chicago Tribune* (as its first black columnist), started one of the first black radio news programs on WJJD, and served as a reporter and anchor for more than 30 years on ABC 7 Chicago. In an interview near the end of his life, he said, "Be willing to always be a scholar; you've got to give whatever it is that you chose your best and then some. Read excessively; I always engaged in overkill and I think that kind of spirit was required then and is still required today to be successful." (Courtesy Hardeman County Multicultural Museum.)

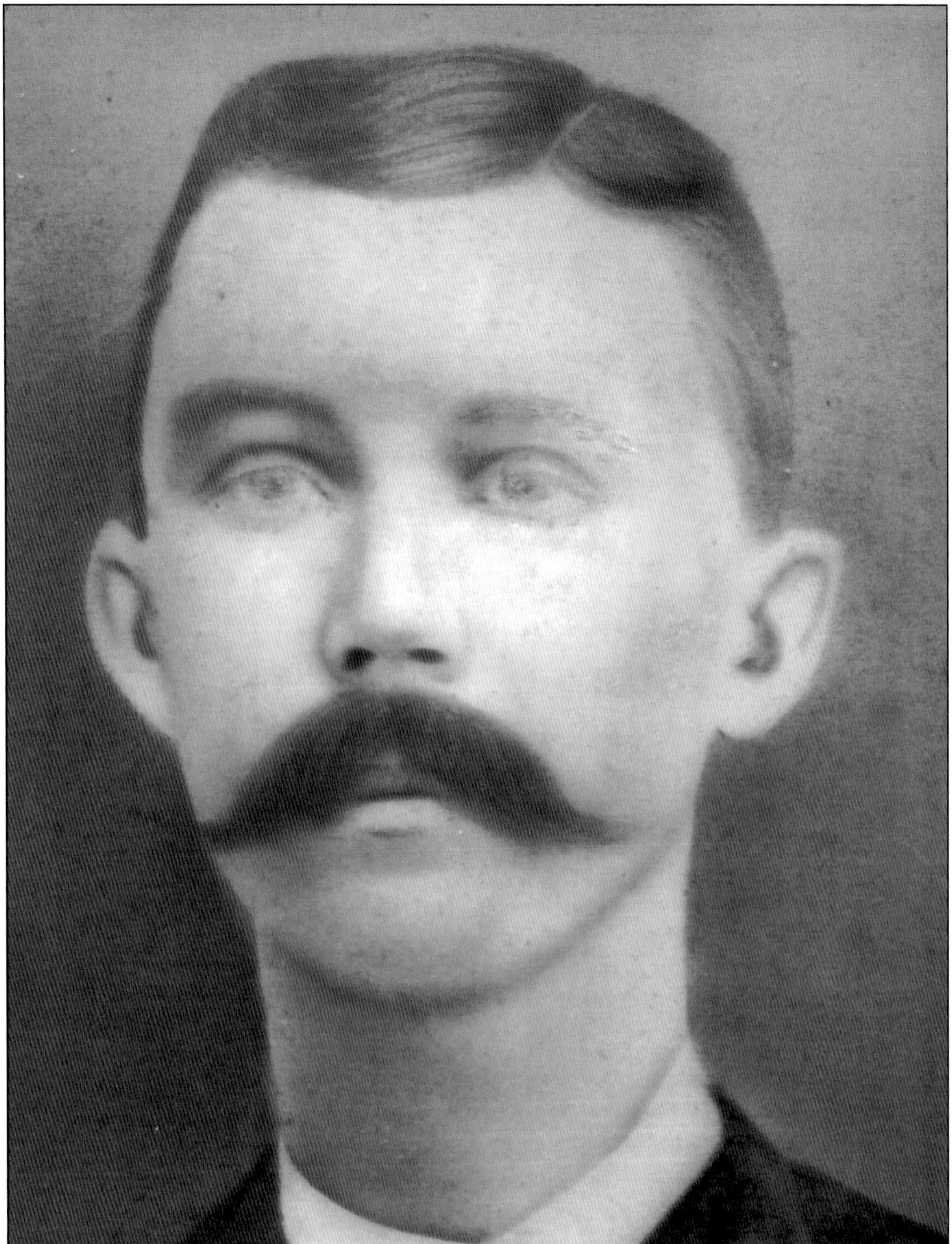

General Price Mills grew up to be a logger and merchant, but almost did not have that opportunity. During the Civil War, the Union army came through the area where he and his family were living and began burning down the family home. Mills's young sister was crying for "my baby," and the general ordered the men to wait so the little girl could go into the house and get what he thought was her baby doll—instead, she returned holding her baby brother. In gratitude for the general's kindness, the baby was renamed "General Price Mills" to honor the man who spared his life. (Courtesy Norma J. West.)

Tennie Lee Lambert Doyle was one of the children of Abner Lambert, who was an early preacher at Hebron Baptist Church. Hebron Baptist Church was long associated with the old Unity Baptist Association and joined the new Hardeman County Baptist Association in 1923. Both Tennie and Abner are buried at the New Hope Church of Christ cemetery. (Courtesy Glenda Doyle.)

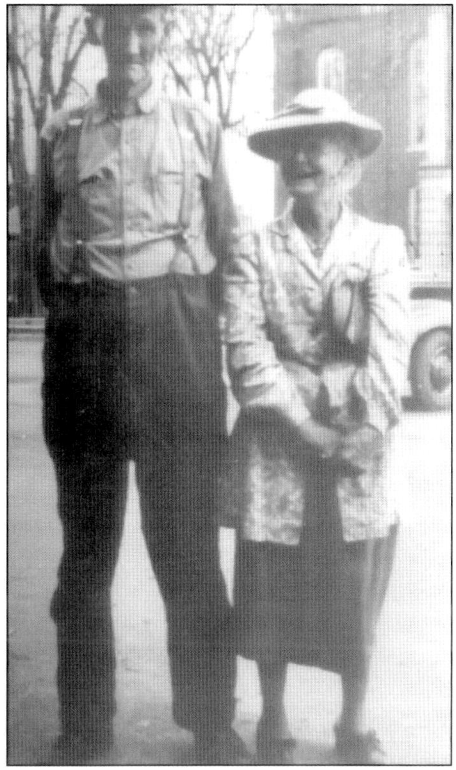

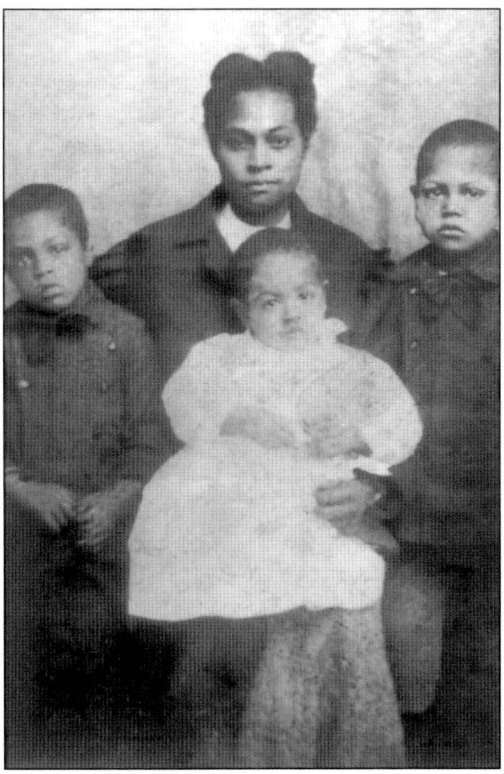

Ada Duncan and her husband, Grandee, were the parents of 13 children born between 1900 and 1916. Grandee Sr. and Ada Miller were married on October 21, 1897, and lived in Hickory Valley. In this 1910 photograph, Ada, age 31, is shown with three of their children, John Lewis (left, age eight), Grandee Jr. (right, age 10), and baby Elizabeth. (Courtesy Mae Duncan.)

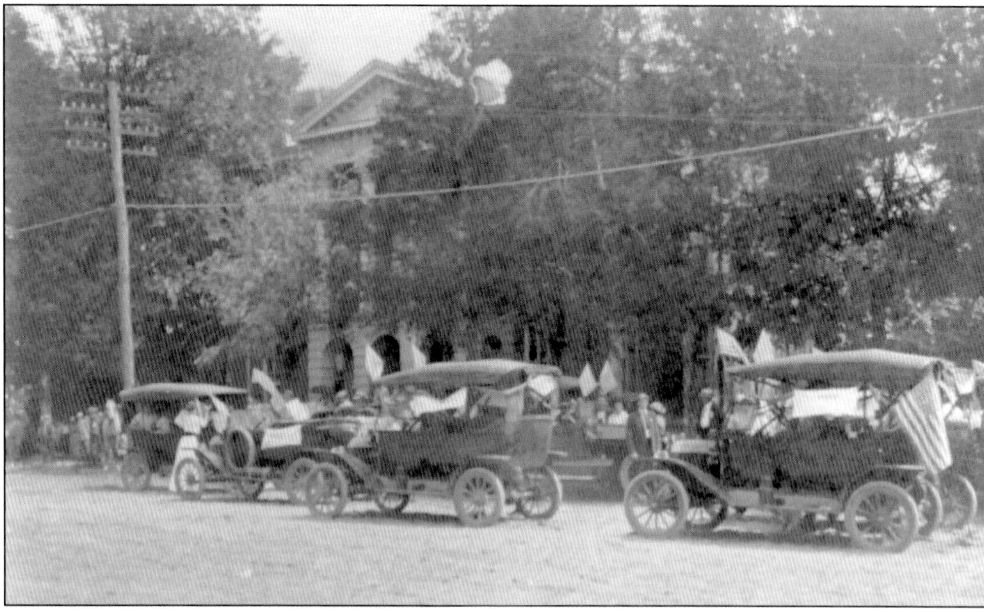

Parades are beloved all over the county, and some of the most popular parades were Easter and May Day parades in the spring, Independence Day parades in July, and of course, Christmas parades. Above, cars and spectators line up in front of the Hardeman County Courthouse for an early-1900s parade (either for May Day or Independence Day). Spectators and vendors anxiously watch and wait on the courthouse lawn. Below, a springtime parade in Middleton in the early 1950s shows boys and girls dressed in their Sunday best as they wait in line to join the parade; moms stand by to make sure everyone stays neat and clean. (Above, courtesy Arthur Jr. and Esther Wheeler family; below, courtesy Gail Mills.)

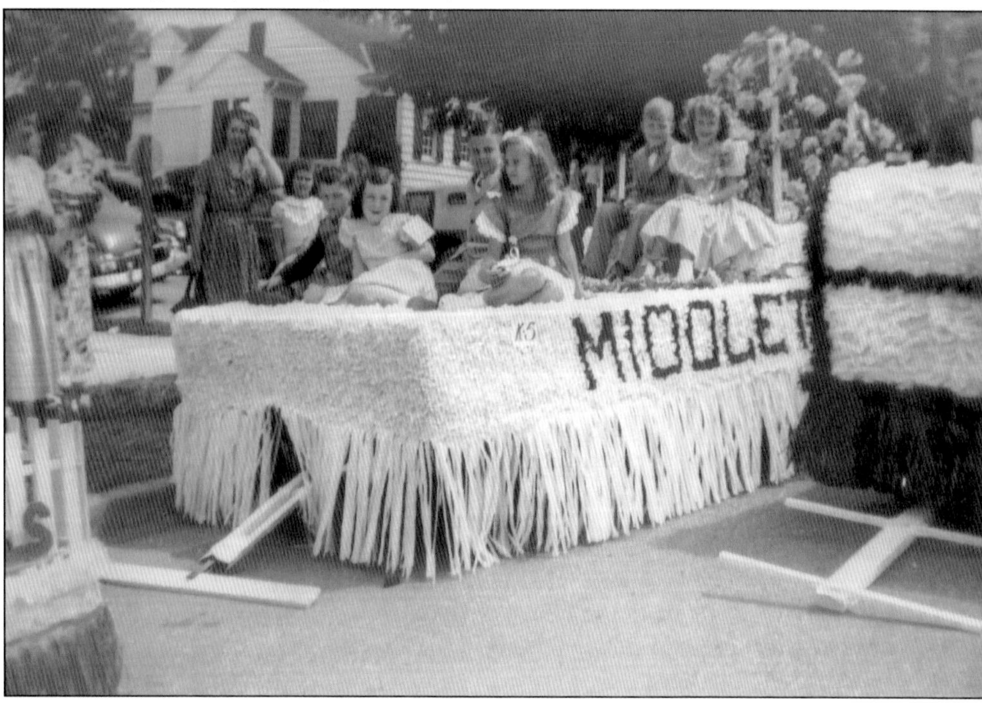

Lewis Miller (born in 1853), or "Pappy Lewis" to his offspring, lived and farmed in Hickory Valley and was often called "The Professor." He had two daughters, Elizabeth (in 1872, with his first wife), and Ada (with his second wife, Lucy Trent). This photograph was taken around 1903, when Miller was about 50 years old. (Courtesy Mae Duncan.)

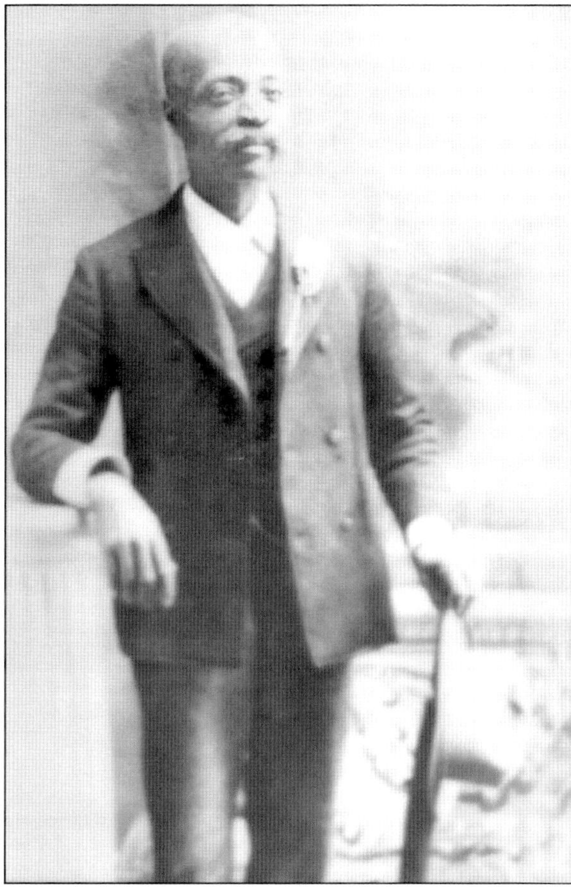

Scoutmaster M.L. Hardin led one of the first Boy Scout troops in the area. Pictured here are, from left to right, (first row) True Redd, Joseph McAnulty, Jack Brewer, Jewell Dorris, Fred Upton, Jack Tate, and Robert Cox; (second row) Tom Emerson, Jasper Smith, Rozwell Redd, Olion Neely, Omer Curlin, Robert McAnulty, and Dewey Whitenton; (third row) Henry Doyle, Carter Sweeton, David Durrett, Tillmon Black, Eugene Savage, Clarence Shearon, Roy Smith, and Robert Mitchell. (Courtesy Hardeman County Genealogical Society.)

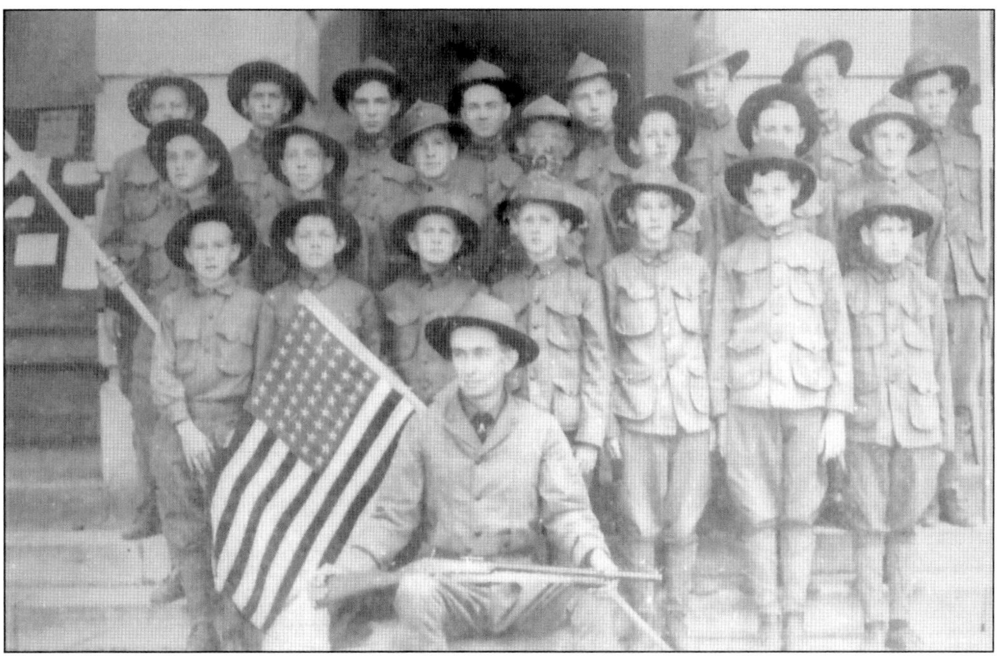

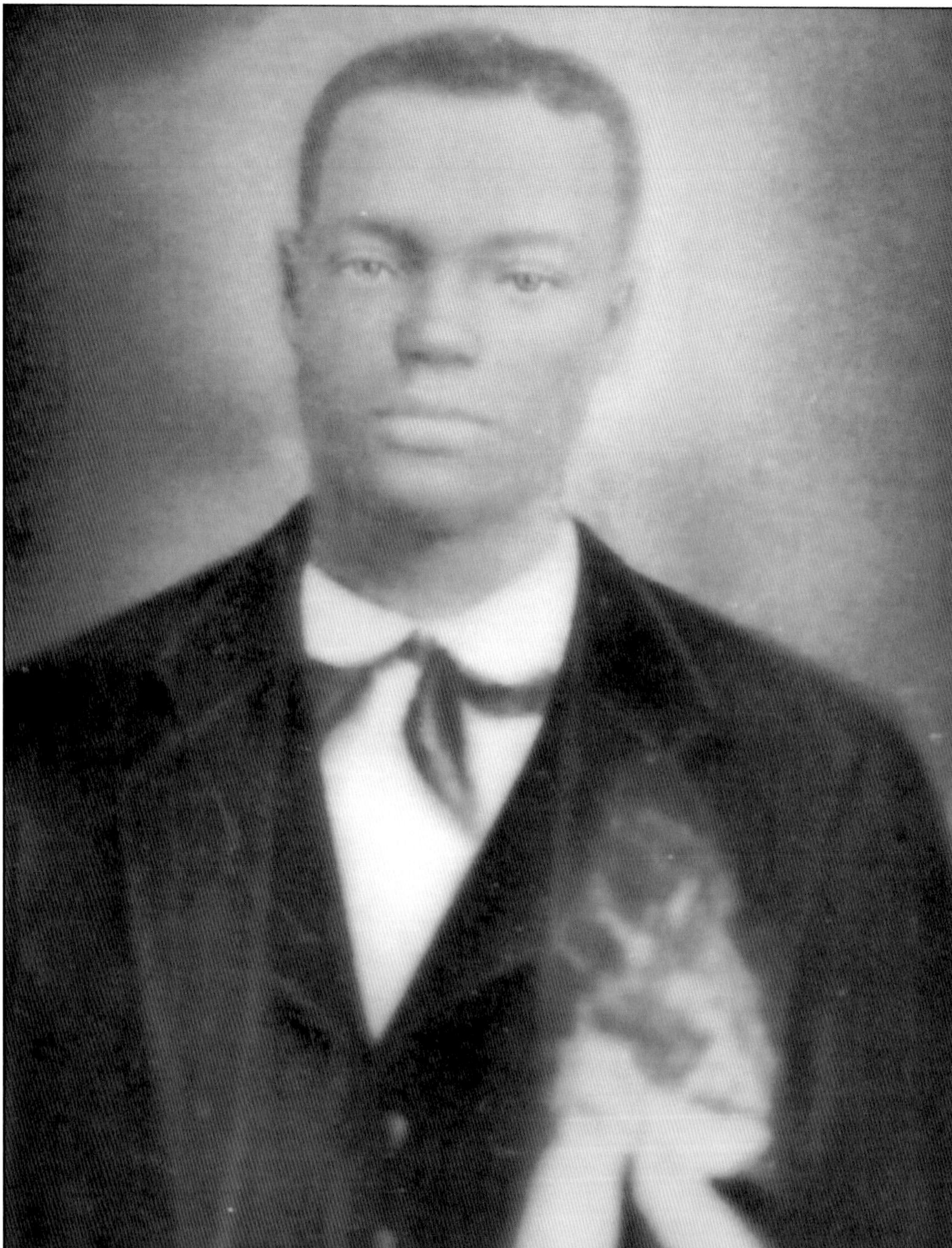

Grandee Duncan (born July 4, 1878, and shown here around age 30), the last son born to George and Mary Hodge Duncan, had an entrepreneurial spirit and found a measure of success. Grandee owned a 200-plus acre home in Hickory Valley with his wife, Ada, and raised and sold vegetables from the back of his wagon. He also made and sold ice cream. He was best known for the "Flying Jenny," a beautifully painted, wooden, hand-operated merry-go-round that he carted everywhere, offering rides to children for 5¢. Grandee Duncan also was one of the founders of the July 4th picnic in Grand Junction. He died on December 27, 1929, and is buried in Woods Cemetery in Hickory Valley. (Courtesy Mae Duncan.)

Louis Tavener Sanderson, born May 11, 1854, near Cloverport, was named for his uncle, James Tavener Toone. He married Lucinda Glidewell on July 25, 1853; they had eight children. Louis was a farmer, producing cotton and corn, and was also a beekeeper. The Sandersons spent their lives in Hardeman County and were members of Maple Springs Baptist Church, where both are buried. (Lisa C. Coleman.)

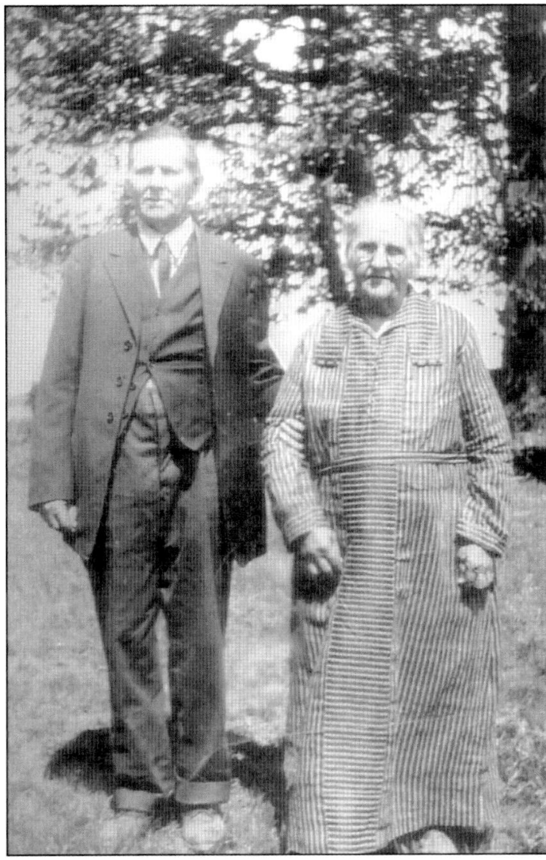

This 1928 photograph captures the just-married Fred Hugh Kiestler and Alma Lee Smith Kiestler. Both were born, raised, and lived their entire lives in Hardeman County—first in Cloverport and later in Bolivar. Hugh was a sharecropper in Cloverport for many years; he later worked for Western State Hospital in several of the hospital's farming operations. Alma was a housewife and mother. (Lisa C. Coleman.)

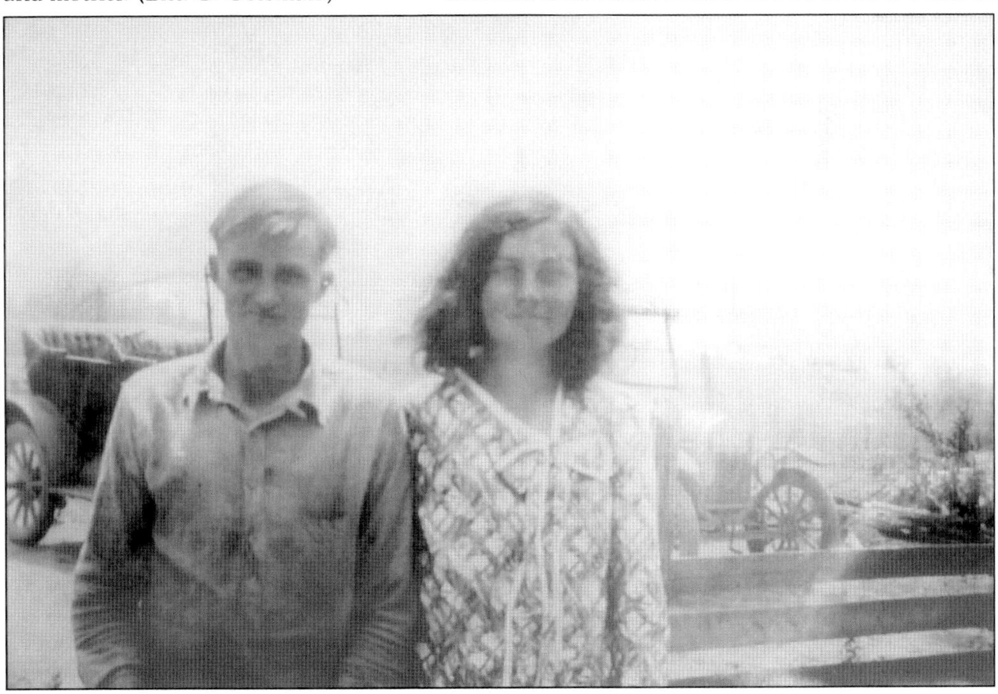

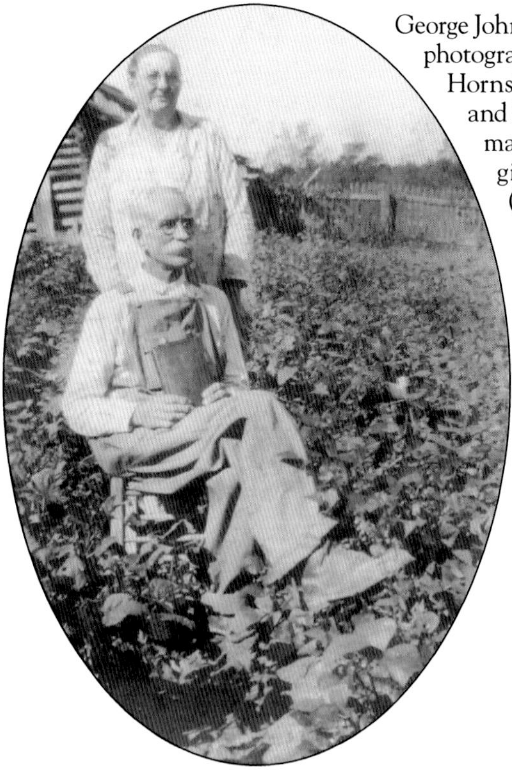

George Johnson and Mary Agnes Hayes Johnson pause for a photograph at their home near the Webb Mill area (near Hornsby). George was a lifelong farmer in Hardeman and McNairy Counties. He is remembered as a kind man who loved children and always had time to give a hug or an encouraging word to a child. (Courtesy Janette Tigner.)

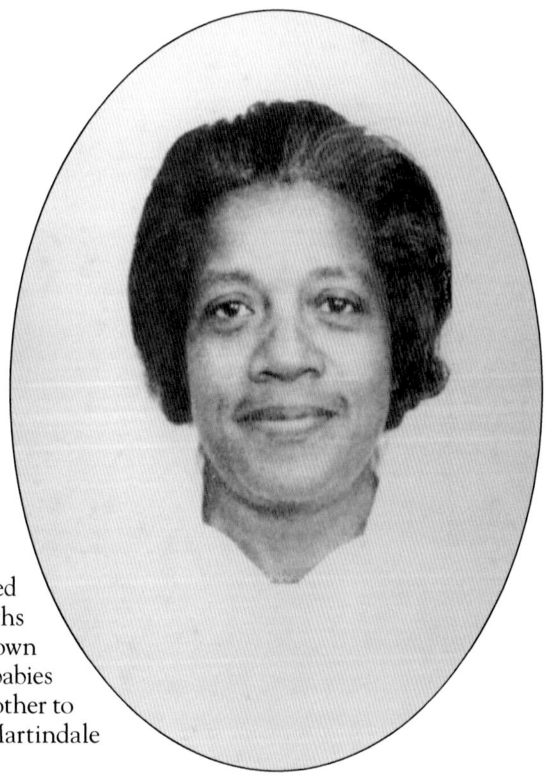

Families who lived far from a doctor and needed a learned and kind hand to assist with births utilized midwives. Midwife Lucille Scott, shown here around age 63, helped deliver over 300 babies in the Grand Junction area. She was also mother to 17 children of her own! (Courtesy Bobby Martindale Memorial Library.)

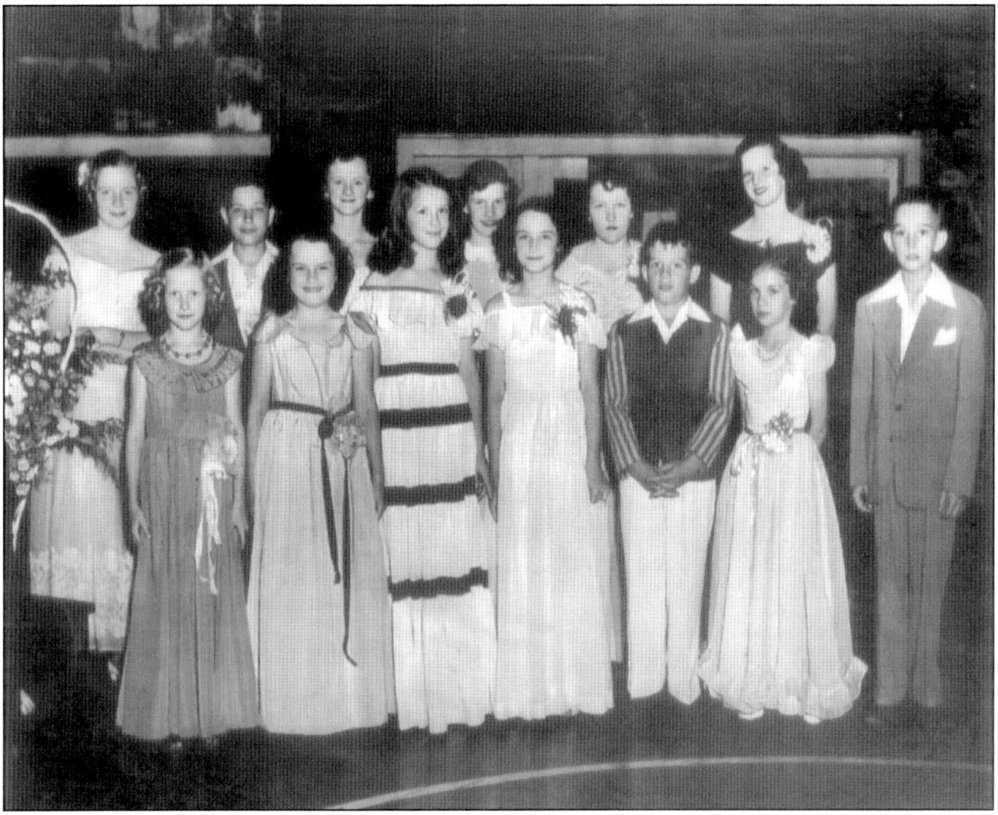

Recitals were much-anticipated yearly events that featured the work of young musicians. Miss Elizabeth Ingram's 1950 recital students pictured here are, from left to right, (first row) two unidentified, Marion Denton, Sandra Williams, Charles "Bunny" Orr, Nancy Orr, and Lee Butler; (second row) Glen Alan Brown, Lee Curtis Lax, and Beverly Denton. The rest are unidentified. (Courtesy Pat Vincent.)

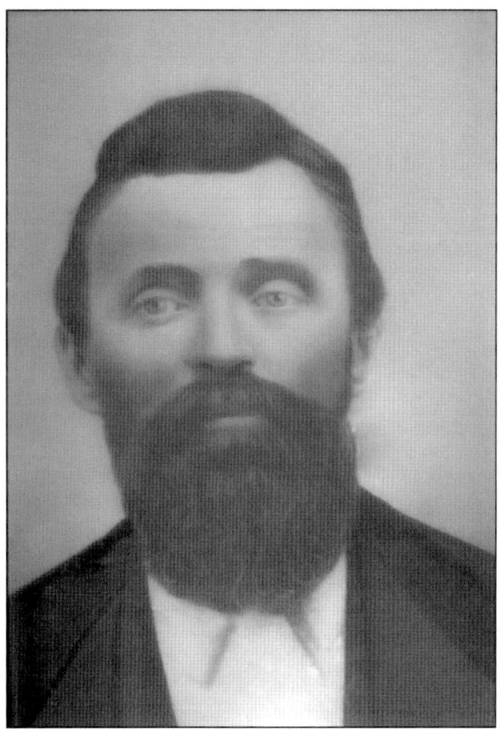

Joseph Alexander Black, born to Amos and Lucy Foster Black on February 20, 1838, was the family's first child born in Tennessee. A meticulous man, he once took over two years to build a house because he would only use the best heart pine boards and inspected each board personally. (Courtesy Ken Kowen.)

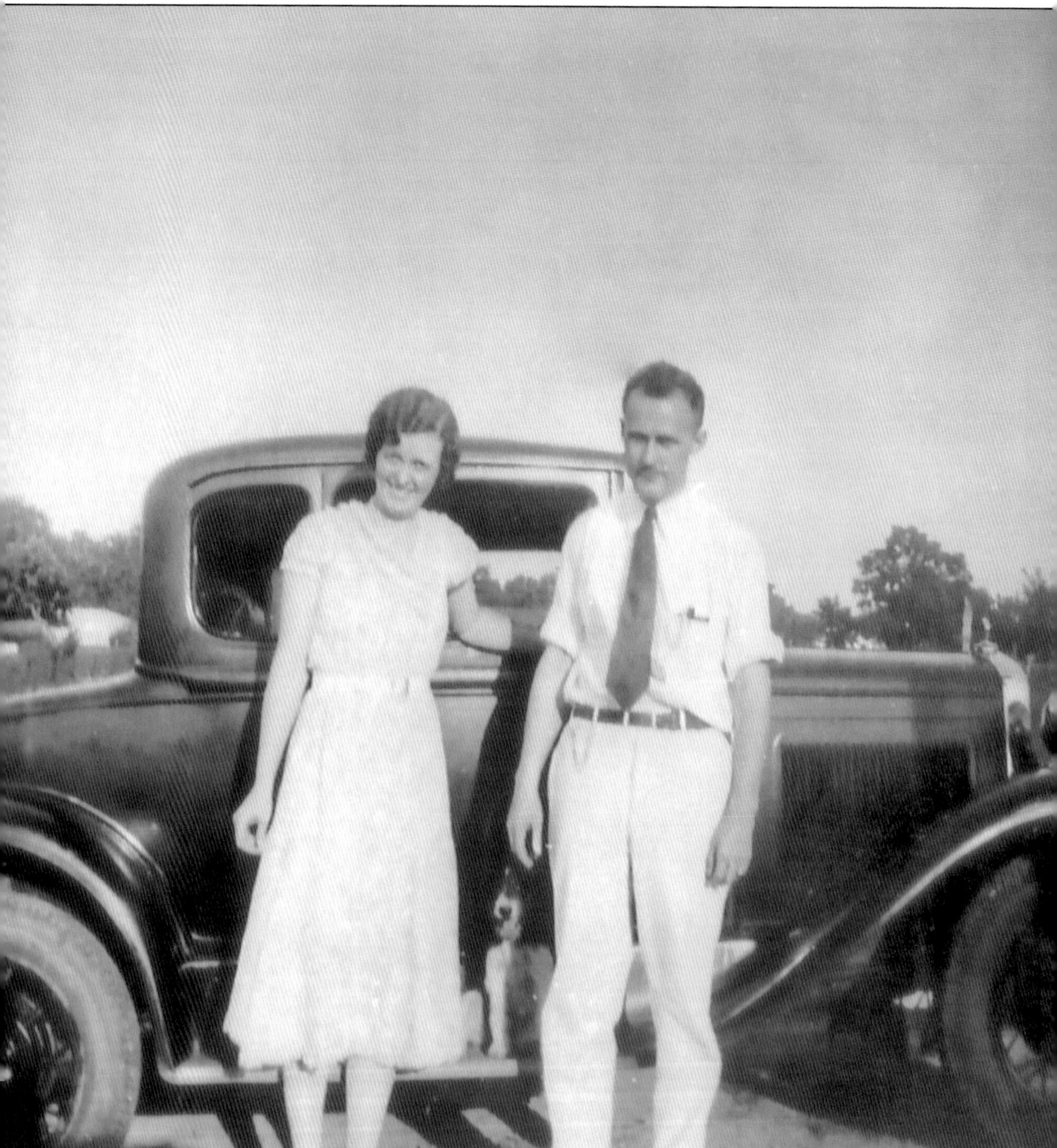

Bedford Forrest McAnulty was named for his mother's cousin, Gen. Nathan Bedford Forrest, and was the son of David Moorman and Willie Beck McAnulty. He graduated from Bolivar Central High School in 1923 and received degrees from Bethel College and the University of Tennessee, returning to Bolivar to set up his medical practice. He married Eva Mae Montgomery in 1931; she was a nurse who graduated from the Baptist School of Nursing. "Dr. Mac" and Eva began their practice during the Great Depression and were often paid with a ham or vegetables. Dr. Mac made many house calls around the county and went to the bedsides of his patients regardless of the weather or time of day or night. He and Eva helped deliver over 2,000 babies before he stopped taking maternity cases in 1960. (Courtesy Hardeman County Genealogical Society.)

“More good deeds and kind words radiated out of the life of this good man than from any life in the history of Hardeman County,” was how Dr. Benjamin Vernon Hudson was remembered in his obituary in November 1949. Born in Vildo, he first worked as a pharmacist in Whiteville and later started his own store in Bolivar, filling an estimated 250,000 prescriptions. He married Maggie Coleman in 1887 and they were the parents of two children, Margie and Vernon Jr. Dr. Hudson was active in civic and church activities and served as the Bolivar Methodist Church Sunday school superintendent for 50 years. This man was so beloved that all town businesses closed on the day of his funeral. He is pictured at right as a young man, around 1887, and below with his family around 1902. (Both, courtesy Anna Laura Bledsoe.)

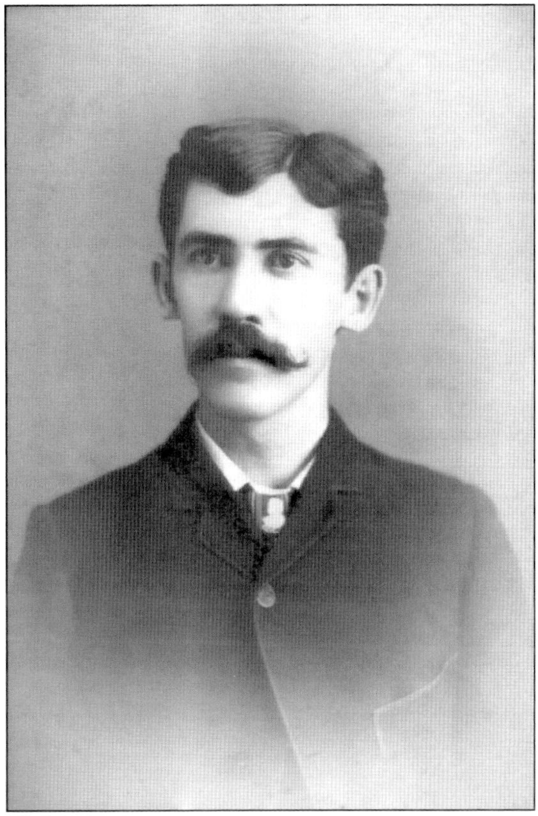

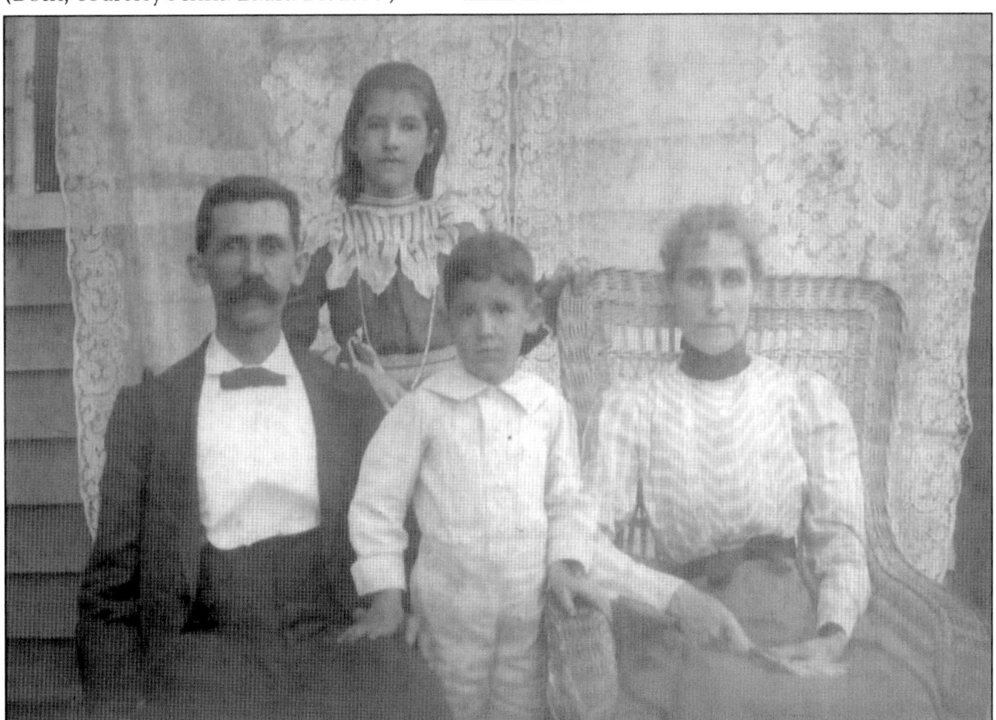

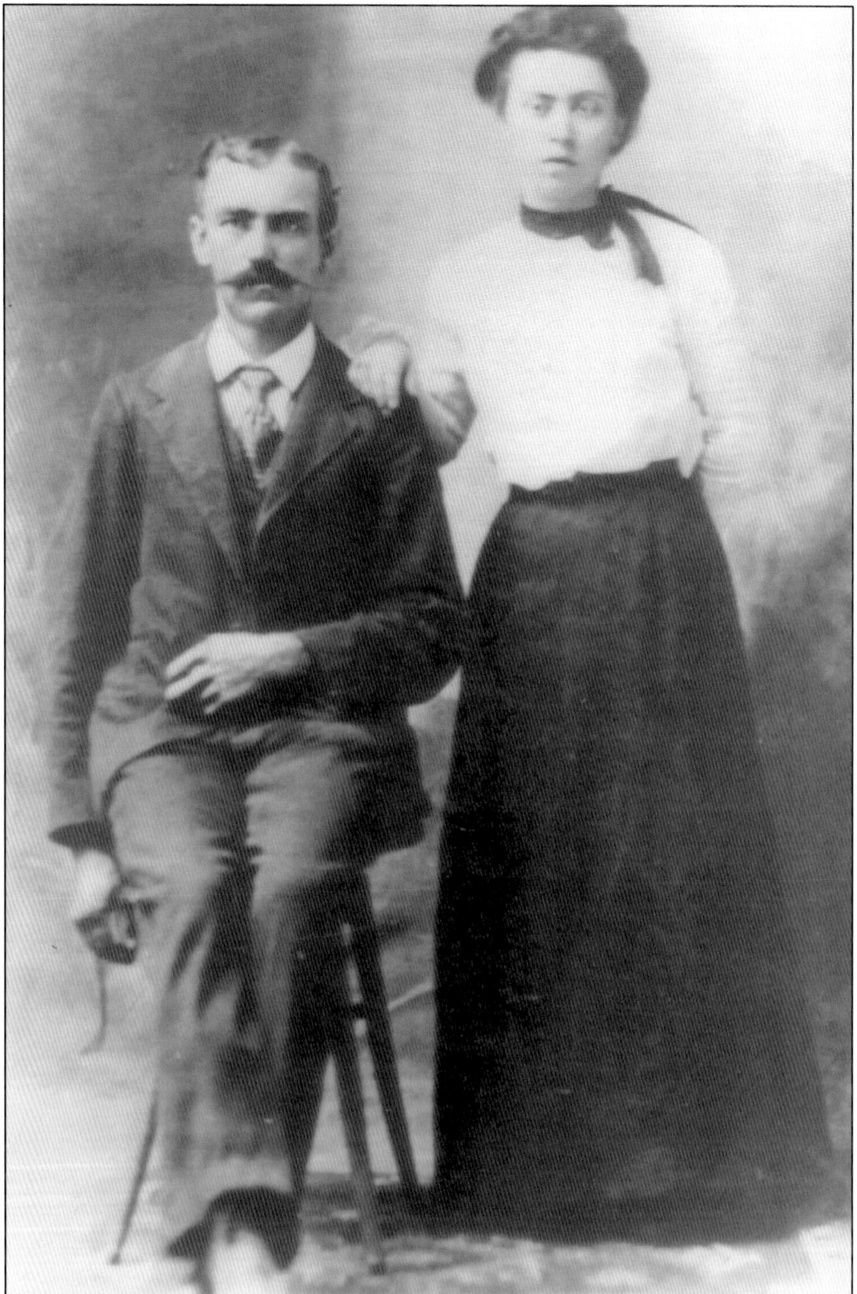

Henry Frederick "Fred" Rixie was the son of German immigrants who came to America in the mid-1850s, settling in Illinois. Fred met and married Roma Ellen (Farris) Rixie in 1881, and in the fall of 1916, Fred, Roma, and their nine children left Rosebud, Illinois, traveling 18 days in a covered wagon to Pocahontas, Tennessee. When they arrived, Fred only had 50¢ in his pocket, and he and eldest son Roy quickly got jobs cutting crossties for the railroad. He later worked as a section foreman for the Gulf, Mobile & Ohio Railroad and was well known for making sorghum molasses, which he sold for 25¢ per gallon. Fred and Roma are buried in the Ebenezer Cemetery near Middleton. (Courtesy Annie Pearl Orman.)

The town of Hornsby, first known as Bright Prospect, began as a small settlement in the Wade's Creek Valley area. Two Revolutionary War veterans, William and Joel Crain, settled in the same area, giving it the later name of Crainsville. Around 1919, when the town was moved closer to the railroad, it was renamed Hornsby because the tracks went through land belonging to Kimbrough Hornsby. The first of the town's nine artesian wells were drilled around 1915; Whitehurst Motor Company had a well on its property that was active until the late 1960s. Below, an unidentified young boy stops for a drink of cool well water; schoolchildren enjoyed drinking well water from an artesian well at the Hornsby School. (Both, courtesy Hardeman County Genealogical Society.)

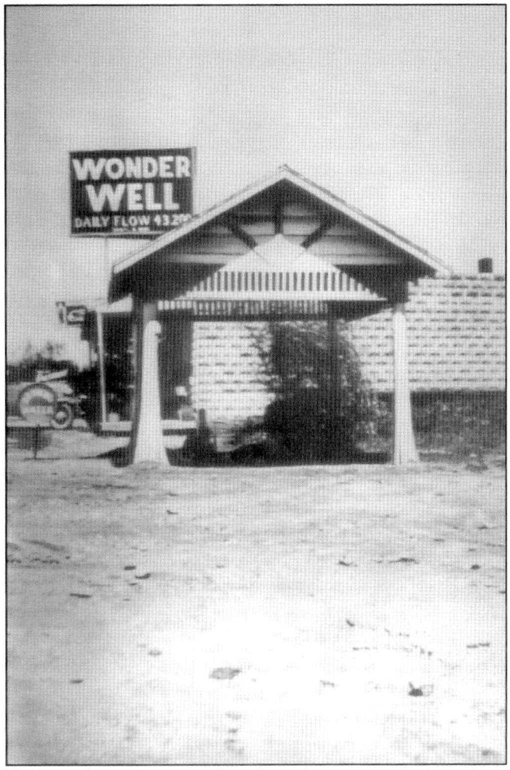

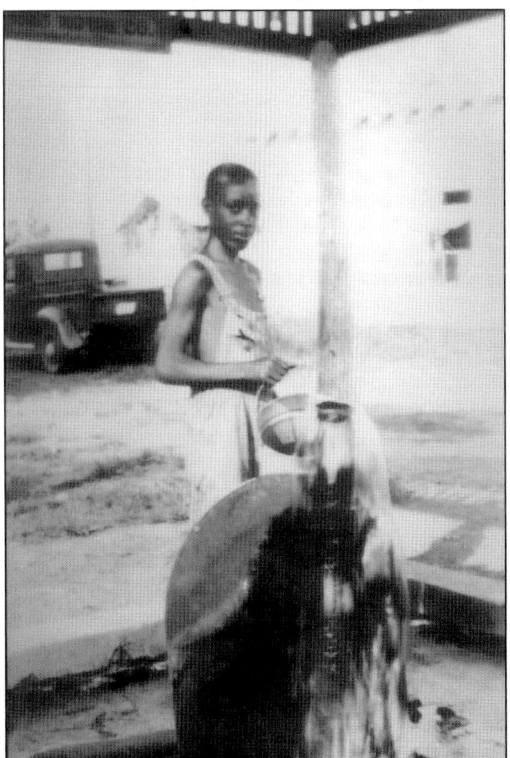

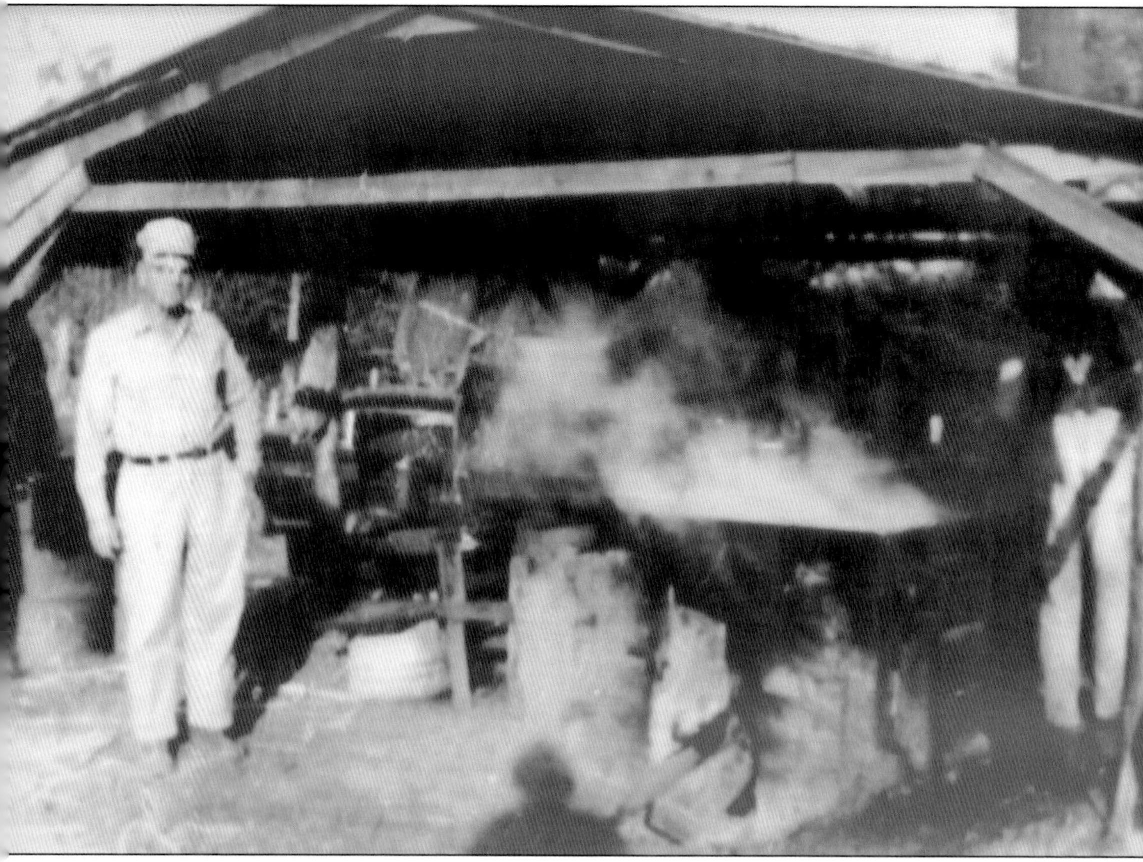

In March 1920, H.H. McMurtree and Luke Wadley built a sassafras mill in Hickory Valley, reportedly the only one of its kind in the United States. Every day that the mill was in operation, a whistle blew at noon that could be heard for many miles around—townspeople depended on this whistle to set watches and clocks. The mill was later sold to J.T. Fawcett, who continued to operate it until the government declared that an ingredient in the sassafras oil was a cancer-causing agent and banned its use in many products. The old Hickory Valley Sassafras Mill was awarded a historical marker on May 17, 1998, and a restored sassafras boiler stands next to city hall today. (Courtesy the Hardeman County Genealogical Society.)

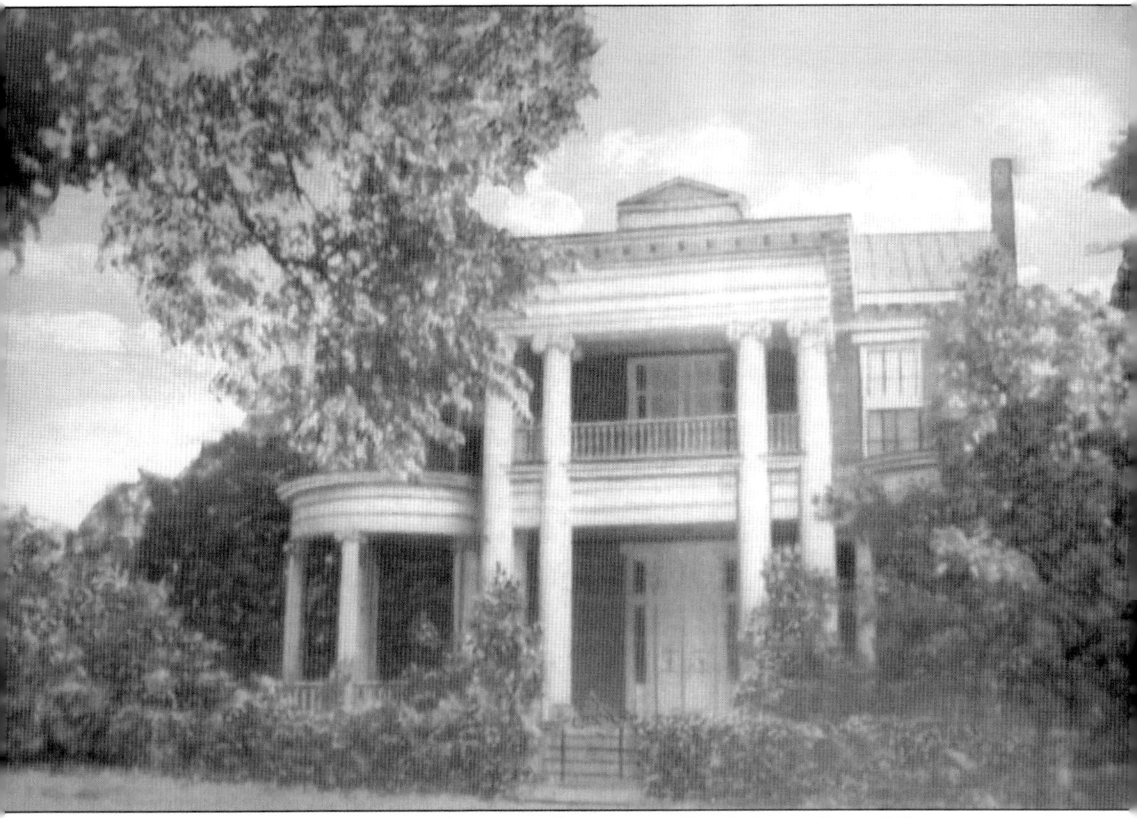

Thomas Smith built this house in Bolivar, now known as "The Columns," in 1860 as a square brick structure with eight rooms. Dr. Archer Allen and Louisa (Neely) Coleman lived in it during the Civil War, when the Union army occupied the house and pressed Dr. Coleman to perform surgeries and care for wounded soldiers on the second floor. The house was later owned by Albert T. McNeal, and then by Thomas Moore, and was sold for the final time to George T. Ingram Sr. in 1909. The house is pictured around 1900 with rounded side porches, which Ingram later removed. To preserve the house for future generations, Elizabeth Ingram established the Bolivar Historical and Community Foundation in the 1970s, donating the house to the foundation and retaining lifetime use of the house and grounds. She was the last Ingram to live in the house and stayed there until her death in 1995 at the age of 101. (Courtesy Gary Fish.)

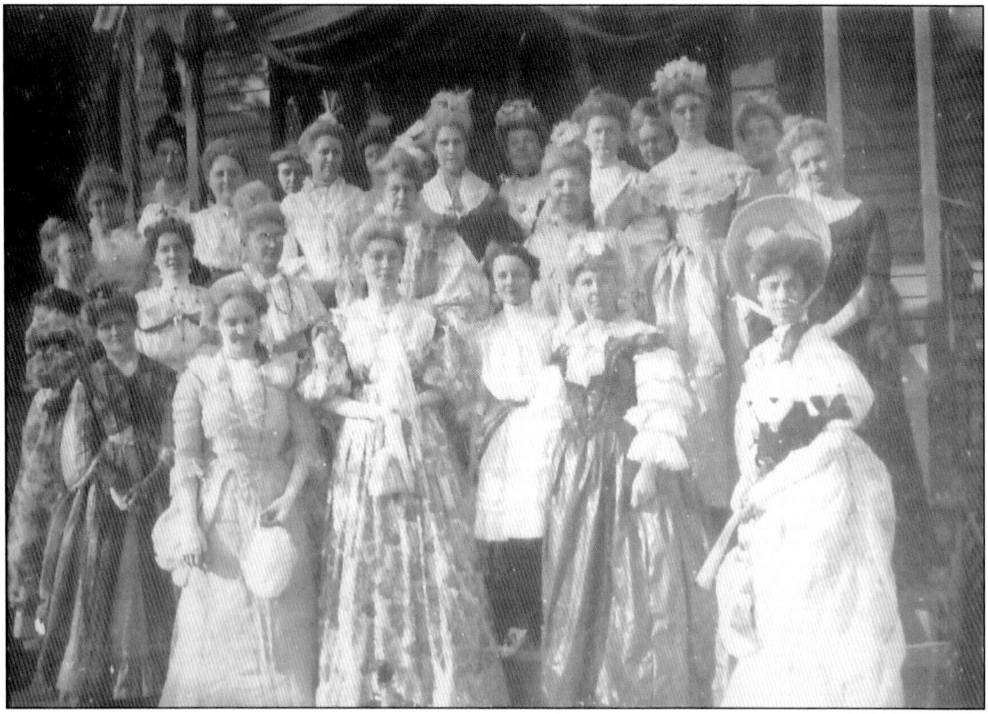

The 1903 Bolivar Society held a Valentine's Day costume party at the home of Mag Dorion. Included in this photograph are Jessie Maddison, Jennie Hardaway, Susie Black, Mary Ingram, Willie Reed, Mary Smith, Mrs. John Wright, Mrs. C.M. Wellons, Mrs. T.M. Moore, Mrs. A.J. Coates, Mrs. Southall Dickson, Mrs. C.D. Durrett, Maria Miller, Mrs. R.W. Tate, and Bessie Ingram. (Courtesy Hardeman County Genealogical Society.)

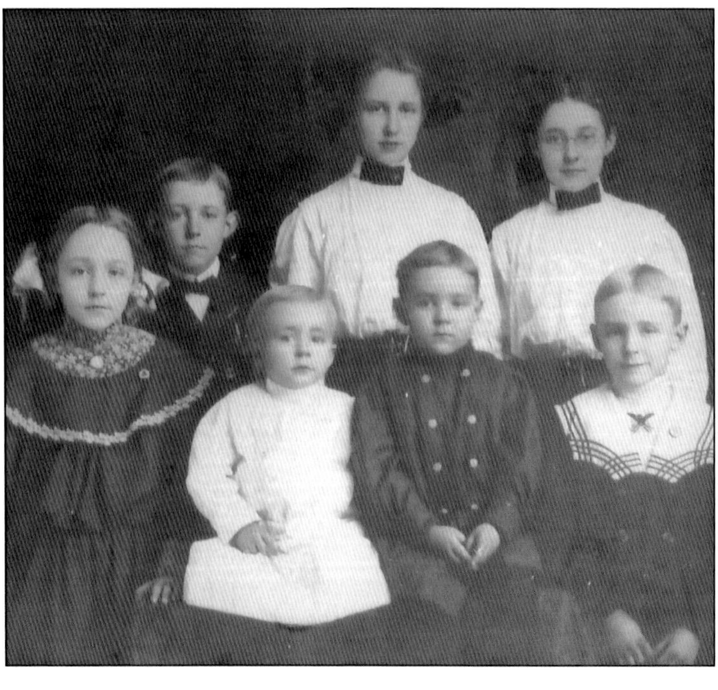

The children of David Moorman and Willie Beck McAnulty pose for a family portrait around 1900. Pictured are, from left to right, (first row, seated) Forrest, Joseph, and Robert; (second row) Margaret, David, Mattie Lou, and Annie Lea. The McAnulty family moved to Bolivar around 1907 and belonged to the Cumberland Presbyterian Church, staying active in town and church activities. (Courtesy the Hardeman County Genealogical Society.)

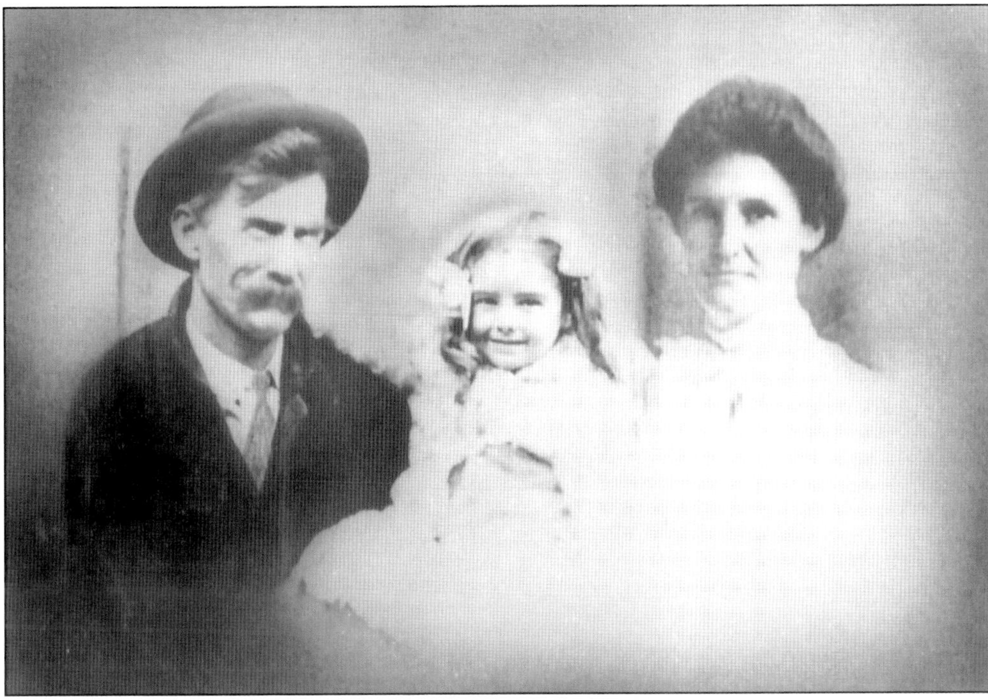

William Henry Hizer was born on September 15, 1866, and married Lillie Etta Jacobs on December 29, 1898, at the home of M.R. and Sara Hizer near Bolivar. In 1900, William and Lillie Hizer moved to Whiteville, where, with his brothers James and George, William organized the Hizer Brothers firm. They sold wagons, buggies, and farm machinery and also operated a repair shop. William and Lillie were the parents of three children, Mary Elizabeth, William Jr., and Inez (nicknamed Girlie). Girlie married Lloyd Hicks Ingram (right), who was a pharmacist in Whiteville. For many years, Girlie was a music teacher and pianist at Whiteville Baptist Church. (Both, courtesy Hardeman County Genealogical Society.)

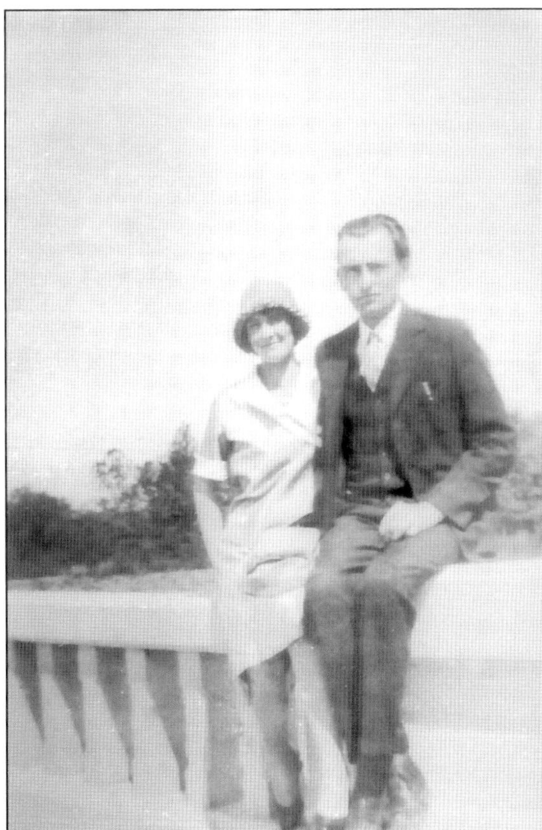

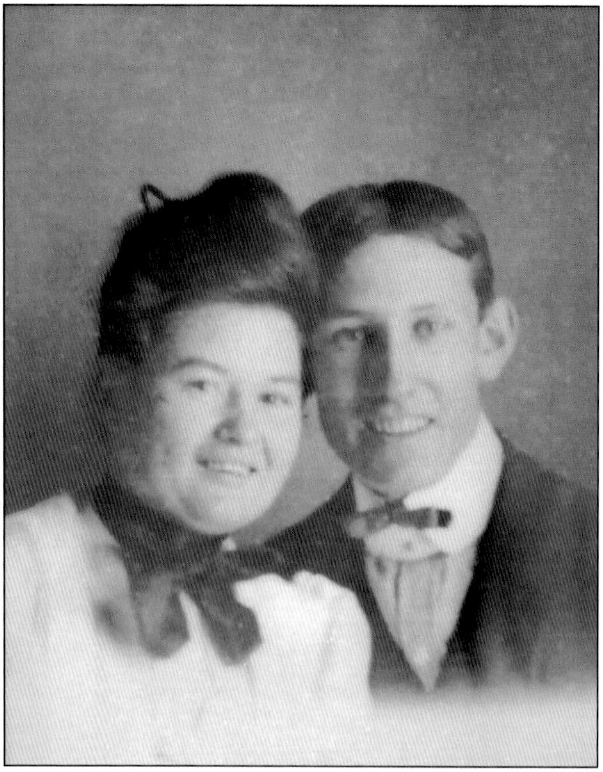

This happy young couple is Sarah "Sallie" Emerson and Edgar Galloway, who were married at the Bolivar First Baptist Church in June 1904. Sarah was the treasurer of the Women's Missionary Union for 50 years and taught Sunday school for 35 years. Edgar was the church's clerk for 29 years and also served as an usher. The Galloways were married for 63 years. (Courtesy Hardeman County Genealogical Society.)

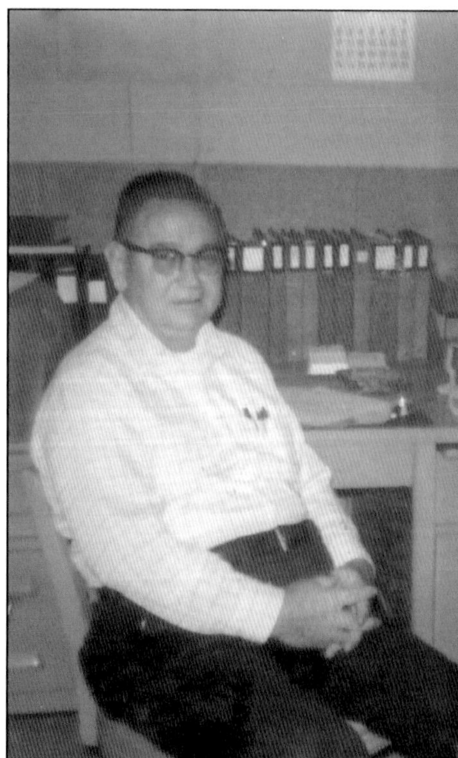

By 1905, rural mail route No. 2 was established from Bolivar to Crainsville (present-day Hornsby), with Alliganey Fulghum as the carrier. The 27-mile route included 132 houses and 508 individuals. Vernon Cox (right) returned from World War II and worked in a local appliance shop before serving as Hornsby's postmaster from 1965 to 1984. (Courtesy Tim Cox.)

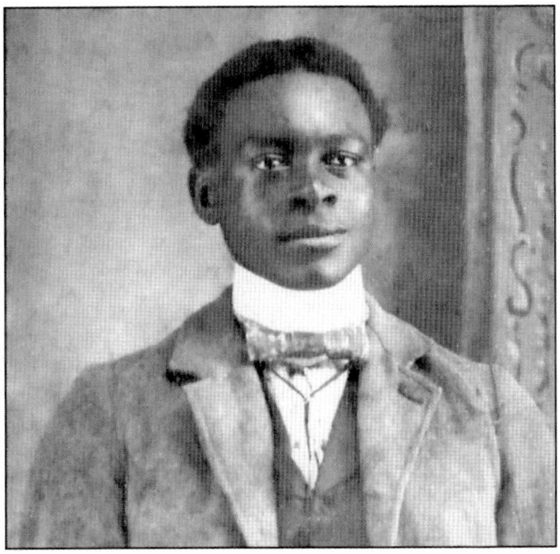 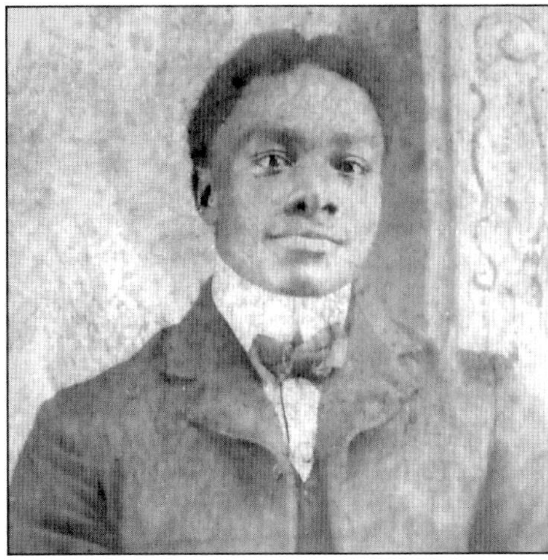

The Lake brothers were the sons and grandsons of former slaves in the Hickory Valley area. Their father, Charlie, was a slave during his youth, and although he never learned to read, he encouraged his children to educate themselves. Charlie's sons James H. and Richard Allen (above) graduated from Alcorn A&M College in Lorman, Mississippi, in 1906 and 1907, respectively, and his other son, Allen (below), graduated from Alabama A&M College in Normal, Alabama, in 1909; all three were teachers in Hardeman County for many years. Each of these photographs was made at the time of graduation as a gift for the boys' father, Charlie. (All, courtesy Hardeman County Genealogical Society.)

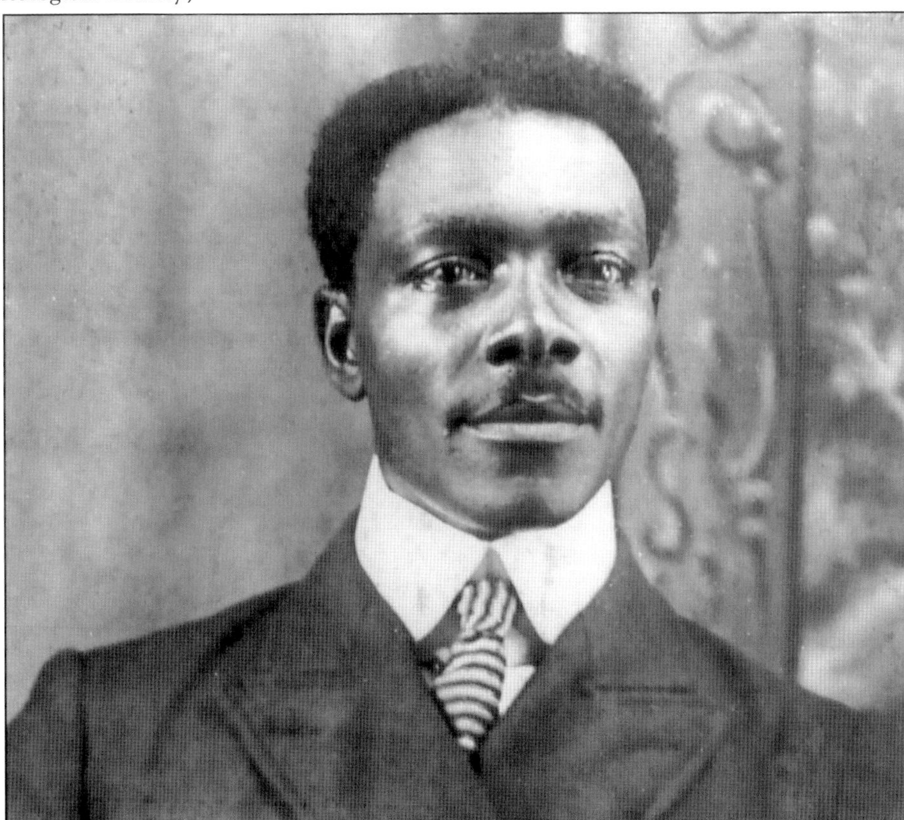

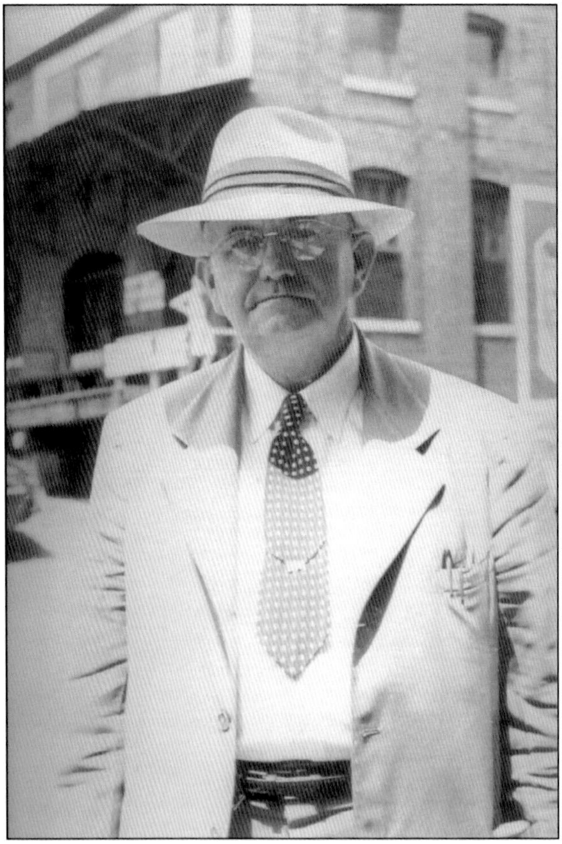

Lester Nelms (left) was elected the sheriff of Hardeman County in 1930 and served for many years. He attended the Southern Tennessee Normal College in Essary Springs, where he met Nancy Ann Elizabeth "Lizzie" Howell—they married in 1910. During the early years of their marriage, he operated a blacksmith shop and garage in Pocahontas. During Prohibition, many of his duties involved enforcing liquor laws and demolishing illegal stills, as shown below. Nelms was serving his eighth two-year term when he died in 1954, and Lizzie, who had helped him with the day-to-day administrative duties of the jail, was named to finish the remainder of his term. (Both, courtesy Pat Murphy.)

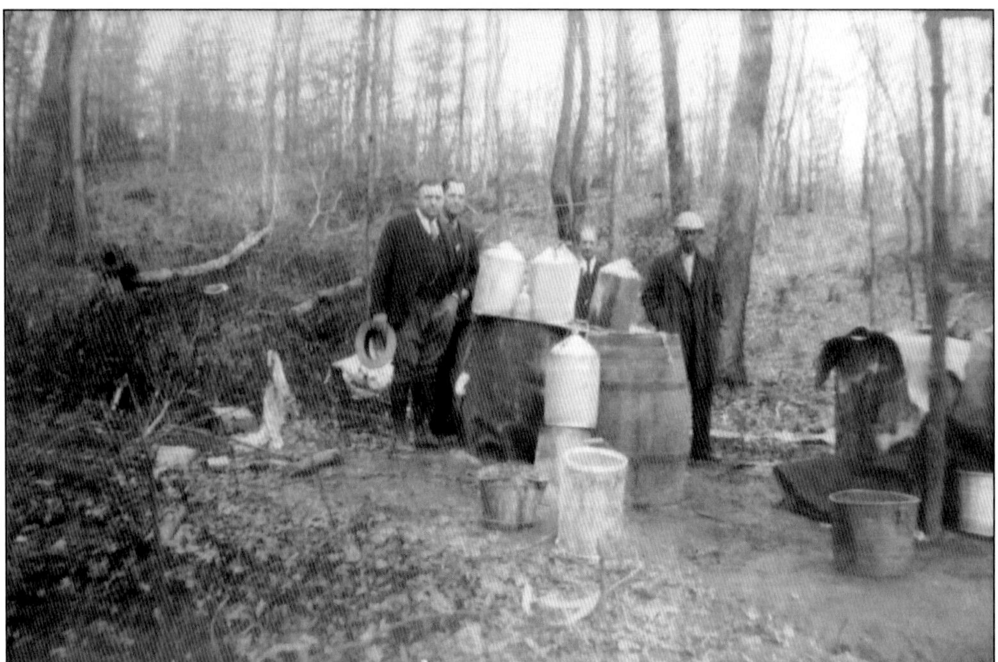

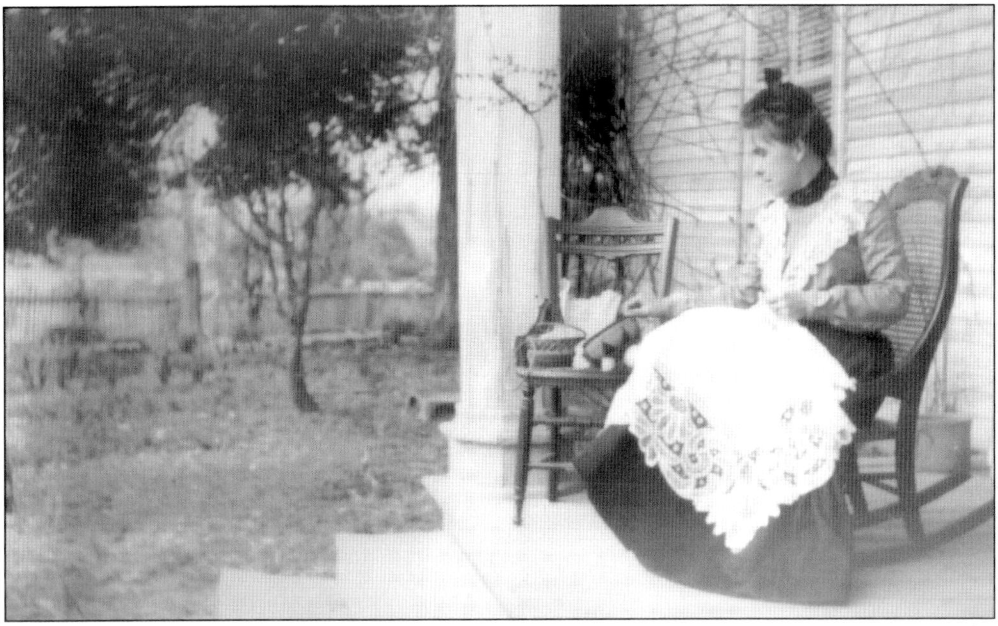

Henryetta Gray Campbell was born on February 27, 1866, and died on April 12, 1926. She greeted friends from the front porch of her home in Pocahontas (above) where she sat to work on delicate handwork sewing. Everyday life in Pocahontas was important to Campbell and was often the subject of her photographs. Visitors who stopped by for lemonade and some of her delicious homemade treats were often photographed in front of her home (below). She was active in the Presbyterian church and played the organ for Sunday services. During World War I, Campbell met every train bringing troops through the small town with a basket of treats and wishes for a safe homecoming. (Both, courtesy Esta Lee Lamberth.)

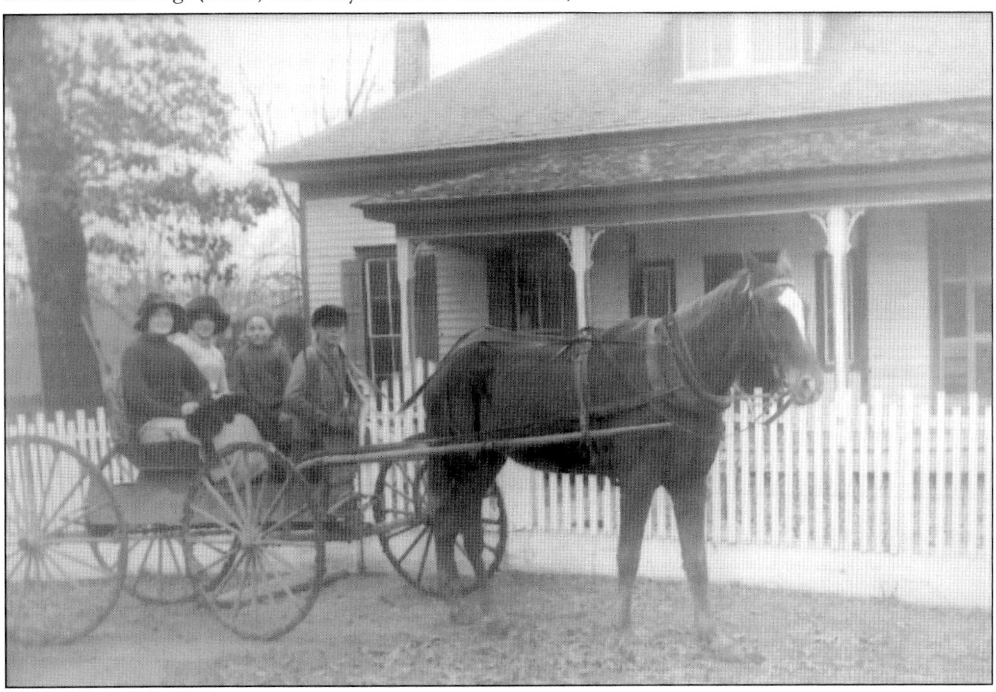

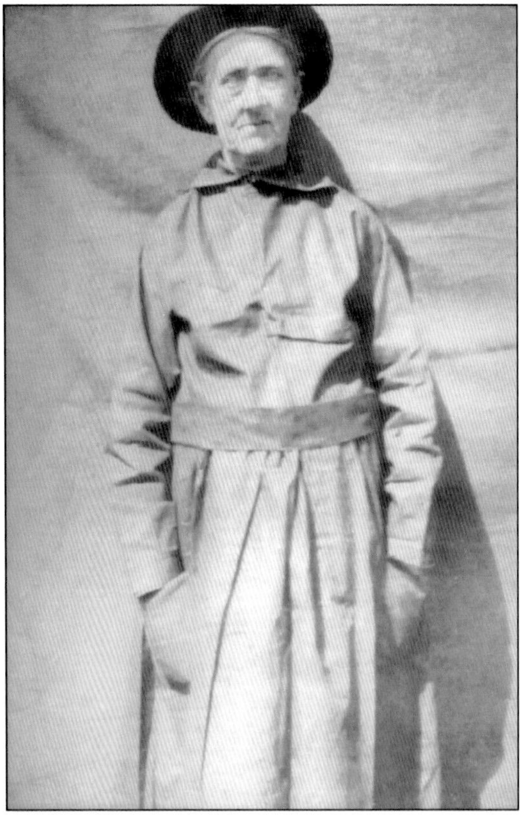

Mary B. Gladden Maples wanted to be sure that everyone had her vital statistics—on the back of this photograph, she wrote, "Mary B. Maples, this is just like me. Age, 81 years old, weight 126 pounds." She married John Maples, from Mercer, and they had several children. Mary Maples is buried in the Ebenezer Cemetery south of Middleton. (Courtesy Larry and Rose Toms Russell.)

Each generation finds its own place to hang out, and in the 1940s in Middleton, that place was the Silver Moon Café, known as *the* meeting place in town. Pictured here from left to right are L.T. Cornelius Sr., Frances Ann Johnson, and an unidentified friend visiting from St. Louis, Missouri. (Courtesy Hardeman County Genealogical Society.)

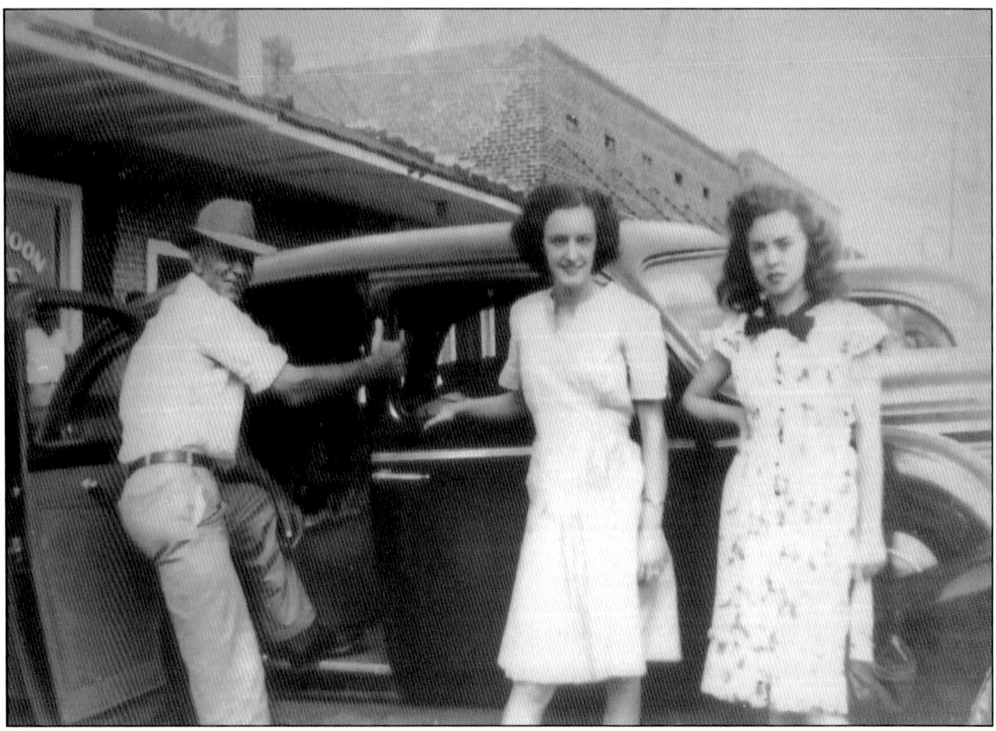

Three pretty, barefoot little girls pose in their best Sunday dresses around 1915. They are Ada Lee (left), age six; Elizabeth (center), age eight; and Elsie Bell, age four. These girls are the daughters of Grandee Duncan Sr. and Ada Miller Duncan, of Hickory Valley. They are the granddaughters of George Duncan, a Civil War veteran who served with the US Colored Troops. (Courtesy Mae Duncan.)

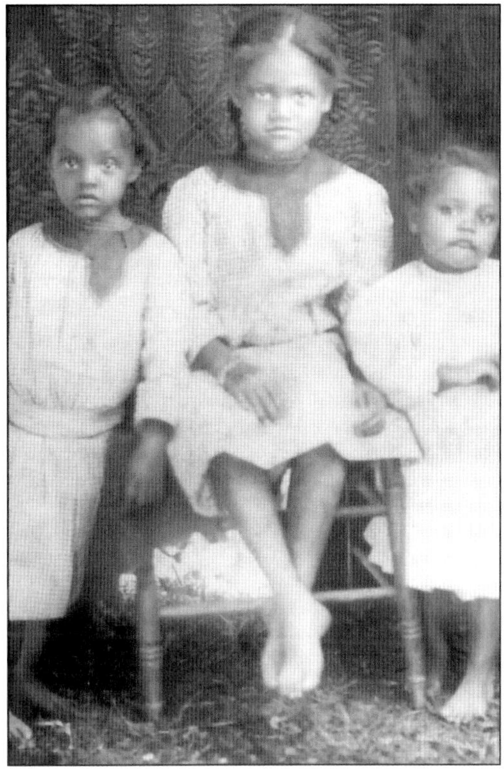

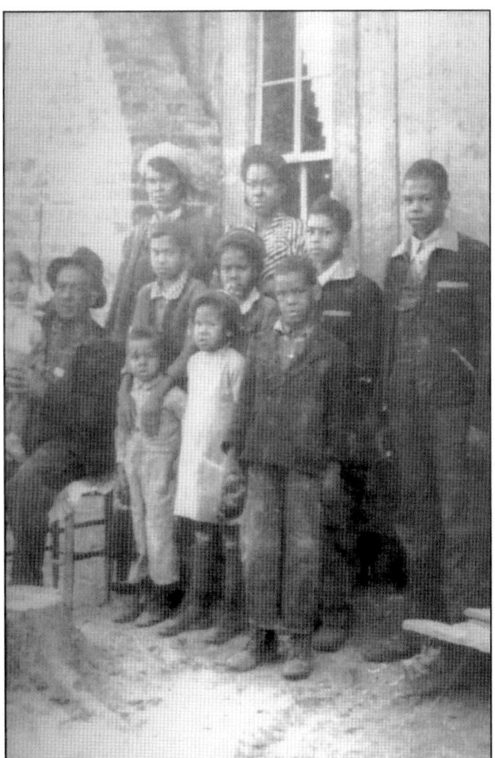

This c. 1942 image shows farmer Eddie Jones and his family at home. They are, from left to right, (first row) Eddie Jones (seated, holding Emogene Jones (Bowden)), Roy Jones, Ruth Jones (McIntosh), and Dempsey Jones; (second row) Ollie Jones (Hatcher) and Lillie Jones (Brady); (third row) Jessie Wilson Beard Jones, Agnes "Dorothy" Jones (Owens), and Samuel "Sammy" Jones. (Courtesy Curtistine Owens Gatlin.)

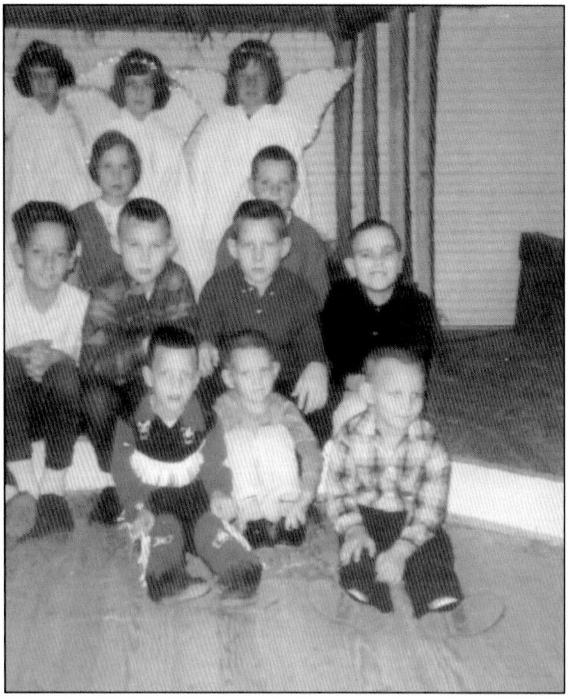

Christmas pageants and programs are a long-standing tradition in Hardeman County. This group of youngsters presented the 1968 program at Powell Chapel Methodist Church. Pictured are, from left to right, (first row) Gary Tigner, Glen Tigner, and Greg Cox; (second row) "Pellie" William Cofe, Drexel Cofe, Steve Cox, and Ricky Tigner; (third row) Brenda Waldrop and Jeff Waldrop; (fourth row) Vicky Tigner, Pat Cox, and Karen Cox (Hunt). (Courtesy Tim Cox.)

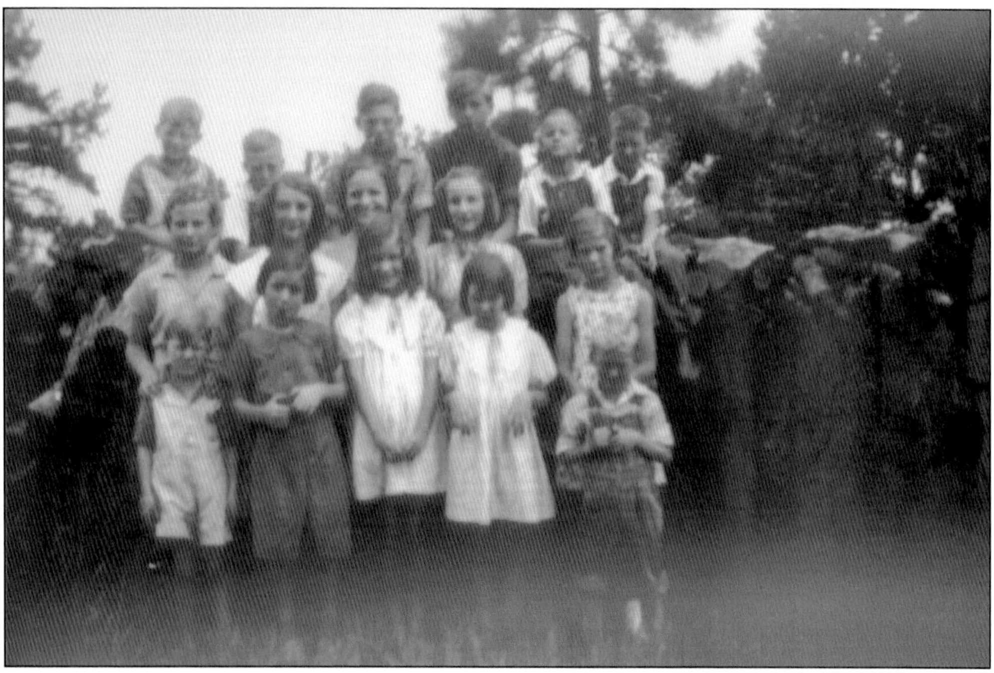

A group of youngsters stand by the woodpile around 1939 or 1940 at the old Chestnut Bluff School House. They are, from left to right, (first row) Billy Toms, Estelle Webb, Dorothy Jean Leadbetter, Ervine Leadbetter, and Donald Russell; (second row) Dovie Durham, Nadine Russell, Romelba Webb, Katie Russell, and Marin Blance Toms; (third row) Cecil "Pete" Toms, Buck Russell, Joe Morris Toms, Sidney Durham, Frank Webb, and Bobby Russell. (Courtesy Larry and Rose Toms Russell.)

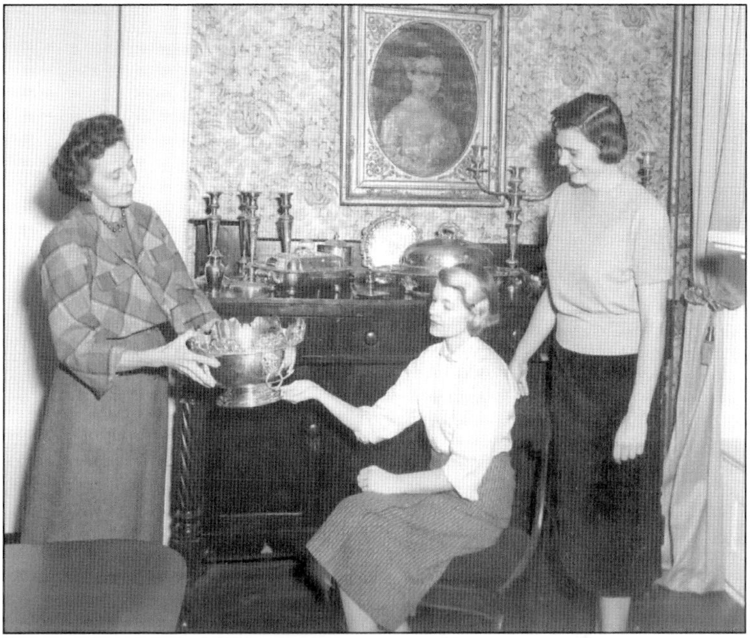

Elizabeth Ingram (left), Evalyn Harris (center), and Peggy Mask admire a piece of old English silver from a collection that was sold in 1956 to benefit St. James Episcopal Church. Other pieces of the collection, displayed in the dining room of the Columns, are visible in the background. (Courtesy Evalyn Mason Harris.)

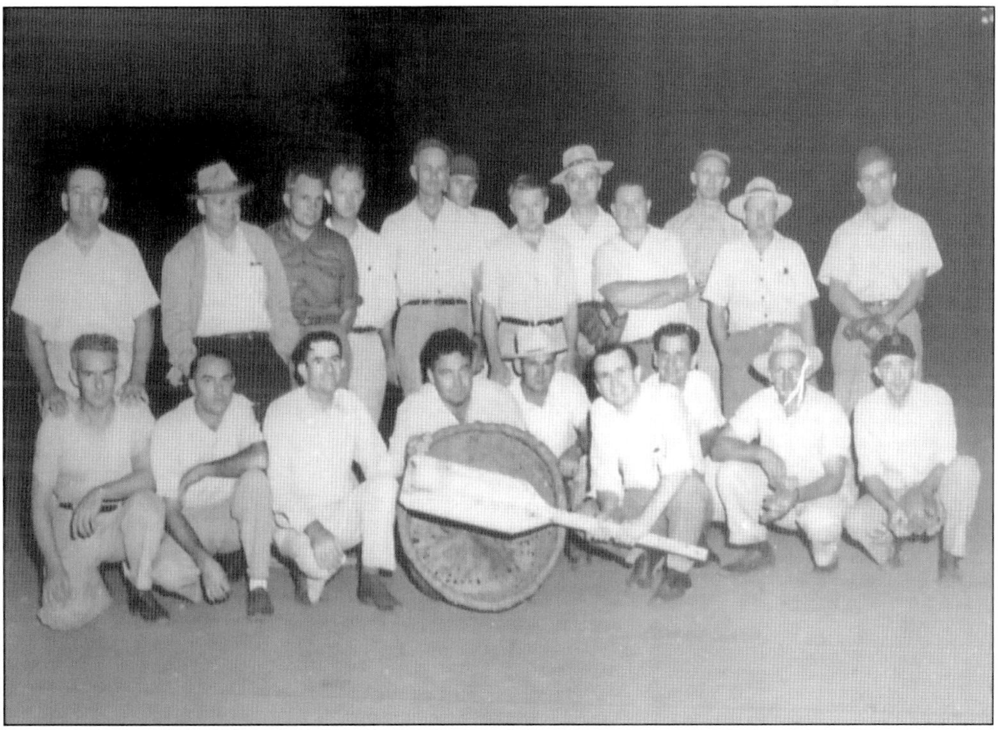

In 1949, Bolivar Rotary Club members formed a team as part of a men's baseball league. Pictured from left to right are (first row) Sam Cross, unknown, Ewing Harris, Hugh Drewery, unknown, W.E. Lawrence, Mahlon Brown, Martin Alpin, and Wilbur Orr; (second row) Harold Carleton, unknown, ? Warner, John Oldham, Curtiss Vaughan, two unknown, Granville Vaughan, Renfro Pruitt, Paisley Shackelford, Tommy Hazlegrove, and Paul Vaughan. (Courtesy Hardeman County Genealogical Society.)

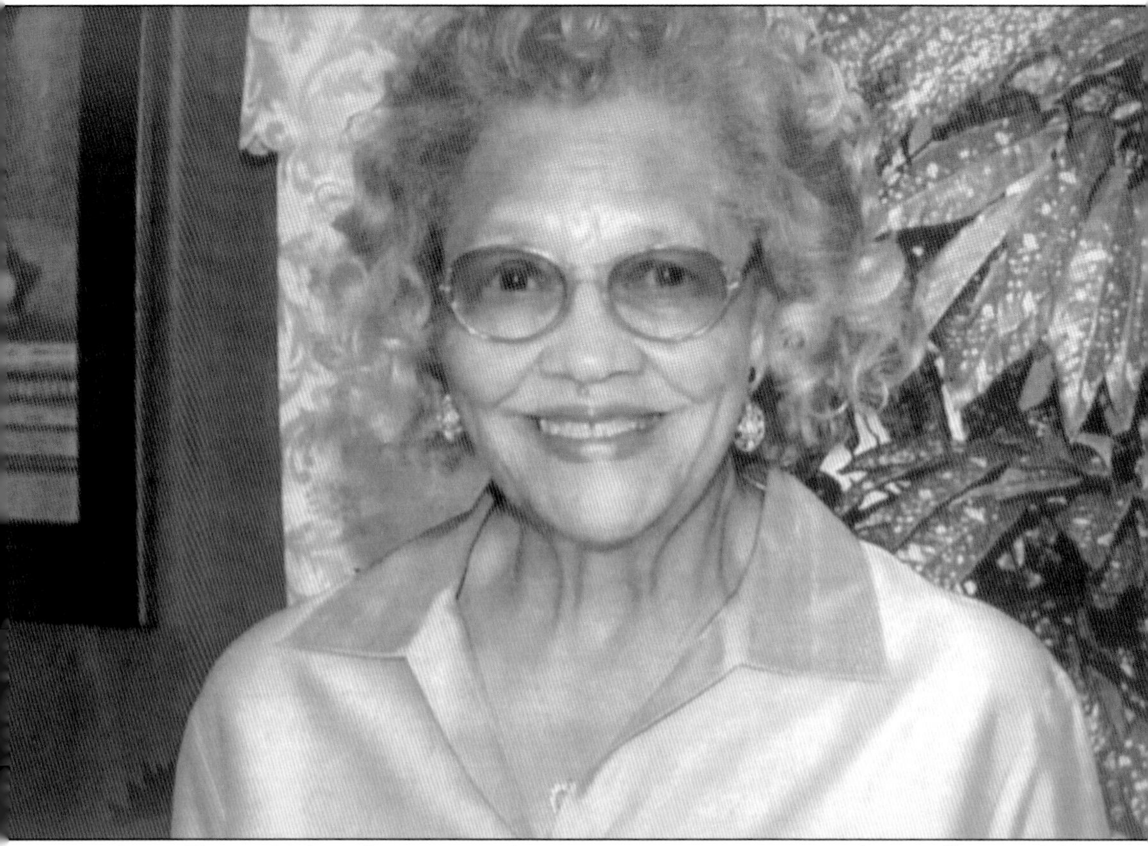

Hattye Thomas Yarbrough grew up in the Prospect community, near Hickory Valley. Her father stressed education for all of his children, and Hattye Yarbrough graduated from Lane College, received certifications as a teacher/librarian from Fisk University, and was one of the first African American students at Peabody College to earn a master's degree in library science after taking classes over the summer. She remembers that, "the obstacles we encountered did not discourage us because we wanted to finish our education and earn those advanced degrees." This education pioneer shared her love of knowledge and reading with students in the Covington, Tennessee, school district for 43 years. (Courtesy Hardeman County Multicultural Museum.)

Young Thomas Edison left home around age 16 to seek his fortune, traveling as a "tramp telegraph operator" throughout the central and southern United States. He worked in Bolivar as a telegraph operator for the railroad for a brief period. Edison returned home ragged and penniless after his telegraph adventures, but his inventions changed the world. (Courtesy Little Courthouse Museum.)

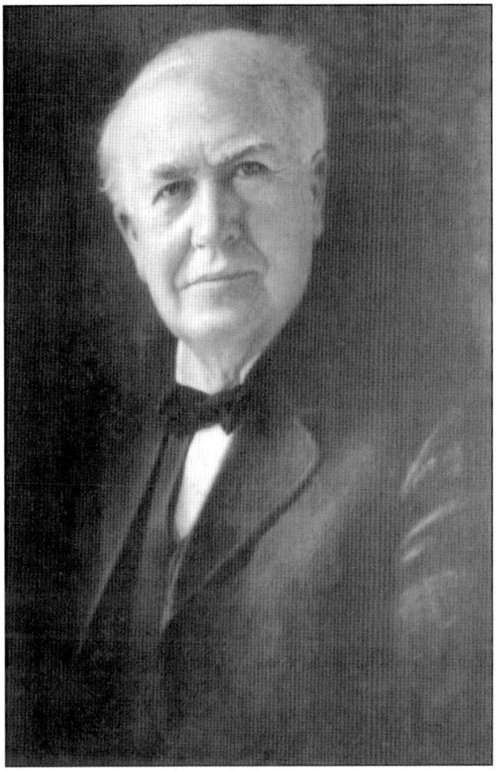

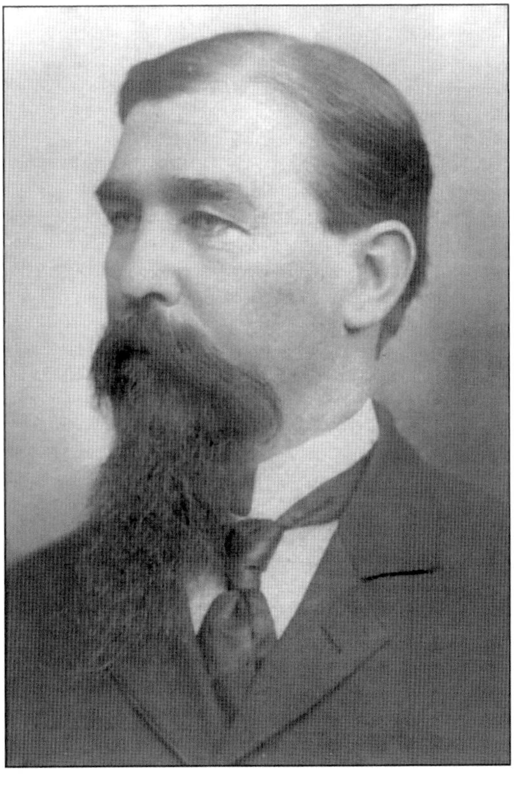

Dr. James Jackson (J.J.) Neely, son of Rufus Polk and Elizabeth Neely, ran away from home at age 14 and joined Company E of the 7th Mississippi Cavalry. After the Civil War, he studied medicine, practicing first in Bolivar and later at the Western State Hospital as one of its first physicians; he also served as the third superintendent of the hospital. (Lisa C. Coleman.)

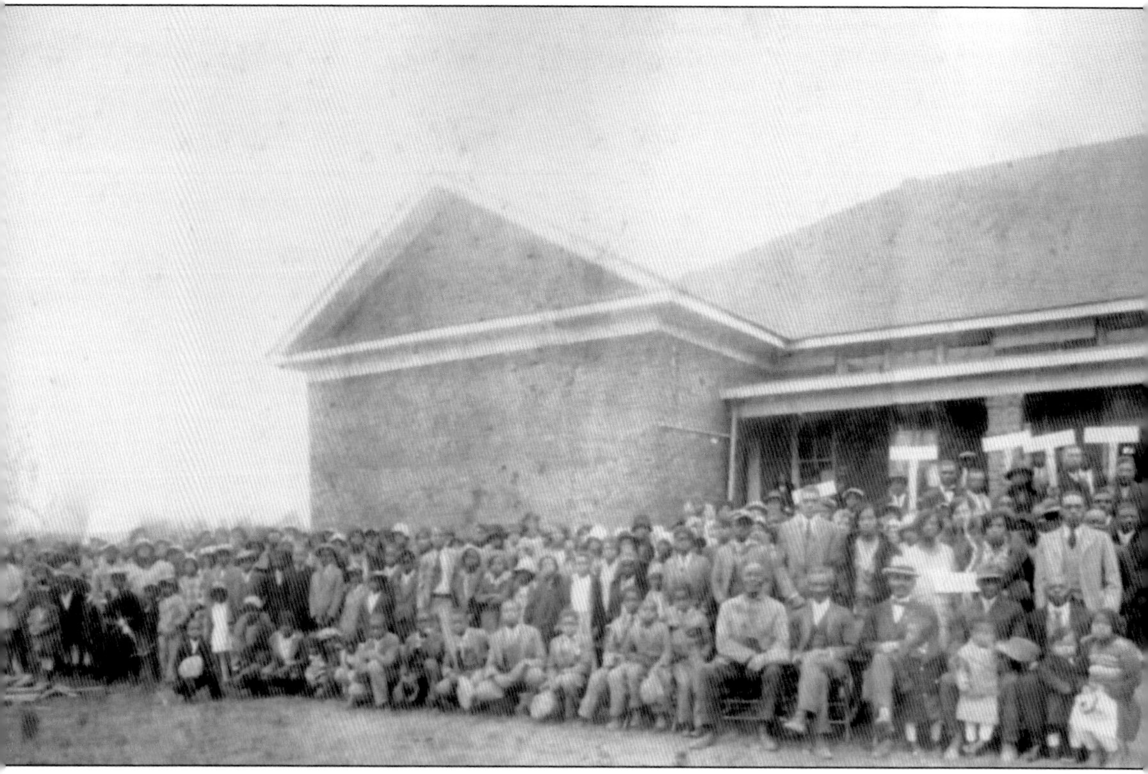

The Allen White High School was established in Whiteville in 1930. It was named for Jessie Christopher Allen and James. H. White and was the only high school for black students in the county. Loans, community donations, and the Julius Rosenwald Foundation funded the school's construction. The school and community held a mortgage-burning ceremony on Thanksgiving Day in 1929. Pupils came from all parts of the county to study, and many of them boarded at

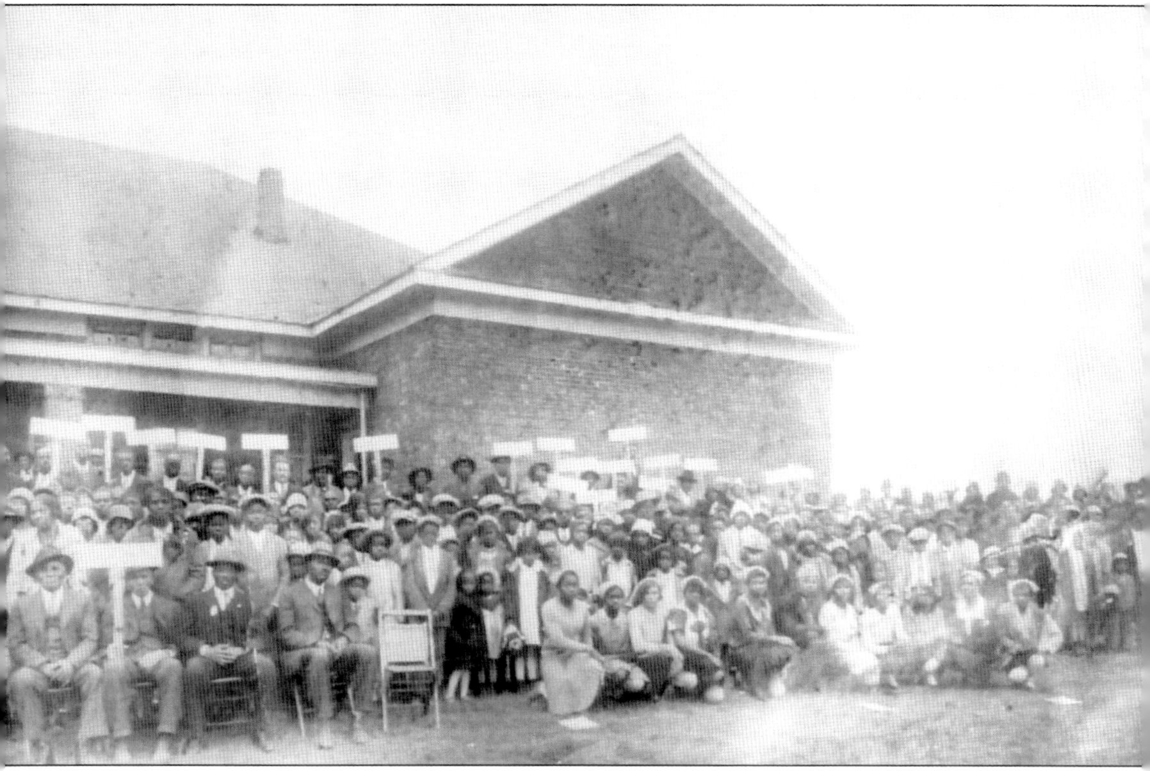

the school. The curriculum included basic studies, with an emphasis on history, science, music, agriculture, and athletics. This small, rural school boasted championship boys' and girls' basketball teams. It closed in 1971, when county schools were fully integrated. (Courtesy Evelyn Robertson Jr. and Hardeman County APTA.)